Lost Loss in American Elegiac Poetry

Reading Trauma and Memory

Series Editors: Aimee Pozorski, Central Connecticut State University, and Nicholas Ealy, University of Hartford

Reading Trauma and Memory offers global perspectives on representations of trauma and memory while examining the tensions, limitations, and responsibilities that accompany the status of the witness. This series attempts to bridge the gap between trauma studies and new directions in the fields of memory studies, popular culture, and race theory and seeks submissions that closely read literature and culture for representations of traumatic wounding, the limits of memory, and the ethical duty to depict historical trauma and its effects.

Given its breadth, this series will appeal to scholars in a number of interdisciplinary fields; given the specific angle of trauma and memory, it will capture those who see ethics and responsibility as key factors in their scholarship. Such areas include: Holocaust studies; war trauma and PTSD; illness and disability; the trauma of migration and immigration; memory studies; race studies; gender and sexuality studies (which has recently had a resurgence with the #MeToo movement); studies in popular culture that take up television and films about witness; and the study of social and historical movements.

We are seeking projects that question how to honor the past through close readings of literature focused on trauma and memory—which would necessarily take on international perspectives. Examples include a consideration of literature and justice in Rwanda through a postcolonial and trauma lens; recent thinking on the phenomenon of "American Crime Story" and the resurgence of interest in the OJ Simpson trial that parallels the narrative of the Black Lives Matter movement; readings of the attempts of popular culture to address issues of historical injustice as exemplified by *12 Years a Slave* and HBO's *Westworld*.

Recent Titles in this Series

Lost Loss in American Elegiac Poetry: Tracing Inaccessible Grief from Stevens to Post-9/11, by Toshiaki Komura

Empathy and the Phantasmic in Ethnic American Trauma Narratives, by Stella Setka

Trauma in 20th Century Multicultural American Poetry: Unmuted Verse, by Jamie D. Barker

Ethics of Witness in Global Testimonial Narratives: Responding to the Pain of Others, by Kimberly A. Nance

The Latinx Urban Condition: Trauma, Memory, and Desire in Latinx Urban Literature and Culture, by Crescencio Lopez-Gonzalez

Literary and Visual Representations of HIV/AIDS: Forty Years Later, by Aimee Pozorski, Jennifer J. Lavoie, and Christine J. Cynn

Occupying Memory: Rhetoric, Trauma, Mourning, by Trevor Hoag

Lost Loss in American Elegiac Poetry

Tracing Inaccessible Grief from Stevens to Post-9/11

Toshiaki Komura

LEXINGTON BOOKS
Lanham • Boulder • New York • London

Published by Lexington Books
An imprint of The Rowman & Littlefield Publishing Group, Inc.
4501 Forbes Boulevard, Suite 200, Lanham, Maryland 20706
www.rowman.com

6 Tinworth Street, London SE11 5AL, United Kingdom

Copyright © 2020 The Rowman & Littlefield Publishing Group, Inc.

All rights reserved. No part of this book may be reproduced in any form or by any electronic or mechanical means, including information storage and retrieval systems, without written permission from the publisher, except by a reviewer who may quote passages in a review.

British Library Cataloguing in Publication Information Available

Library of Congress Cataloging-in-Publication Data Available

ISBN 978-1-7936-1262-5 (cloth)
ISBN 978-1-7936-1264-9 (pbk)
ISBN 978-1-7936-1263-2 (electronic)

Contents

Introduction	1
1 Wallace Stevens's Elegiac Mode: Creating Fictions of Loss	35
2 Sylvia Plath's Poems of 1963: Dysthymia and Subterranean Loss	73
3 Elizabeth Bishop's *Geography III*: Un-losing Lost Loss	97
4 Sharon Olds's *The Dead and the Living*: Distant Loss and Ethical Empathy	125
5 Post-9/11 Elegiac Poetry: The Unsaid	149
Conclusion & Afterword: Lost Loss beyond American Elegiac Poetry	175
Bibliography	189
Acknowledgments	211
Index	215
About the Author	217

Introduction

It is a truism that the human mortality rate is 100 percent. It is also a truism that we generally have significant relations that we will lose over the course of our lives. This book, however, is not about the grief of losing a specific someone. This book is about the distance, diffusion, or detachment within dispossessive experiences—the sense that those losses feel "lost" to us. There is a subset of modern and contemporary American elegiac poetry that gives shape to elusive feelings of tenuous and inconclusive losses: losses that are semi-, half-, sub-, or unconscious, unrecorded, forgotten, unacknowledged, denied, or repressed. While the American elegy of the twentieth and twenty-first centuries has often been characterized as intense and direct in its expression of loss,[1] elusiveness manifests in a segment of the lamentative poetry of this period, as evidenced by the poems studied in this book, which are selected from the oeuvres of Wallace Stevens, Sylvia Plath, Elizabeth Bishop, Sharon Olds, Louise Glück, and others. Their ambiguous grief takes many different forms. Some losses may be characterized as imaginary; one mourns the unrealized possibilities that one could imagine but that did not materialize. Other losses can be classified as distant; when the relationship between the deceased and the mourner is tenuous, the mourner cannot claim the loss and, in such inability, is left with an indeterminate feeling of emptiness. Still others are proleptic; these are losses that have not yet come to actuality but that one can anticipate will likely occur in the future. Loss may be left unacknowledged; the mourner perceives the occurrence as loss, whereas society at large would not. There are also subtle privations overshadowed by more apparent and visible ones. And some types of loss can feel so profound and overwhelming that they cannot be conceptualized, like the sun too blinding for us to see with our own eyes.

These inexpressible feelings of unrecognized or unrecognizable dispossession embody a phenomenon that this book names "lost loss": a privative state in which a specific loss is either absent, ineffective, or inaccessible, or has become a stand-in or screen for some other inarticulable loss. This concept requires its own distinct sub-category, for, in lost loss, the dispossessive experience itself becomes the object of denial, skepticism, oblivion, or other kinds of unavailability, complicating its effects on us in ways that deviate from the dominant theorization of loss. If loss is typically defined as the state of not having something anymore, lost loss queries precisely this state of not having; it calls attention to the fragility of the concept of loss itself, exposing what it leaves out.

Poetry of lost loss simulates the muted dejection, a type of characteristically less intense but more chronic, ambiguous, and surreptitious despondency that persists in the background of one's psyche; it contrasts with the intense grief of explicit loss that has been the focus of previous elegy studies. The aim of this book is to codify a new subgenre of elegiac poetry where loss itself is the target of contention. The intended contributions of this project are twofold: in the narrower scope of elegy studies, this theorization of lost loss proposes an alternative explanation for the ambiguous despondency that becomes more visible in modern and contemporary poetry; and in the larger scope of literary studies, this concept provides an explanation for several social and psychological phenomena, such as how unacknowledged loss dilutes mourning, facilitates a proliferation of fictive beliefs as consolatory philosophies, or generates a desire to reconstruct and reclaim what one imagines has been dispossessed. The poems discussed in this book perform the elegiacs of equivocation; they parry and muddle their grief and grievances, in the process of giving shape to the tenuous loss that they strain to elucidate.

Exemplification proves instructive in clarifying an unfamiliar concept; I begin with the following two poems as illustrations of lost loss. One is a poem entitled "Cellars and Attics" by an American Yiddish poet, Malka Heifetz Tussman. The speaker of this poem is a second-generation Holocaust survivor; the poem details her conversation with a friend named Teddy, who talks about his children playing in his elderly parents' old house with its attic and cellar. Attics and cellars are the spaces where old clothes, photographs, and other mementos of one's ancestors are kept; they represent family history. The friend describes how his children take joy in opening the trunks full of "[g]reat-great possessions"—the vestiges of their great or great-great grandparents—and then asks a question that the speaker is unable to answer:

"So much history, tradition
In old attics!
Children should know where
They come from. . . ."

And Teddy asks,
"Where is your old house—
Your cellar and your attic?"
And I answer in a Jewish way—
A question with a question,
"Indeed, where is
My grandfather's old house?" (63–66, 109–115)[2]

For the descendants of Holocaust survivors, everything earlier exists only in memory, since there are few inherited objects from before their parents emigrated;[3] this condition is particularly poignant to the second generation, who might conceivably have had tangible access to prior generations, had the genocide not taken place. The speaker, having lost her ancestors, does not have the "cellars and attics" that are material symbols of family history and tradition, the commemorations of the life or death of the ancestors. Unlike the first-generation survivors who intimately knew their deceased parents, grandparents, siblings, and friends as living beings, second-generation survivors would be bestowed no evidence of those people's deaths other than their stories. It is a loss that feels itself out of one's grasp—a loss that is sufficiently abstract that one feels presumptuous, and hence hesitates, to call it a loss.

Tussman's "Cellars and Attics" is not about the acute trauma of the Holocaust, which is expunged from the poem's consciousness altogether: all that remains in the poem is the unease of answering a question with a question, an irresolvable question after an unanswerable question. As the indefinite plural of "cellars" and "attics" suggests, the lyric-speaker of this poem is bereft of those reminders of past dispossessions that she could claim as her own. The speaker, for whom the original loss is inaccessible because she did not exist at the time of the Holocaust, tries to express a feeling of double-privation, by creating a phantom ideation of cellars and attics and querying where her grandfather's old house could be. This loss of loss is signaled by the indeterminate feeling of having been deprived of something but not knowing what exactly it is. The inarticulate unsettlement expresses itself in the speaker's open-ended question that concludes the poem: is the speaker lamenting the absence of her grandfather, his old house, the fact that she had neither of those, or something else?

Another model case of lost loss is Theodore Roethke's "Elegy for Jane." Given that this poem has achieved canonical status as a teacher's elegy for a memorable student and that its critical discussion has focused more around the question of whether the lament is more personal or universal,[4] "Elegy for Jane" may seem counter-intuitive as an example of unrecognized loss. But while it is widely known that the occasion of this elegy is the death of one of Roethke's students, Roethke's biography suggests that he had not known her well.⁵ This non-intimate status with the deceased urges us to reinterpret the poem as an inquiry into how we may cope with the loss of people whom we know but have little right to claim personal proximity to. The death of a colleague or acquaintance may not sink us into the acutest depression as it may with a family member or a close friend, but it nonetheless is unsettling and discomforting to us. "Elegy for Jane" is a case study of what we may call "distant loss": a loss of someone with whom we have not yet established a close enough relationship to be able to assert the right to grieve. After all, one cannot be seen to have lost what one does not possess. Mourning is delimited by the nature of the relationship; the strength of the tie must be seen to be quantifiably equivalent to the degree of sorrow, and deviations from this formulation disenfranchise the grief. The loss of a chance to get to know someone elicits a type of dejection that has not yet been given an adequate name.

Roethke's elegy addresses this conundrum of the loss that we feel toward an individual who has gone before any prospect of a significant relationship. In object relations, the absence of the lost object complicates the normative mourning process of consolation and recovery. The concluding lines of the poem offer sufficient evidence of the speaker's diffidence and ambivalence about claiming the student's death as his personal loss:

If only I could nudge you from this sleep,
My maimed darling, my skittery pigeon.
Over this damp grave I speak the words of my love:
I, with no rights in this matter,
Neither father nor lover.   (18–22)⁶

By introducing the traditional figures of personal proximity—father, lover—as negations, the stanza creates a clash between the figures of speech and the content of the speech. Even as the poet-speaker insistently uses the possessive for the lost object—such as "My maimed darling," "my skittery pigeon," "my love," starting in the third stanza with "My sparrow" (14), in a deliberate shift from the initial use of indefinite articles like "a wren" (5)—he realizes that he has no "rights" to grieve, being neither a father nor a lover. The poem's use of the possessive coincides with its shift to the direct second-person address in a turn away from the subdued third-person address of the earlier stanzas. As William Waters points out, "for a poem to say *you* is in every case a complex act."⁷ The poet-speaker struggles to express his sorrow; the words elude the thoughts, and the thoughts themselves elude thinking. The sensation is almost like writer's block—the inadequacy of the language, the unspeakable, the unsayable that lurks within and evades us. The highly conflicted language becomes, in a sense, a makeshift expedient to grope blindly through the incomprehension of this unplaceable grief, one about which the poet-speaker does not know how to speak. "Elegy for Jane" is a poem about the indeterminacy of lost loss—the loss of an opportunity to know someone well enough to say that one has "lost" her.

The feeling of dejection arising from these unarticulated losses remains irresolute, keeps echoing persistently and pervasively in the background, and is difficult to locate; even when this faint echo of privation is registered, its expressive tropes diffuse the sense of dispossession. The sentiment is akin to that of looking at the cashbox-skyline of present-day Chicago full of modern skyscrapers, a city that chose to make itself new, rather than restore itself, after the devastating fire. There is a faint feeling that something else was once there and that this something else is gone, but that the present landscape betrays few signs of what had been wiped out; as a result, it leaves little to be mourned for, since no history of loss is found there. Likewise, not having an old house with a cellar and attic or not knowing a person well enough to have rights to grieve evokes only a dull, attenuated, half-conscious sorrow that detaches itself from the missing object, prolonging its melancholy without closure. It is a specific type of denied grief, in which the experience of loss is itself questioned or questionable.

What these examples tell us is that loss is amorphous, as well as pervasive. Whether it is a wasted hour in the waiting room, the separation from the mother's womb in the process of birth, or the death of a distant other we only read about in the news, some experiences of loss barely register in our mind. There are also kinds of dispossessions that are placed outside or at the margins of the cultural norms of grief, such as pet loss, early stage miscarriage, or prolonged bereavement; these losses have the tendency to be left without proper recognition, as they are seen to be less consequential by society even as they afflict the mourner. Even significant, well-acknowledged losses fade over time; remembrances of past deaths and devastations, as compelling as they once may have been, grow distant as time passes. Recent disasters can quickly turn into the past, divorced from present immediacy and overwritten by other, newer calamities. Whether through repression, irrecognition, acceptance, resilience, or passage of time, the feelings of dispossession dissipate and retreat into the background in the hurry-scurry of the fast-paced modernity. Still, they continue to haunt, in the absence or obfuscation of actual object-loss, like water turning into invisible vapor but sustaining its presence in the airy void.

DEFINING ELEGY: CONVENTIONAL ELEGY, MODERN ELEGY, AND THE ELEGIAC POETRY OF LOST LOSS

This book begins as a study of elegiac poetry because it is a genre that has been closely entwined with the theorization of loss. One of the challenges that any study of elegiac poetry encounters is the question of definition: what is "elegy"? What constitutes an elegy is an unsettled matter. *The Oxford Handbook of the Elegy*, the landmark compendium on elegy studies edited by Karen Weisman, proclaims that her book "emphatically does not seek to establish a simple definitive definition" of the genre, presumably because it is difficult and perhaps even fruitless to try to codify it.[8] There are formal definitions: as formulated in T. V. F. Brogan's *The New Princeton Handbook of Poetic Terms*, elegy has traditionally been read as a poem of mourning that "frequently includes a movement from expressed sorrow toward consolation."[9] Mark Strand and Eavan Boland's *The Making of a Poem* defines the genre as expressive of a lament in which the poem "mourns for a dead person, lists his or her virtues, and seeks consolation beyond the momentary event," and is "not associated with any required pattern or cadence or repetition."[10] Generally, conventional definitions of the genre point to its lamentative character and its movement toward consolation as the common denominators.

At its historical origin, the word "elegy" comes from Ancient Greek, and the word and its derivatives were used in two senses: in one, the singing of a sad and mournful song; and in the other, the rhythm of two particular verses combined, referred to as the elegiac couplet.[11] Some of the original impulses of the genre have atrophied; for instance, the genre is no longer associated with any particular formal characteristics, such as the elegiac couplet that defined the genre through antiquity. Other characteristics have survived, even if their incarnations are variegated by eras and regions. Few scholars would dispute that elegy expresses lament, even if the poets of different periods have invariably complicated its formulaic movement from grief to consolation. Self-reflexivity has been a staple of the genre since its conception, whether it manifests as Petrarchan self-reflection, Victorian skepticism, or postmodern metacognition. So is the custom of questioning, such as is seen in the complaints of Lamentations and Psalms or in the self-scrutiny of E. A. Robinson's "Richard Cory." Beyond the few commonalities, however, expansiveness and fluidity define the genre: the name has encompassed variations that range from the classical love elegy of Ovid, the pastoral elegy of Spenser and Sidney, the war elegy of Wilfred Owen, to the hospital elegy of Thom Gunn.

The elasticity of the genre owes in part to the sometimes-deliberate and sometimes-unintentional confusion between the genre and the mode: according to John Frow's classification, the elegy as a genre is "specifically concerned with the act of mourning a particular person," whereas the elegiac mode "is a matter of view—of reflective melancholy or sadness."[12] Since the early romantic period, elegy has come to lean more toward a mode of approaching reality,[13] even as it has continued to retain its legacy as a genre that involves a lament for a particular individual, to be salvified by a move toward consolation. What we refer to as elegy today is an untidy mixture of the "genre" and the "mode"; this oscillation between the two is at the root of the malleability of the present-day conception of elegy.

Precisely when the prototype of the conventional elegy in the English language started to coalesce is open to debate. One signpost, however, is the funeral elegy in early modern Britain. The elegy of this period is notable for its integration of three concerns—lament, praise, and consolation—which vivifies the complexities and paradoxes involved in making art out of mortality, particularly around the notion of consolation.[14] The scholarship on traditional elegiac poetry has codified the consolatory mechanism: namely, a normative mourning that successfully concludes with a philosophical consolation as its destination, often as a result of finding the elegy itself to be a sign that offsets the loss of the beloved.[15] This idea of substitutive restitution often anchors the consolatory philosophy of conventional elegies.[16] Since Jahan Ramazani's *Poetry of Mourning*, however, modern elegies have frequently been studied against this paradigm; modern elegies tend to enact failed or "melancholic" mourning, which subverts the therapeutic efficacy of the compensatory mechanism. If the aspiration toward the compensatory consolation of normative mourning defines the classical elegy, melancholic mourning that eschews compensation has become a key feature of the modern elegy,[17] even as there continues to be resistance toward this view of the genre.[18] While the question of what makes elegy conventional or modern remains far from being settled, one useful distinction remains that the former leans toward instrumental grieving—which often involves converting one's feelings into physical or cognitive activities, with the aim to "get over" one's grief—while the latter aligns more with intuitive grieving—the adaptive strategies of which gravitate more toward retaining and sharing one's feelings, with a recognition that grief work is an ongoing, valuable process.[19]

This development follows a wave of reinterpretations of Sigmund Freud's work, including his own concession in a 1929 letter to his friend Ludwig Binswanger, acknowledging that there really are no substitutes for the lost object:

> Although we know that after such a loss the acute state of mourning will subside, we also know we shall remain inconsolable and never find a substitute. No matter what may fill the gap . . . it nevertheless remains something else. And actually this is how it should be. It is the only way of perpetuating that love which we do not want to relinquish.[20]

As exemplified in this letter, Freud himself began to question both the possibility and desirability of the "successful" severing of ties with the lost beloved.[21] Healthy skepticism accompanies claims of compensatory restitution as grounds for consolation.[22] These reappraisals of Freud's earlier work have prompted recent elegy scholarship to regard mourning through the lens of new critiques of "Mourning and Melancholia," particularly in terms of the ethics of the possibility and desirability of freeing oneself emotionally from the lost beloved.

Since the 1990s when Ramazani's *Poetry of Mourning* introduced the concept of anti-elegy,[23] modern elegies have frequently been associated with eruptive violence, emotional surges, and rejection of consolation. Some of the famed examples include John Berryman's radical denunciation of his dead father in "Dream Song #384"—"I spit upon this dreadful banker's grave / who shot his heart out in a Florida dawn" (7–8)[24]—and Sylvia Plath's no less bitter rant on her dead father in "Daddy," which concludes, "Daddy, daddy, you bastard, I'm through" (80).[25] Whether as a counter-narrative or as resistance against the classical compensatory consolation paradigm, modern elegies have been defined and studied through the lens of the poetics of melancholia; as Diana Fuss observes in *Dying Modern*, melancholia "has become the new consolation."[26] These critiques suggest that melancholia has its own consolatory potentials, whether as a type of respect, loyalty, or ethical stance toward the deceased.

The project of this book, however, revolves around a study of more subdued, veiled dejection of what may be described as dysthymia, rather than traumatic major melancholia that represents earlier studies of the modern elegy. Clinically speaking, dysthymia falls under the umbrella of chronic depression, and it is distinguished from acute or major depression by such characteristics as low-grade chronicity, insidious onset with unclear origin, and persistence and intermittence.[27] In the protraction of dysthymia, afflictions express themselves so faintly that they elude linguistic and cognitive apparatuses; their sources become untraceable, and efforts at closure beset with resistance. The dysthymia of inarticulate losses differentiates itself from the melancholia of expressly lamentative elegies. Poems of dysthymia do not so much attack the loss-consolation paradigm of traditional elegies but rather present a divergent paradigm in which feelings of dispossession continue to haunt in the absence, obfuscation, or denial of object-loss. The faint echoes of privation in these poems cannot easily be exorcised because they are masked and made inaccessible. What poems of dysthymia reveal to us is that we do not necessarily hold onto losses as adamantly as we are thought to do, but we also do not always accept or resolve them, either; sometimes, they simply fade, become inaccessible except as traces, and remain in the background of our psychic landscape, unsettling but unknown.

Dysthymia is an apt emblem of lost loss: both lend themselves to a mood that is faint, irresolute, persistent, and difficult to access. Modern and contemporary elegiac poetry is not merely represented by melancholic poetry of loss;

it also contains dysthymic poetry of lost loss. In this sense, the contribution of this book is envisioned to be two-pronged: first, to present and explicate this notion of "lost loss" by exploring the ambiguous despondency of modern-day elegiac poetry; second, to delineate how this dysthymic diffusion of loss functions to create various emotional effects, which include creation of fictive cognitions, tenacity of irresolution, emergence of a desire to "un-lose" distanced loss, accidental forging of empathy with strangers, and effacement and swifter leaving-behind of catastrophic losses, even while the sense of diffusion prolongs the feeling of disconsolation. Insofar as obliqueness becomes the trademark of the poems discussed in this book, they move away from the previous interpretive paradigms that have been dominant in the studies of elegiac poetry, such as compensatory consolation, anti-elegiac resistance, or community-making. Poetry of lost loss enacts the elegiacs of equivocation.

In addition to this focus on equivocation, this book also critically diverges from previous elegy studies, in that it adopts an even more liberal approach to the terms "elegy" and "elegiac poetry." Many of the poems examined in this book are at the periphery of the genre and may not count as "elegies" in the strictest sense of the word, even if, as Andy Orchard suggests, "the particular identification of individual poems as 'elegies'" is often "a tendentious business."[28] John B. Vickery's *The Modern Elegiac Temper* comments on the instructiveness of the broadening focus of the modern elegy; it deals with many types of losses, including lives, loves, families, marriages, civilizations, cultures, philosophies, and selves.[29] Not all elegies respond to the death of a specific individual or group of individuals, and there is value in uncovering elements of elegy in poems that are not conventionally regarded as such.

The history of elegiac poetry is one of progressive admission; it is the inclusion of the lived experiences of various forms and stages of privation that had been left out and left behind by previous, more restrictive definitions. In *American Citizenship: The Quest for Inclusion*, Judith Shklar suggests that American politics has provided a forum for a quest for inclusion, a process through which out-groups have, with varying degrees of success, pressed their case for full and equal citizenship.[30] A similar mechanism of inclusion inheres in elegiac poetry, for it is a genre that traditionally records and retains lives and memories that can otherwise be disremembered: various forms of excluded losses demand admission to the social and cognitive mourning process. For my purpose, the use of the term "elegiac poetry" encompasses poems that are plaintive, mournful, reminiscent, or expressive of some type of sense of loss—in particular, a type that contains a degree of ambiguity within itself—but irrespective of the presence or absence of actual death, consolatory rhetoric, communal mourning, or other defining features associated with many of the previous definitions of elegy.

Loss is an elastic and ambivalent concept. For some readers, the inexistence of the cellars and attics in the Tussman poem may not count as "loss." Some may argue that it is not a loss at all, since you cannot "lose" what you do not have. And others may argue that it is more absence than loss.[31] But this restrictiveness—and its resultant exclusion—is what this study resists. In the Tussman poem, the sorrow is too palpable to disregard, and the word "absence" is inadequate to convey the fullest impact of the nonexistence of cellars and attics. Those enclaves full of ancestral goods could have existed had it not been for the Holocaust; they do exist for other people whose life histories are different from the speaker's; and the speaker can imagine a life with them—a life she might have had. The same applies to the Roethke poem; the death of a student we barely know could trigger a surge of grief, in the absence of any Catullian context, when we think of future possibilities that could have awaited her but are lost without having ever come close to realization. Imagination is an illusion, but merely to call it absence undersells the force of forged relational ties, which, while perhaps more tenuous than actually existent ones, nonetheless constitute a significant portion of our psychic landscape.

THEORIZATION OF LOSS AND LOST LOSS

The interventions of this project reflect the climate change in the study of loss since the last century. The general premise of this newer development is that concepts like absence and presence are not absolutes; there are many different shades and gradations of grief that remain questioned, unrecognized, unrecorded, or socially unaccepted. Advancement in theorization of loss, as seen in Freud's work of mourning theory, Elisabeth Kübler-Ross's model of the stages of grief, or George Bonanno's four trajectories of grief, has informed our understanding of disasters and tragedies in the twentieth century and into the twenty-first century. As the next stage of this development, what is becoming imperative now is the theorization of lost loss.

Grief resulting from a loss that cannot be acknowledged, socially validated, or publicly mourned can be characterized as disenfranchised.[32] The disenfranchising of grief can occur in a number of ways. Sometimes, the loss is registered as significant on a personal scale but insignificant in terms of social norms, and this gap alienates the griever from the grieving process. Pet loss, for instance, had not gained citizenship until its psychological impact on pet owners became widely known in ways that legitimized the grief caused by it; the same principle applies to miscarriage, as well as bereavements that are seen to last longer than they should. In other scenarios, a sense of shame could inhibit the public validation of grief, a phenomenon observable in such instances as the AIDS crisis in the 1980s and the general silence of family members of those who commit suicide.³³ In addition to the disenfranchisement that occurs in personal tragedies that are placed outside of the social grieving norms, there are phenomena that leave us perplexed as to how we should grieve, or whether or not we can grieve. In *Precarious Life: the Powers of Mourning and Violence*, Judith Butler devises a concept of "ungrievable life" to discuss the precarity of refugees, immigrants, foreigners, and those who would be classified as the "other" and whose deaths have a tendency to be overlooked.³⁴ In *Ambiguous Loss: Learning to Live with Unresolved Grief*, Pauline Boss gives the name "ambiguous loss" to complications in relational disruptions, which are largely divided into two categories: psychologically present but physically absent loved ones, such as people who went missing while families wait in hopes that they might return someday; and physically present but psychologically absent loved ones, such as those suffering from Alzheimer's disease, dementia, and other types of personality deaths.³⁵ Studies like Butler's and Boss's indicate that ambiguity confounds the experience of mourning and coping, as the grievers are flummoxed by the fundamental question: what can qualify as loss? Can we properly lament when a loss is socially unacknowledged or unacceptable? And if something or someone may not technically be dead, is it appropriate to grieve, a process culturally normalized to be a response to death?

Multiple scholars—Joseph Jacobs in "The Dying of Death," Philippe Ariès in *The Hour of Our Death*, among others³⁶—have noted the phenomenon they call the "disappearance of death" in the modern era: namely, when people started fearing death in earnest at the advent of modernity, they stopped talking about it, for cultural anxieties about death "crossed the threshold into the unspeakable, the inexpressible."³⁷ Given the numerous representations of death in various media as well as continuous attention to death studies, the disappearance of death in modern society approaches the level of overstatement. At the time of this writing, the news of COVID-19 deaths reverberates throughout television and the Internet; many of us are being made aware of our own fragilities. Nonetheless, what these studies of disenfranchisement, ambiguity, and disappearance tell us is that there still remain many types of concealed loss. Lost loss is proposed as a term for previously little-understood experiences of under-acknowledged loss, which affect us unaware; in this condition, the presence, recognition, or legitimacy of dispossession becomes the object of query. Proximate theories such as ambiguous loss and disenfranchised grief have been gaining citizenship in related fields; this book delves into those concepts, as well as other varieties, including imaginary, distant, and phantom loss.

In theorizing lost loss, I reference several key texts and their concepts, and one of those is Jacques Derrida's formulation of proleptic loss, which he proposes in *The Work of Mourning*, a 2001 collection of his writings on dead writers. This collection encompasses materials ranging from letters of condolence addressed to family members to eulogies read at the grave site, words of tribute first published in newspapers in the hours immediately following a death, and memorial essays read at colloquia a few or even many months after the death. In those texts, Derrida suggests that any relational ties, whether with the beloved, friends, acquaintances, or imaginary beings, contain within them an anticipation of their loss. Derrida explains this idea through his use of the plural form to address the "deaths" of Roland Barthes:

> How to reconcile this plural? . . . I can scarcely bear the apparition of a title in this place. The proper name would have sufficed, for it alone and by itself says death, all deaths in one. It says death even while the bearer of it is still living. While so many codes and rites work to take away this privilege, because it is so terrifying, the proper name alone and by itself forcefully declares the unique disappearance of the unique—I mean the singularity of an unqualifiable death (and this word, "unqualifiable" already resonates like a quotation from one of Roland Barthes's texts I will reread later). Death inscribes itself right in the name.[38]

As Derrida's editors comment, we "prepare for the death of a friend; we anticipate it; we see ourselves already as survivors, or as having already survived. To have a friend, to call him or her by name and to be called by him or her, is already to know that one of the two of you will go first, that one will be left to speak the name of the other in the other's absence."[39] Loss is inscribed at the start of the relationship, right at the moment of learning each other's name. Ruptures are anticipated; one's deaths are performed continually at each encounter, all the way up to the final death: hence, the plurality. A deeper implication of this phenomenon lies in the following phrase: "so many codes and rites work to take away this privilege [of the living deaths of the name-bearer], because it is so terrifying."[40] Derrida suggests that the screening mechanism of our mind obstructs our recognition of the proleptic dispossession inscribed in the name of the name-bearer. This loss is lost in the interference by the "codes and rites" that obfuscate the ghastly anticipation. This concealed privation barely registers in our mind, but it nonetheless profoundly affects our interpersonal relationships.

Ideas like Derrida's anticipatory grief are more familiar and intuitive, and as such, they lay the groundwork for other, more subterranean forms of elusive loss. The theoretical formulation of lost loss is anchored by concepts from Nicholas Abraham and Maria Torok's *The Shell and the Kernel*. This post-Freudian psychoanalytic text has been influential in many fields, but its theories of the phantom, secrets, and cryptic mourning prove to be particularly instructive in understanding the dysthymia of unrecognized dispossession. Like nonexistent cellars and attics, phantasmal hauntings symbolize the imagined trace of inaccessible loss.

In their refashioning of Freudian psychoanalysis, Abraham and Torok designate as "secret" a type of trauma that is entombed and consigned to internal silence, albeit unwittingly, by the sufferers themselves.[41] The secret is an intrapsychic enclave of denied or excluded reality, which triggers melancholia, failed introjections, and other similar malaises. There are two ways in which this theory of the secret becomes instructive for the present project: first, it provides a model of reading the mood of the poems as an expressive trace of the repressed reality, a reminder of the secret, or what Abraham and Torok refer to as the "phantom"; and second, it formulates a model of reading the poetic language, such as that of allegory and other interpretive expressions, as a kind of cryptonymy that reveals the presence of shut-away objects through its layers of obfuscation and equivocation. Equivocation becomes itself a type of communication. This denied reality is produced not only in cases of traumatic grief but also in cases of subdued, disenfranchised sorrow, where cognition lags behind the emotional impact. Given the role of consciousness as a mechanism to protect us against stimuli by screening and blocking out their excess,[42] a blander dysthymia could well signal the presence of excluded psychic enclaves.[43] Abraham and Torok's theory of the phantom affords us with one more apparatus through which to create a tentative shape for the vague expression of lost loss.

Using this theory of the secret, one may read elegiac poetry for symptoms of the phantom. According to Abraham and Torok, the phantom is a type of sealed-off sorrow in inaccessible mental graves. It is a wraith coming out of the psychic crypt, which reveals itself through linguistic unintelligibility or concealment, often entailing inventions of particular forms of obfuscation, which they call "cryptonymy."[44] Abraham and Torok explicate the concept of phantom as follows:

> [A phantom] points to. . . a memory. . . buried *without legal burial place*. The memory is of an idyll, experienced with a valued object and yet for some reason unspeakable . . . . Between the idyllic moment and its subsequent forgetting . . . , there was the metapsychological traumatism of a loss . . . . This leads to the establishment of a sealed-off psychic place, a crypt in the ego. Created by a self-governing mechanism we call *inclusion*, the crypt . . . is a form of anti-introjection, a mechanism whereby the assimilation of both the illegitimate idyll and its loss is precluded.[45]

Here, the loss is revealed to have two layers: initially, the unspeakable memory is turned into an idealized, pastoral context of "idyll"; then it is sealed off outside of the "legal burial ground." The "illegitimate idyll" is orphaned, along with the memory it symbolizes; it gets secluded in a psychic "crypt" that had been created by the mechanism of repression. In effect, memories are forgotten twice. In the first oblivion, the idyll is forgotten. In the second occurrence, the fact of forgetting is itself forgotten. Because it cannot be integrated into our conscious memory, the unassimilated, isolated memory becomes a phantom, which returns to haunt us upon instigation.

As Abraham and Torok acknowledge, the phantom is a human invention, a necessary contrivance intended to help us conceptualize what eludes conceptualization:

> It is a fact that the "phantom," whatever its form, is nothing but an invention of the living. Yes, an invention in the sense that the phantom is meant to objectify, even if under the guise of individual or collective hallucinations, the gap produced in us by the concealment of some part of a love object's life. The phantom is therefore also a metapsychological fact: what haunts are not the dead, but the gaps left within us by the secrets of others.[46]

The phantom is not so much the dead themselves but rather the "gaps" left within us; the dead are not actually coming back from the grave to haunt us, but the gaps left in our cognitive reality after a loss do. It is an expressive medium of the left-behind memory.

The fundamental premise in this mode of reading poetry is that poetry is a way of giving voice to something that does not yet have a voice. In the case of the dysthymic strain of elegiac poetry, what it gives voice to is the sealed-off enclave of privation: things that are left out, shut away, or unnoticed in one's process of readjusting or reorganizing one's self and reality in the aftermath of disturbances to those. In literary works, this loss of loss manifests itself in various incarnations: as a kind of equivocation; as a screen for or obfuscation of some unsayable dispossession; in a mode of hide-and-seek, hiding to reveal; as expressions of vague melancholy.

LOST LOSS IN THE AMERICAN AND BRITISH ELEGIAC TRADITIONS

In order to discern the tentative expressions of lost loss, readers are tasked with the labor of sorting through the strata of their obfuscation. For this endeavor, it proves instructive to examine a few premodern examples, both to uncover the lost loss that often lurks beneath explicit, recognizable ones and to understand the modern forms through cognition of difference.[47] Loss is a transhistorical phenomenon; so is lost loss, its unacknowledged twin. The contention of this book is not so much that lost loss is a strictly modern phenomenon, but rather that it has become more visible and hence can be more fruitfully studied in the current era. The newer developments in the theorization of loss, such as the aforementioned *The Shell and the Kernel*, help provide partial answers to the questions raised by modern and contemporary elegiac poetry.

Elegy is by its nature a veiled speech, for the fact that, regardless of whether it is traditional, modern, or experimental, it often says what it does not mean; when the voice of Ben Jonson's speaker in "On My First Son" displays the deepest sadness, it is in his paralipsis, in the denial of his dejection: "For why / Will man lament the state he should envy?" (5–6).[48] It is reductive to say that elegy navigates the questions of life and death, one of the most fundamental opposites; as W. David Shaw claims in *Elegy & Paradox*, to "commemorate death rightly is also to magnify the life and love that make death terrible."[49] As a genre entwined with the task of expressing or attempting to reconcile antitheses—whether it is a wish for some form of revival or life in death, or a discovery of consolation in times of disconsolation—elegy constructs various forms of fiction that are rife with contradictory elements, triggering cognitive dissonance.

Despite the rise of what scholars call "anti-elegies" in the modern era, the characteristics of melancholic or intuitive grieving, such as the eulogy-denial impulse, self-reflexivity, questioning, and indeterminacy, are deep-rooted in the elegiac tradition. These traits are observable in many major elegies prior to the twentieth and twenty-first centuries. The infectiously popular landmark poem of the Graveyard School, Thomas Gray's "Elegy Written in a Country Churchyard" has been received as a paradigmatic pastoral elegy. Gray's poem, however, does not mourn for a specific, singular individual, and its lamentation derives primarily from his own imagination: the unknown lives, buried in unmarked graves, of rustic souls who Gray fancies might have been as courageous as John Hampden or as brilliant as John Milton; and the anticipation of his own death, the imagining of what people might say about him after he dies. The feeble melancholy of the closing lines—"No farther seek his merits to disclose, / Or draw his frailties from . . . / The bosom of his Father and his God" (125–26, 128)—is diffusive;[50] its failure to comfort leads readers to search elsewhere for a consolatory philosophy, whether it is "in the tears of things" or in the reader's recognition of "the endurance of the English poetic canon."[51]

Likewise, the American tradition also espouses many instances of inquiries into the complexities of loss. Anne Bradstreet's "Here Follows Some Verses upon the Burning of Our House, July 10, 1666. Copied out of a Loose Paper" is about the trauma of losing one's home and property. The experience is, however, not a mere material dispossession: along with the house and the goods, the memories of the past as well as the prospects of the future—guest visits, dinner conversations, and the comfort of just sitting and lying in the home environs—too are taken away. Lines 17–18—"It was His own, it was not mine, / Far be it that I should repine" (17–18)—sound, on the surface, like a quintessential Puritan consolation, the rejection of earthly fulfillment as a step toward a hope for eternal bliss.[52] Material possessions belong to God, not humans, and therefore, one has no grounds to grieve or fret; one's "hope and treasure lies above" (54). Beneath this stoicism, however, lies self-reflexive uncertainty: how could one lose what one does not have—was this experience really a loss? For Puritans, excessive grieving for the departed was tantamount to doubting Christ's ability to save them.[53] When grief itself becomes a sin, an elaborate doctrine—such as exemplified by what English Puritan Richard Sibbes calls "spiritual mourning"—is, by necessity, tapestried to obscure the delegitimized feeling of loss. In this reading, the burned house becomes less an embodiment of a lost object than a reminder of the cognitive manacles that compel an unauthorized burial of unsanctioned emotions.

This sense of instability around the idea of loss abounds in the elegiac canon, manifesting itself in various forms. In William Cullen Bryant's "Thanatopsis," it is the diminution of one's own selfhood that attenuates the melancholic mood: after a person is dead, all other people, happy ones or unhappy ones, will simply trudge onward with their lives as they always have. It is an irony that Bryant describes the goal of people's lives as an illusory "phantom" (64).[54] The somber dejection of the poem stems from the lyric-speaker's immersion in proleptic, imaginary loss: everyone is a ghost, living his or her own death. In both "O Captain! My Captain!" and "When Lilacs Last in the Dooryard Bloom'd"—elegies occasioned by the death of Abraham Lincoln—Walt Whitman leaves Lincoln unnamed; if the readers did not know about Lincoln, they would glean few details about him from these poems. On the one hand, this namelessness reflects the elegiac tradition of the time; after the nineteenth century, the elegy's representations of the dead and mourners have generally moved away from the categorical and universal to the intimate and particular.[55] On the other hand, the anonymity of the deceased anchors the sublimatory absorption of the individual into the universal; its effect is similar to the sanitization of obituaries of disaster victims. One recalls Nancy Miller's disbelief at the homogenous narrative in the portraits of lives lost in 9/11 from which "all traces of unhappiness were banished";[56] Lincoln becomes a symbolic vessel of the national tragedy, devoid of personality other than as a captain or as a fallen star. At the same time, the hypervisibility of a singular loss often dwarfs the numerous other deaths of less-known people: many of those in attendance as Lincoln's coffin passes through the lanes and streets—"crape-veil'd women" and "the silent sea of faces and the unbared heads" (6.4, 6)—must have lost their loved ones as well,⁵⁷ but those losses are subsumed into the tragic death of the president, like the brilliance of the lodestar obscuring the lesser stars around it. This indeterminacy complicates one's cognition of grief.

Three more canonical works, in particular, deserve a sustained analysis of the lurking shadows of lost loss in elegies before the twentieth century: John Milton's "Lycidas," William Wordsworth's "Peele Castle" elegy, and Emily Dickinson's "The missing All, prevented Me." Milton's "Lycidas" is a pastoral elegy that has been critically regarded as the quintessence of its tradition: a memorialization of a loved one, through a pastoral cycle of death and regeneration, drawing from the literary heritages that date back to Theocritus. The elements of the conventional elegy, such as the theological complaints of "How can it be?" and the formulaic movement from lament, praise, to consolation, are also represented in it. Explicit diatribes like the bitter invective against nature that "slits the thin-spun life" (75) had, by Milton's time, become a part of elegiac convention, albeit as moments of doubts that the mourner must overcome in his or her progress toward a conclusive, triumphant consolation.

In this context, "Lycidas" reveals glimpses of its anti-commemorative skepticism, even in a supposedly consolatory passage:

Bring the rathe primrose that forsaken dies . . .
And every flower that sad embroidery wears:
Bid amaranthus all his beauty shed,
And daffadillies fill their cups with tears,
To strew the laureate hearse where Lycid lies.
For so to interpose a little ease,
Let our frail thoughts dally with false surmise.   (142, 148–53)⁵⁸

This depiction of the flowery rewards of consolation for Lycidas remains irresolute, undercutting nature's salve. The fragility of the "rathe primrose that forsaken dies" refers primarily to the preciousness of early primrose—in economics, the rarity of an object increases its value—but hints, secondarily, at the frailty of consolation it symbolizes. And while the undying, unfading "amaranthus" shedding "his beauty" as a reward for Lycidas feels like an ultimate sacrifice that attests to Lycidas's worthiness, one need not be particularly perverse to detect a certain ominous tone in this dying of an immortal flower. The poetic technique here is similar to a photographic technique of semi-silhouette backlight: a half-negative framing that adumbrates the object and adds, through the shadowy contrast, a sense of depth to the portraiture.

In addition to the descriptive ambivalence of this passage, line 153 reminds the readers that this scene of consolation is based on "false surmise"; by doing so, the poem highlights the dejection it wants to mask. Since Lycidas's body has been lost to the sea and is not here to receive the floral tributes, the scene simultaneously becomes an intimation of the loss of the evidence of loss: a double-loss that parallels the inexistence of cellars and attics in the Tussman poem. Milton's choice of the verb "dally"—in favor of other more comforting verbs like "embrace" or "trust"—further underscores his ambivalence over this consolation. The phrase "false surmise" anticipates William Wordsworth's *Essays upon Epitaphs* and its premise that epitaphic writing is primarily "tender fiction."[59] The poem, in other words, is convincing in its lack of conviction. It reveals that, beneath the false solace, there are many traces of losses that the elegy cannot retrieve or salvage, which are metonymically represented by the unreturned body of Lycidas, the idealized figure of Milton's deceased friend, Edward King.

Another instance of canonical elegies that exhibit elegiac dissonance is William Wordsworth's "Elegiac Stanzas, suggested by a picture of Peele Castle, in a storm, painted by Sir George Beaumont." "Elegiac Stanzas" was, as the full title of the poem indicates, inspired by George Beaumont's painting, and is known to be an elegy for John Wordsworth, Wordsworth's brother who was the captain of the ship when he died in a shipwreck. Commonly referred to as the "Peele Castle" elegy, this Wordsworth poem places itself in the genealogy of elegies where the identity of the person who occasions the poem is suppressed—an elegiac tradition that has been in conflict with its function as a remembrance of the deceased. Like the "Lines" of Tintern Abbey, "Elegiac Stanzas" is an opaque generic title that offers little insight into its subject. That the poem is an ekphrasis creates an additional layer of indirection between the poem and the object of its portraiture. A significant portion of the poem focuses on the description of the painting and remembrance of the castle, near which Wordsworth lived for four summer weeks.

The Peele Castle elegy refers to John Wordsworth only once. That sole reference occurs as an object pronoun "Him" in line 42,[60] in a stark contrast to Wordsworth's friend and the painter of the picture, Sir George Beaumont, who is mentioned by name both in the title and in line 41 of the poem; without knowledge of the Wordsworth biography, one would be hard-pressed to discern, from the poem itself, that the poem is about John Wordsworth.[61] It is also notable that the painting itself leaves out most human traces except for a few brushstrokes that one almost needs a magnifying glass to see. In fact, the name of George Beaumont, when placed side by side with the suppression of John Wordsworth, adumbrates the unspecified and absented loss, evoking a feeling of discomfort that something should be there in a place where nothing is.

Plausibly because of this reticence, there is considerable critical disagreement over precisely what the Peele Castle elegy mourns. For many years, the accepted view was that what has been lost is Wordsworth's faith in Nature.[62] Geoffrey Hartman, however, argues that the loss was "definitely not his faith in nature" but rather a "capacity for generous error and noble illusion."[63] In Marjorie Levinson's view, "the subject of Wordsworth's lament is neither John Wordsworth nor a Nature experienced as a constant and nurturing . . . [nor] his former 'capacity for generous error and noble illusion.' The subject of this elegy—the loss deplored—is that binary apparatus whereby Mind redeems itself," which is to say, Napoleon and the hope and promise he had inspired.[64] Other critics argue that the loss represented in "Elegiac Stanzas" is the collection of all prior losses, which include the death of John, the deaths of Wordsworth's parents, the experience of being orphaned, and the separation from Dorothy, among others.[65]

Critical proliferations occur to fill the void of inconclusion. In *Ruins and Empire*, Laurence Goldstein investigates Wordsworth's fascination with "monumental 'Piles' in country areas," which, like epitaphs, are "symbolic structures which bind together past and present, death and life."[66] In the Peele Castle elegy, the castle is the epitaph. As a structure that binds together binaries like past and present, death and life, an epitaph represents a liminal space, which, because it resists facile comprehension, opens itself up to interpretations. Epitaphs, therefore, become a site of transference for readers with their own thoughts and preoccupations. Life coaches often tell us, "life is what you make of it"; in elegy studies, one might say, "death is what you make of it," for the dead has no mouth to speak back to us. There is ample biographical evidence that there were various newspaper and pamphlet accounts offering inconsistent and even inaccurate reports of the shipwreck that "tended to throw discredit on [John Wordsworth's] conduct and personal firmness,"[67] and that those aspersions prompted Wordsworth to write many letters to various people seeking information and defending his brother's behavior.[68] In the silence of death, there are no truths to be uncovered, as the dead becomes a manipulatable object, subjected to projections and transferences of the living who take the liberty to become its mouthpiece. In death, there are only interpretations.

The castle—a ruin that is a silent receptacle of transferred emotions and thoughts—becomes an appropriate emblem of the dead John Wordsworth, for whom there was little verifiable evidence of his last actions, whose body was never recovered, and who became a socially unmentionable figure, having suffered the dishonor of causing a shipwreck and inflicting tremendous financial damage to cargo owners. In "Captain John Wordsworth's Death at Sea," Richard Matlak points out that there is a discrepancy between Beaumont's representation of the sinking vessel and that of the actual event, which transforms accident and human frailty into destiny.[69] That has led to a view that the Peele Castle elegy functions as a means of historical denial.[70] But the real loss that occurs in this circumstance is the interpretive erasure of the actual person of John Wordsworth, compounded by the oblivion that visits society in due time.

In some cultures, people are said to die twice. The first time, they physically die, and the second time, they "die" as people forget about the dead. Total erasures are enacted when memories of the dead are no longer, and Shakespearean lines like "So long as men can breathe, or eyes can see, / So long lives this, and this gives life to thee" give voice to this anxiety,[71] for the flip side of this implication is that once readers are gone, the objects of commemoration also lose their afterlife. The Peele Castle elegy was written one whole year after the shipwreck. In one year's time, the incident would suffer multiple deaths: physical death, interpretive annihilation, and death through oblivion. The accident would be half-forgotten by many of the writers of newspapers and pamphlets who had assailed the character of John Wordsworth; it might even be outside of Wordsworth's daily thoughts. Like the way the loss of the passengers on the boat is expunged from the painting, the disappearance of his brother would begin to feel hollow to Wordsworth. In this sense, the painting of a landscape with an almost empty boat and uninhabited castle becomes a congruous vehicle that captures the tenor of John Wordsworth's life after death: the Peele Castle elegy is an allegory of second death.

The poems discussed so far all epitomize various aspects of lost loss: consolatory fiction and its dilution of privation in "Lycidas"; the irresolute melancholy of unsanctioned grief in "Here Follows Some Verses"; the loss of unknown lives in "Elegy Written in a Country Churchyard"; a story of "second death" in "Elegiac Stanzas"; the deprivation of an opportunity to get to know a person in "Elegy for Jane"; the inexistence of the mementos of ancestral deaths in "Cellars and Attics"; and so on. Emily Dickinson's "The missing All, prevented Me" concludes this catalog:

The missing All, prevented Me
From missing minor Things.
If nothing larger than a World's
Departure from a Hinge
Or Sun's Extinction, be observed
'Twas not so large that I
Could lift my Forehead from my work
For Curiosity.   (1–8)[72]

The most common reading of this poem is that it expresses Dickinson's puritanical concentration on her work. The speaker is so focused that not even the disappearance of species or the destruction of the world would tempt her to look up from her desk. In one's tunnel vision, one becomes oblivious to the loss of peripheral things.

Recent scholarship on Dickinson historicizes pain as the predicament and signature topic of nineteenth-century women poets and explores how Dickinson's poetry represents "the nineteenth-century poetics of misery, or lyric sentimentalism";[73] in this view, Dickinson herself becomes the "missing all," a historical person whose individuality has been tragically erased in the course of its critical appropriations.[74] The condition of "The missing All, prevented Me" becomes an effigy of lost loss: an all-encompassing sense of hollowing that consumes and overshadows individual instances of loss. When one is entrenched in the experience of calamitous loss, all other losses that are seen to be minor compared to that catastrophe are absorbed into it, and what is left of them consolidates into a vague feeling of privation; when a tsunami washes away one's entire house, it becomes too taxing to enumerate and catalog all of the lost items. When smaller aggressions chipping away at one's emotional health accumulate to the point of general exhaustion, it becomes harder to remember specific grievances.

The purpose of these examinations of older elegiac poems is to demonstrate that poetry of lost loss resides on the underside of poetry of loss. While I identify modern and contemporary periods as the most fertile ground for the study of unrecognized loss, it does not mean that poetry of previous periods is devoid of it. Elegiac poetry has historically betrayed the ambivalence between an adherence to and skepticism of the belief in substitutive consolation. Elegy is a genre beset with contradictory elements, such as one's professed attachment to the deceased and eventual, necessary detachment from it, or one's desire for consolation and one's susceptibility to disconsolation. Canonical elegies contain within them heterogeneity and resistance to oppressive normalization just as the modern counterpart does; their embedded countertexts not only anticipate the modern elegy but also constitute a resource on which modern elegists draw.[75] The main difference between the older elegies and the modern ones, then, is not the absence of effaced loss or elegiac skepticism in the former, but rather the degree to which the evidence of those—namely, the deployment of fictive narratives, cognitive dissonance triggered by them, the dysthymic mood, or the cognition of the amorphousness of loss—is foregrounded. When applied to modern and contemporary elegiac poetry, the theory of lost loss helps elucidate the sense of unexplainable melancholy that constitutes a portion of the postmodern sensibility. Otherwise, the argument of this book remains both historical and transhistorical.

CHAPTERS

Poems such as Dickinson's "The missing All, prevented Me," Wordsworth's "Peele Castle" elegy, Roethke's "Elegy for Jane," and Tussman's "Cellars and Attics" speak in the equivocal mode, which emerges prominently in the specific poets and poems studied in this book. I begin with Wallace Stevens in chapter 1, entitled "Wallace Stevens's Elegiac Mode: Creating Fictions of Loss." Chapter 1 analyzes Stevens's allegorical elegies as exemplification of lost loss, and concretizes the theoretical underpinning of this book. The theories that explore hidden and transient phenomena include Nicholas Abraham and Maria Torok's phantom, D. W. Winnicott's transitional object, and Jacques Derrida's proleptic loss. Stevens becomes an apt starting point for this study; his poems are elegiac, but he is not regarded as an elegist because of the relative scarcity of formal elegies in his oeuvre. Generally, scholars count only "The Owl in the Sarcophagus" and "To an Old Philosopher in Rome" as formal elegies.[76] This reputational gap is one of the signs that the poet engages with ambiguity of loss. Stevens's elegiac poetry does not often fit into the criterion of formal elegies because the losses that his poems speak of are often not explicit or specific. Beyond the eulogistic "To an Old Philosopher in Rome," the chapter highlights "The Owl in the Sarcophagus" in particular as a paradigmatic case of a poem that unveils the phenomenon of lost loss. The ensuing investigation of Stevens's later poems, including "Final Soliloquy of the Interior Paramour" and "As You Leave the Room," confirms and develops this core concept: when one senses emptiness in the void of lost objects, one is compelled to create fictive narratives of grief. Fakeries turn into the salve: even if one knows it to be fiction, sometimes it is all that one can hope to have, and that one must have.

As chapter 1 maps out the fundamental concepts, subsequent chapters examine various manifestations of them. Chapter 2, entitled "Sylvia Plath's Poems of 1963: Dysthymia and Subterranean Loss," examines Sylvia Plath's 1963 poems as works of ambivalent loss that simulate the mood of dysthymia, where no immediate loss is in sight and only the faint echoes of amorphous privation are detectable; in the discussion of lost loss, dysthymia and its quieter gloom prove to be a more appropriate insignia than the acute afflictions of major melancholia. Plath is similar to Stevens in that she is not considered to be a conventional elegist: Plath wrote few formal elegies—many of her poems that are classified as elegies are more apt to be called anti-elegies—but a large body of her work has been frequently characterized as elegiac. Whereas Plath's work has been extensively discussed through the lens of melancholia, I propose that her later poems are better conceived as being more dysthymic than melancholic. In particular, the chapter focuses on the poems of 1963. The poems of 1963 have variously been characterized as "cycle of death poems"[77] or "poems read as epitaphs,"[78] but unlike the eruptive violence of *Ariel* anti-elegies like "Daddy" and "Lady Lazarus," the quieter desolation of the 1963 poems offers verisimilitude of ambivalent grief, the origins of which have been disremembered. The effect is similar to that of what Pauline Boss refers to as "ambiguous loss," where, because of the indeterminacy of the loss, one feels uncertain how one should process or cope with one's sorrow. In this context, the chapter discusses the poems of 1963, alongside pre-1963 poems, including "Sheep in Fog," "The Munich Mannequins," "Edge," and "Parliament Hill Fields," as instances of poems portraying losses that are themselves absent or equivocated.

Chapter 3, entitled "Elizabeth Bishop's *Geography III*: Un-losing Lost Loss," explores poems from Elizabeth Bishop's *Geography III*, which portray how lost losses, as they are acknowledged and given shape, trigger one's desire to "un-lose" them. *Geography III* is Bishop's final collection of poetry before her death in 1979; along with precursors in *Questions of Travel*, Bishop's *Geography III* poems brim with feelings of subdued melancholy and grief that often betray few traces of identifiable origins, hidden beneath the illusion of neutrality.[79] "In the Waiting Room" salvages a sense of dispossession and subjective catastrophe that could have otherwise been lost to the child's irrecognition.[80] "Crusoe in England" details the chronicle of displacement and isolation, whereby the acknowledgment of past losses becomes the task of the present. "Poem" discusses a painting by a deceased great-uncle whom Bishop had never known: the painting becomes a symbolic embodiment of the great-uncle, who is related to but had not meaningfully existed for the poet. "Poem" describes how she comes to know this previously unknown great-uncle through the shared vision of the painted landscape—a process that facilitates the "un-losing" of the long-lost relative. Likewise, "The Moose," "The Night City," "The End of March," and other poems from the collection redeem the loss of things that Bishop would not have known about and would not have been able to record, if not for the newfound cognition of those privations. With the recent influx of materials from Bishop's life, ranging from letters, essays, to new biographies,[81] we have come to discover the biographical details that underlie the seemingly ambiguous melancholy of many of her poems. Between the suppression and uncovering of Bishop's life circumstances, one can more fruitfully study the *Geography III* poems as elegiac equivocations that prompt both the losing and un-losing of loss.

Building on the previous chapter's thesis that deaths of distant others could turn into lost losses if not for poetic efforts to record and restore them, chapter 4, entitled "Sharon Olds's *The Dead and the Living*: Distant Loss and Ethical Empathy," takes a social turn to study the "Public" section of part I of Sharon Olds's collection, *The Dead and the Living*. When it comes to elegies, Olds is better known for the book-length elegy about her father's cancer, *The Father*,[82] but the interest of this chapter is to delve into the question of how the deaths and sufferings of people whom we do not know well affect us—people to whom we are connected only through the news and photos, the out-group that is often excluded from our parochial concerns. The sequence of poems in the "Public" section of part I of *The Dead and the Living* is comprised of ekphrases based on photographs of mostly historical disasters and atrocities, often in remote or foreign locales; those include the Russian famine of 1921, the Armenian genocide in the early twentieth century, the Rhodesian Bush War, and the Tulsa race massacre. These poems depict the plights of people located beyond multiple barriers; the subjects are usually the temporal, geographical, or ethnic "other"—those who often fall into the category Judith Butler calls "ungrievable"—and they are doubly mediated through photography and poetry. Even though the public section of *The Dead and the Living* has garnered tepid reception as political poetry,[83] these poems reveal more insights when reexamined as poetry of empathy, rather than as poetry of social protest. In this enterprise of engaging with the distant other, Olds's *The Dead and the Living* becomes ideal because her poems project not so much the eyes of an activist in the mode of Carolyn Forché and Margaret Randall, but rather those of an ordinary person viewing the news or photos, removed from the targets of sympathy. Given that degrees of relational separation can dilute one's emotional response—because of the variability in people's sensitivities, one's grief can be socially sanctioned but can feel personally inauthentic, or vice versa—this chapter inquires what impact these distant losses have on average people with no specific relational ties beyond the humanistic level, and how one can ethically develop empathic responses to them, whereby one recognizes tragedies as they are but does not usurp or exploit them for one's own consumption.

Chapter 5, entitled "Post-9/11 Elegiac Poetry: The Unsaid," continues with the broader theme of distant loss, but in this chapter, it specifically relates to 9/11: a disaster that was globally witnessed but did not implicate all viewers directly and personally, the gap out of which the complication of grief was born. After the whole community is impacted by a catastrophe, two competing impulses customarily surface: a desire to chronicle the tragedy and a concomitant revulsion toward it. Many of the artistic responses to 9/11 elicited critical repudiations, some of which cited Theodor Adorno's famous dictum that there can be no poetry after Auschwitz. In the first half of the chapter, I observe how taboos—the unsaid and the unsayable—are formed in the midst of those two thrusts, and how, in this process, losses are diverted and made into inaccessible "lost loss." Some of the seminal "falling man" poems, such as Wisława Szymborska's "Photograph from September 11," have been criticized as being offensive, and yet even those leave some things out of the ekphrastic camera frame. In examining the process in which a definitive sorrow of collective mourning turns into undefined melancholy of suppressed grief, the chapter switches its focus in the second half to poems written a while after 9/11, in which the catastrophe is represented obliquely, rather than explicitly. A poem that was heralded as a welcome respite from the medusa enthrallment of 9/11, Louise Glück's "October" becomes the primary target of analysis, alongside other poems from her collection *Averno*. Glück's poems dissect the mechanism of equivocation, which gives voice to the afterimages of 9/11 while also effacing them at the same time.

EXIGENCIES

As a summation of the literary and theoretical discussions, the question of utmost import must be asked: why study lost loss? The impetus behind elegy studies is generally encapsulated by the inevitability of grief. Its project is to mourn and to console. It is to understand, explain, and contain the mystery of irrevocable parting; if death is unavoidable, all one can do is to try to tame it. "We need elegies," Countee Cullen writes in the closing line of a poem entitled "Threnody for a Brown Girl" published in 1925.[84] Cullen speaks in terms of need, because consolation is a necessity. This book does not entirely sidestep the discourse of healing and consolation, while acknowledging that reasonable people can be fatigued with the scholarly focus on traumatic grief or with the melancholic attachment to the deceased, however ethical or not.[85] The knowledge that is produced in this book, however, focuses on the complications of suppressed grief; those involve various forms of attenuated, subterranean, distant loss in which the experience of dispossession is itself an object of skepticism. This enterprise is hatched in response to the following questions: what does it mean to lose loss, how do literary responses to it differ from those of undeniable loss, and what effect does this condition have on us?

The ensuing chapters aim to answer these questions by exploring the psycho-literary implications of the poetry of lost loss: the poems studied in those chapters, ranging from Stevens's "The Owl in the Sarcophagus" to Louise Glück's "October," are case studies of elegiac poetry that add to the still as-yet nascent inquiry into the effects of denied dispossession. As an illustration of the imperative of these questions, I will end this introduction with a confession of their personal applicability and an attestation that this study has not only theoretical but also practical implications. To be personal in a scholarly work is to risk embarrassment, but to take that risk, I confess to growing up feeling that something was always missing in my life: a sentiment that I had lost something but that I did not know what it was. My upbringing was solidly middle class; my parents were a teacher and a housewife, and I was the second of three children. There were few visible signs of relative or absolute poverty, and no major mishaps had befallen us. The sentiment of personal displacement was no doubt partially stirred by the sense of fracture experienced in my childhood immigration to the United States—for many immigrants, the life before America often becomes an idyll that is dutifully buried and made inaccessible—but even that relocation came as a result of my father's desire to study in the United States, rather than out of any need to flee from oppression or crises. An analyst in me has produced several theories why I have been haunted by this anxiety of some unknown and unknowable loss—such as that my months-long hospitalization and separation from parents in my infancy, during which a large portion of the basis of human personality is said to be formed, may be responsible—but one hypothesis that I find myself coming back to is that practically all of my father's side of the family had died during or in the aftermath of World War II. I grew up with a full set of extended family on my mother's side, and only a few distant ones on my father's side. For much of my childhood, I did not know what that meant: war was merely a vague idea, and since I had never even seen any photographs of the deceased relatives, their deaths were more an abstraction than a real absence. In particular, two of my father's older brothers had, apparently, died of starvation on one of the southern islands to which the Japanese force had sent their soldiers with few rations or supplies. Most of those soldiers died of malnutrition, rather than in combat. Their remains were largely never recovered, and not much is known about what actually happened to them; there is scant possibility of ever knowing, given the dearth of evidentiary traces and the general lack of interest in the ungrievable World War II losses. The only thing that remains of them is that my father had taken parts of their names and put them together in my name. Their loss is inscribed in me, but I do not know what that loss is.

Whether it is imagined absence, unexperienced loss, anticipatory sorrow, the deaths of distant others, phantom, second death, disenfranchised grief, repression, ungrievable death, or relative deprivation, the losses that we fail to notice—the losses that we lose—creep up on us; we live among those, but have little idea how they affect us. My hope is to create a language to speak of these losses that remain inaccessible, unrecognizable, or unrecognized. For cognition can blunt the opacity of their vague melancholy. The project of this book is to identify and define this amorphous concept that I name lost loss, and to observe its various effects through the psycho-literary reading of modern and contemporary elegiac poetry.

NOTES

1. Stephen Regan, "The Art of Losing: American Elegy since 1945," in *American Poetry since 1945*, ed. Eleanor Spencer (Basingstoke: Palgrave, 2017), 184. The present book offers a counter-narrative to the dominant view of modern and contemporary American elegies as intimate and explicit.

2. Malka Heifetz Tussman, "Cellars and Attics," in *American Yiddish Poetry: A Bilingual Anthology*, ed. Benjamin Harshav and Barbara Harshav (Berkeley: University of California Press, 1986), 607–11.

3. Lori Hope Lefkovitz, "Inherited Memories and the Ethics of Ventriloquism," in *Shaping Losses: Cultural Memory and the Holocaust*, ed. Julia Epstein and Lori Hope Lefkovitz (Champaign: University of Illinois Press, 2001), 20.

4. As a sampling of critical reception, Jay Parini universalizes the poem's grief by contending that "the poet's feelings of grief and pity transcend the occasion" (*Theodore Roethke: An American Romantic* [Amherst: University of Massachusetts Press, 1979], 138), while Lynn Ross-Bryant individualizes the occasion by characterizing the loss as one "expressed in terms of a uniquely human relationship" (*Theodore Roethke: Poetry of the Earth, Poet of the Spirit* [Port Washington: Kennikat Press, 1981], 75). Kenneth Burke champions the poem as a "greater individualizing of human relations" ("The Vegetal Radicalism of Theodore Roethke," in *Theodore Roethke*, ed. Harold Bloom [New York: Chelsea House Publishers, 1988], 36). Jeffrey Meyers interprets the poem as an expression of "the traditional themes of the genre by contrasting the age of the poet to the youth of the dead girl, emphasizing the injustice of death and suggesting a love motif—which goes back to Catullus" ("The Background of Theodore Roethke's 'Elegy for Jane,'" *Resources for American Literary Study* 15, no. 2 [Autumn 1985]: 139). Laurence Perrine introduces the poem as "a pure and delicate emotional appreciation of an older man for a young girl" (Laurence Perrine and James M. Reid, *100 American Poems of the Twentieth Century* [New York: Harcourt Brace, 1966], 205). In Sandra Gilbert's *Inventions of Farewell*, the poem is classified as that of friendship (*Inventions of Farewell: A Book of Elegies* [New York: W. W. Norton, 2001], 288).

5. Allan Seager, *The Glass House: The Life of Theodore Roethke* (Ann Arbor: University of Michigan Press, 1991), 193.

6. Theodore Roethke, *The Collected Poems* (New York: Doubleday, 1975), 98. This stanza is at the root of the aforementioned critical debate over whether to interpret this poem as an expression of universal grief or of personal lament, and it has been read in varying ways: some see it as the poet being neither father nor lover but claiming to be a little of each, in effect becoming a universal mourner (Richard Blessing, "Theodore Roethke: A Celebration," *Tulane Studies in English* 20 [1972]: 174); others see it as an ambiguous romantic-paternal feeling that "many teachers would feel" toward an intelligent student and justify "the words of . . . love" by remarking on Jane Bannick's striking resemblance to Beatrice O'Connel whom Roethke had married (Meyers, "The Background," 140); and still others suggest the presence of another female student, Lois Lamb, whom Roethke had known well, as the inspiration of the poem (Seager, *The Glass House*, 193). My proposal is to read it

as what it is: the loss of someone one had not known well, and the concomitant difficulty of expressing sorrow for the loss of an opportunity to get to know someone.

7. William Waters, *Poetry's Touch: On Lyric Address* (Ithaca: Cornell University Press, 2003), 12.

8. Karen Weisman, "Introduction," in *The Oxford Handbook of the Elegy*, ed. Karen Weisman (Oxford: Oxford University Press, 2010), 2.

9. T. V. F. Brogan, *The New Princeton Handbook of Poetic Terms* (Princeton: Princeton University Press, 1994), 66.

10. Mark Strand and Eavan Boland, ed., *The Making of a Poem: A Norton Anthology of Poetic Forms* (New York: W. W. Norton, 2001), 167.

11. Gregory Nagy, "Ancient Greek Elegy," in *The Oxford Handbook of the Elegy*, ed. Karen Weisman (Oxford: Oxford University Press, 2010), 13.

12. John Frow, *Genre: The New Critical Idiom* (New York: Routledge, 2006), 132.

13. Morton W. Bloomfield, "The Elegy and the Elegiac Mode: Praise and Alienation," in *Renaissance Genres: Essays on Theory, History, and Interpretation*, ed. Barbara Keifer Lewalski (Cambridge: Harvard University Press, 1986), 148.

14. Lorna Clymer, "The Funeral Elegy in Early Modern Britain: A Brief History," in *The Oxford Handbook of the Elegy*, ed. Karen Weisman (Oxford: Oxford University Press, 2010), 170, 184.

15. In *Placing Sorrow*, Ellen Zetzel Lambert highlights the relation between elegiac consolation and pastoral landscape by commenting that some form of regeneration, such as is found in nature, can also be at work in human losses (*Placing Sorrow: A Study of the Pastoral Elegy Convention from Theocritus to Milton* [Chapel Hill: University of North Carolina Press, 1976], xvii). Peter Sacks's *The English Elegy* examines elegies as works of mourning that guides the grieving mourner toward a compensatory consolation for the loss (*The English Elegy: Studies in the Genre from Spenser to Yeats* [Baltimore: Johns Hopkins University Press, 1985], 4–10).

16. In Sacks's *The English Elegy*, the compensatory restitution model of elegy studies derives from several of Sigmund Freud's writings, most prominently from his essay "Mourning and Melancholia," and from the *fort-da* episode in *Beyond the Pleasure Principle*. The game of "*fort-da*" refers to the one played by Freud's grandson, in which the child, who had lost his mother, throws away ("*fort*," or "away") and then retrieves a wooden spool in order to rehearse the disappearances of his mother (Sigmund Freud, *Beyond the Pleasure Principle*, trans. James Strachey [London: Hogarth Press, 1950], 11–16).

17. Patricia Rae, *Modernism and Mourning* (Lewisburg: Bucknell University Press, 2007), 14.

18. Neil Roberts, "English Elegies," in *A Companion to Poetic Genre*, ed. Erik Martiny (Hoboken: Wiley-Blackwell, 2011), 91. Roberts notes that "compensation is still a possible element" in modern English elegies and that "elegy is a genre which answers to one of the profoundest and most permanent human needs, and as such is it likely to continue to challenge any totalizing account of it."

19. Anne K. Mellor, "'Anguish No Cessation Knows': Elegy and the British Woman Poet, 1660–1834," in *The Oxford Handbook of the Elegy*, ed. Karen Weisman (Oxford: Oxford University Press, 2010), 443. Mellor derives the distinction between

instructive and intuitive modes of grieving from Terry Martin and Kenneth J. Doka's *Men Don't Cry . . . Women Do: Transcending Gender Stereotypes of Grief* (Philadelphia: Brunner/Mazel, 2000), 37, 40, 53. Mellor is careful to circumvent gender essentialism, noting that Martin and Doka acknowledge that these grieving patterns "are influenced by gender but not determined by it" (Martin and Doka, 2) and that any given male or female may be either an intuitive or an instrumental griever (Mellor, "Anguish," 444). The question of gender and mourning is largely outside of the scope of this particular book, but it is a fruitful inquiry that has been explored expertly in works such as Lauren Berlant's "The Female Complaint" (*Social Text* 19/20 [1988]: 237–59), Adela Pinch's *Strange Fits of Passion: Epistemologies of Emotion, Hume to Austen* (Stanford: Stanford University Press, 1996), Melissa F. Zeiger's *Beyond Consolation: Death, Sexuality, and the Changing Shapes of Elegy* (Ithaca: Cornell University Press, 1997), and Anita Helle's "Women's Elegies, 1834-Present: Female Authorship and the Affective Politics of Grief," in *The Oxford Handbook of the Elegy*, ed. Karen Weisman (Oxford: Oxford University Press, 2010), 463–80, among others.

20. Sigmund Freud, *Letters of Sigmund Freud*, ed. Ernst L. Freud, trans. Tania and James Stern (New York: Basic Books, 1960), 386.

21. For further studies on Freud's changing views on successful mourning, one may refer to Kathleen Woodward, "Late Theory, Late Style: Loss and Renewal in Freud and Barthes," in *Aging & Gender in Literature: Studies in Creativity*, ed. Anne Wyatt-Brown and Janice Rossen (Charlottesville: University of Virginia Press, 1993), 84–89, and John E. Baker, "Mourning and the Transformation of Object Relationships: Evidence for the Persistence of Internal Attachments," *Psychoanalytic Psychology* 18, no. 1 (Winter 2001): 58–59.

22. For instance, R. Clifton Spargo's *The Ethics of Mourning* finds value in melancholia itself; the book asserts that there is, in elegy, an insistence on the "other's uncancellable and unassimilable value" as the basis of one's refusal of the substitutive valuation of the dead, and suggests that melancholic mourning, for its valuation of the singular over the collective, is more ethical (*The Ethics of Mourning: Grief and Responsibility in Elegiac Literature* [Baltimore: Johns Hopkins University Press, 2004], 13). Other scholars have sought consolation to be deriving from the elegiac confirmation and development of communal relations. Judith Butler reminds us that loss makes "a tenuous 'we' of us all" and that the function of grief is to bring "to the fore the relational ties" (*Precarious Life: The Powers of Mourning and Violence* [London: Verso, 2004], 20, 22). Max Cavitch claims that "the telos of American elegy is not consolation for the deaths of others, but fulfillment of a specifically political, shared happiness that 'loss' misnames" (*American Elegy: The Poetry of Mourning from the Puritans to Whitman* [Minneapolis: University of Minnesota Press, 2007], 24). In *Grief & Meter*, Sally Connolly notes the elegy's ability to "make something happen" in elegies written for ancestral poets (*Grief & Meter: Elegies for Poets after Auden* [Charlottesville: University of Virginia Press, 2016], 2). The debate continues to this date: if the rejection of consolation is viewed to be ethical toward the dead, it may be unethical for the living. As Diana Fuss asks in *Dying Modern: A Meditation on Elegy*, "Who is an elegy for: the dead or the living?" ([Durham: Duke University Press, 2013], 5). In a living-centric view, mourning functions as a balm because it

provides an occasion for the bereaved to form a collective bond of fellowship with other human beings.

23. Jahan Ramazani, *Poetry of Mourning* (Chicago: University of Chicago Press, 1994), xi.

24. John Berryman, "Dream Song #384," in *The Dream Songs* (New York: Farrar, Straus and Giroux, 2014), 406.

25. Sylvia Plath, "Daddy," in *The Collected Poems*, ed. Ted Hughes (New York: HarperPerennial, 1992), 223.

26. Fuss, *Dying Modern*, 5.

27. Hagop S. Akiskal and Giovanni B. Cassano, ed., *Dysthymia and the Spectrum of Chronic Depressions* (New York: The Guilford Press, 1997), 11. In *The Diagnostic and Statistical Manual of Mental Disorders*, Fifth Edition, published in 2013, dysthymia has been subsumed into persistent depressive disorder; I am reviving the term here as an instructive emblem of a poetic mood, not as a clinical diagnosis.

28. Andy Orchard, "Not What It Was: The World of Old English Elegy," in *The Oxford Handbook of the Elegy*, ed. Karen Weisman (Oxford: Oxford University Press, 2010), 104.

29. John B. Vickery, *The Modern Elegiac Temper* (Baton Rouge: Louisiana State University Press, 2006), 1.

30. Judith Shklar, *American Citizenship: The Quest for Inclusion* (Cambridge: Harvard University Press, 1991), 3.

31. Dominick LaCapra, "Trauma, Absence, Loss," *Critical Inquiry* 25, no. 4 (Summer 1999): 696–727.

32. Kenneth J. Doka, ed., *Disenfranchised Grief: Recognizing Hidden Sorrow* (Lexington, Massachusetts: Lexington Books, 1989), xv.

33. Mark E. Hastings, et al., "Shame, Guilt, and Suicide," in *Suicide Science: Expanding the Boundaries*, ed. Thomas Joiner and M. David Rudd (Berlin: Springer, 2002), 67–79.

34. Butler, *Precarious Life*, xiv.

35. Pauline Boss, *Ambiguous Loss: Learning to Live with Unresolved Grief* (Cambridge: Harvard University Press, 1999), 7–9.

36. Joseph Jacobs, "The Dying of Death," *The Fortnightly Review* 66 (August 1899): 264. Jacobs writes the following: "Perhaps the most distinctive note of the modern spirit is the practical disappearance of the thought of death as an influence directly bearing upon practical life . . . . The fear of death is being replaced by the joy of life . . . . Death is disappearing from our thoughts." Also, Philippe Ariès notes that in "industrialized, urbanized, and technologically advanced areas of the Western world, except for the death of statesmen, society has banished death" (Philippe Ariès, *The Hour of Our Death* [New York: Vintage Books, 1982], 560).

37. Ariès, *The Hour of Our Death*, 405–6. More recently, Brandy Schillace writes that "in the Western world we don't live with the idea of death": "We refrain from thinking about it, we avoid reflecting upon it, and death is something most of us simply don't talk about" (*Death's Summer Coat: What the History of Death and Dying Teaches Us about Life and Living* [New York: Pegasus Books, 2016], 2).

38. Jacques Derrida, "The Deaths of Roland Barthes," in *The Work of Mourning*, ed. Pascale-Anne Brault and Michael Naas (Chicago: University of Chicago Press, 2001), 34.

39. Pascale-Anne Brault and Michael Naas, "Editors' Introduction," in *The Work of Mourning*, ed. Pascale-Anne Brault and Michael Naas (Chicago: University of Chicago Press, 2001), 13.

40. Derrida, *The Work of Mourning*, 34.

41. Nicolas Abraham and Maria Torok, *The Shell and the Kernel*, Vol. 1, ed. and trans. Nicholas Rand (Chicago: University of Chicago Press, 1994), 99–100.

42. Walter Benjamin, "On Some Motifs in Baudelaire," in *Walter Benjamin: The Selected Writings*, Vol. 4, ed. Michael Jennings (Cambridge: Belknap, 2003), 317, 319.

43. In addition to this notion of psychic enclave, what Abraham and Torok's theory of secret contributes to the reading of elegiac poetry is their view of language: their treatment of speech as cryptonymy, a type of concealment in language. Abraham and Torok follow Freud in regarding language as a product of psychic processes, and consider disruptions of language as an expressive medium that reveals the fact of its obfuscations. This view of the language as symptoms that have meanings to be unpacked can prove to be instructive, especially when we analyze poems that have the air of "resistance"—a "poet's desire to sequester herself" as James Longenbach describes (*The Resistance to Poetry* [Chicago: University of Chicago Press, 2004], 8)—or that engage in a sophisticated game of hide-and-seek, or allusive, allegorical, or equivocating indirections, as D. W. Winnicott explores ("Communicating and Not Communicating Leading to a Study of Certain Opposites," in *The Maturational Processes and the Facilitating Environment* [New York: International Universities Press, 1965], 179–92).

44. Abraham and Torok, *The Shell and the Kernel*, 17–19.

45. Abraham and Torok, *The Shell and the Kernel*, 140–41.

46. Abraham and Torok, *The Shell and the Kernel*, 171.

47. Human cognition functions by means of detecting differences (Georg Simmel, "The Metropolis and Mental Life," in *Rethinking Architecture: A Reader in Cultural Theory*, ed. Neil Leach [New York: Routledge, 1997], 70).

48. Ben Jonson, *Epigrams and the Forest* (New York: Routledge, 2003), 43.

49. W. David Shaw, *Elegy & Paradox: Testing the Conventions* (Baltimore: Johns Hopkins University Press, 1994), 6.

50. Thomas Gray, "Elegy Written in a Country Churchyard," in *The Making of a Poem: A Norton Anthology of Poetic Forms*, ed. Mark Strand and Eavan Boland (New York: W. W. Norton, 2001), 183.

51. Helen Deutsch, "Elegies in Country Churchyards: The Prospect Poem in and around the Eighteenth Century," in *The Oxford Handbook of the Elegy*, ed. Karen Weisman (Oxford: Oxford University Press, 2010), 204.

52. Anne Bradstreet, "Here Follows Some Verses upon the Burning of Our House, July 10th, 1666. Copied Out of a Loose Paper," in *The Making of a Poem: A Norton Anthology or Poetic Forms*, ed. Mark Strand and Eavan Boland (New York: W. W. Norton, 2001), 179.

53. Jeffrey Hammond, "New World Frontiers: The American Puritan Elegy," in *The Oxford Handbook of the Elegy*, ed. Karen Weisman (Oxford: Oxford University Press, 2010), 214.

54. William Cullen Bryant, "Thanatopsis," in *The Norton Anthology of American Literature*, Shorter Eighth Edition, Vol. I, ed. Nina Baym (New York: W. W. Norton, 2013), 494.

55. Ramazani, *Poetry of Mourning*, 18–19.

56. Nancy Miller, "Reporting the Disaster," in *Trauma at Home: After 9/11*, ed. Judith Greenberg (Lincoln: University of Nebraska Press, 2002), 46.

57. Walt Whitman, "When Lilacs Last in the Dooryard Bloom'd," in *The Norton Anthology of Modern and Contemporary Poetry*, Third ed., Vol. 1, ed. Jahan Ramazani, et al. (New York: W. W. Norton, 2003), 25.

58. John Milton, "Lycidas," in *The Norton Anthology of English Literature*, Ninth ed., Vol. 1, ed. Stephen Greenblatt (New York: W. W. Norton, 2012), 1795.

59. William Wordsworth, *Essays upon Epitaphs* in *The Prose Works of William Wordsworth*, Vol. 2, ed. W. J. B. Owen and Jane Worthington Smyser (Oxford: Clarendon Press, 1974), 60.

60. William Wordsworth, "Elegiac Stanzas, Suggested by a Picture of Peele Castle, in a Storm, Painted by Sir George Beaumont," in *The Norton Anthology of English Literature*, Ninth ed., Vol. 2, ed. Stephen Greenblatt (New York: W. W. Norton, 2012), 344.

61. Shaw, *Elegy & Paradox*, 118: The oblique naming of John Wordsworth has been interpreted as part of Wordsworth's evasion "of dark truths."

62. Leon Waldoff, *Wordsworth in His Major Lyrics: The Art and Psychology of Self-Representation* (Columbia: University of Missouri Press, 2001), 147.

63. Geoffrey Hartman, *Wordsworth's Poetry, 1787–1814* (New Haven: Yale University Press, 1964), 284–85.

64. Marjorie Levinson, *Wordsworth's Great Period Poems: Four Essays* (Cambridge: Cambridge University Press, 1986), 113.

65. Waldoff, *Wordsworth in His Major Lyrics*, 148. Also, Thomas McFarland, *Romanticism and the Forms of Ruin: Wordsworth, Coleridge, and Modalities of Fragmentation* (Princeton: Princeton University Press, 1981), 161.

66. Laurence Goldstein, *Ruins and Empire* (Pittsburgh: University of Pittsburgh Press, 1977), 178.

67. William Wordsworth, *The Letters of William and Dorothy Wordsworth, Vol. 1: The Early Years, 1787–1805*, ed. Ernest de Selincourt and Chester L. Shaver (Oxford: Clarendon Press, 1967), 557. Various criticisms directed toward John Wordsworth assert that he "had failed to have the ship's boats hoisted out, thus causing unnecessary loss of life" and "that he made no effort to save his own life" (Waldoff, *Wordsworth in His Major Lyrics*, 132).

68. Waldoff, *Wordsworth in His Major Lyrics*, 132.

69. Richard E. Matlak, "Captain John Wordsworth's Death at Sea," *The Wordsworth Circle* 31, no. 3 (2000): 132.

70. Kurt Fosso, *Buried Communities: Wordsworth and the Bonds of Mourning* (Albany: State University of New York Press, 2004), 261.

71. William Shakespeare, "Sonnet #18," in *The Norton Shakespeare*, ed. Stephen Greenblatt (New York: W. W. Norton, 1997), 1929.

72. Emily Dickinson, "The missing All, prevented Me," in *The Poems of Emily Dickinson*, ed. R. W. Franklin (Cambridge: Belknap Press, 1999), 415.

73. Virginia Jackson, *Dickinson's Misery: A Theory of Lyric Reading* (Princeton: Princeton University Press, 2005), 209.

74. Magdalena Zapedowska, "Dickinson's Delight," *The Emily Dickinson Journal* 21, no. 1 (2012): 4.

75. Zeiger, *Beyond Consolation*, 168: "contemporary elegies provide a way of locating and reading earlier elegiac counterdiscourses."

76. Ramazani, *Poetry of Mourning*, 87. Also, Charles Berger, "The Mythology of Modern Death," in *Wallace Stevens: Modern Critical Views*, ed. Harold Bloom (New York: Chelsea House Publishers, 1985), 166.

77. Marjorie Perloff, *Poetic License: Essays on Modernist and Postmodernist Lyric* (Evanston: Northwestern University Press, 1990), 187.

78. Susan Bassnett, *Sylvia Plath* (Basingstoke, Hampshire: Macmillan, 1987), 136.

79. Alice Bolin, "Map Quest," *The Paris Review*, September 4, 2012, https://www.theparisreview.org/blog/2012/09/04/map-quest/.

80. In "How to Lose Things: Elizabeth Bishop's Child Mourning," Diana Fuss argues that an autobiographical story like "In the Village," which describes the events surrounding Gertrude Bulmer Bishop's breakdown, shows that to Bishop's own best recollection her childhood mourning was actually no mourning ("How to Lose Things: Elizabeth Bishop's Child Mourning," *Post 45*, September 23, 2013, http://post45.org/2013/09/how-to-lose-things-elizabeth-bishops-child-mourning/). Upon this premise, one surmises that, in "In the Waiting Room," the mourning that Bishop did not feel in childhood is reconstructed in the child Bishop with the aid of the adult Bishop, as an effort to "un-lose" the loss.

81. Among them are Elizabeth Bishop's *Edgar Allan Poe & The Juke-Box: Uncollected Poems, Drafts, and Fragments*, ed. Alice Quinn (New York: Farrar, Straus and Giroux, 2006); *Words in Air: The Complete Correspondence between Elizabeth Bishop and Robert Lowell*, ed. Thomas Travisano and Saskia Hamilton (New York: Farrar, Straus and Giroux, 2006); the collected volume of *Poems, Prose, and Letters* (New York: Library of America, 2008), which includes a considerable number of previously unpublished letters; and recent biographies such as Megan Marshall's *Elizabeth Bishop: A Miracle for Breakfast* (Boston: Houghton Mifflin Harcourt, 2017).

82. Discussions of Olds's elegies for her father include Iain Twiddy, *Cancer Poetry* (Basingstoke: Palgrave Macmillan, 2015), 54–78, and Russell Brickey, *Understanding Sharon Olds* (Columbia: University of South Carolina Press, 2016), 30–54.

83. Linda Gregerson, *Negative Capability: Contemporary American Poetry* (Ann Arbor: University of Michigan Press, 2001), 37.

84. Countee Cullen, "Threnody for a Brown Girl," *Poetry* 26, no. 2 (May 1925): 78–80.

85. Esther Schor, *Bearing the Dead: The British Culture of Mourning from the Enlightenment to Victoria* (Princeton: Princeton University Press, 1994), 3: "I interpret mourning as a phenomenon of far greater extension and duration than an individual's traumatic grief."

Chapter 1

Wallace Stevens's Elegiac Mode
Creating Fictions of Loss

In response to a request for a biography by the publishing staff of Perspectives USA, which was to accompany a reprinting of *The Auroras of Autumn*, Wallace Stevens writes that his "work suggests the possibility of a supreme fiction, recognized as a fiction, in which men could propose to themselves a fulfillment . . . . There are many poems relating to the interactions between reality and the imagination, which are to be regarded as marginal to this central theme."[1] One of the guiding preoccupations in Stevens's works, particularly in his later poems, is the concept of fiction.[2] Professing to be a poet who "lives in the world of Darwin and not in the world of Plato,"[3] Stevens sought, and desired to create, a "supreme fiction" that would take the place of defunct grand narratives.[4] One may trace early indications of Stevens's interest in the concept of fiction from early poems in *Harmonium* and *Ideas of Order*; examples include "The Comedian as the Letter C" and its "introspective voyager" trying to recover a "mythology of self,"[5] as well as "The Idea of Order at Key West" and its protagonist as the "artificer of the world" creating the story of herself through her song.[6] This fixation culminates in two major poems in *Transport to Summer*, "Esthétique du Mal" and "Notes toward a Supreme Fiction," which are often read as a part of "Stevens's lifelong attempt to give art the position of religion."[7] Creation of fiction is a key cog in the poetry of lost loss: when a loss is felt to be ambivalent and tenuous, it triggers the need for reinforcement, namely a fictive narrative that legitimizes the loss and gives it shape.

Stevens's work elucidates this mechanism of loss-salvaging through fiction-making. Stevens pronounces this concept of fiction most succinctly in the following passage from *Adagia*:

> The final belief is to believe in a fiction, which you know to be a fiction, there being nothing else. The exquisite truth is to know that it is a fiction and that you believe in it willingly.[8]

The statement echoes the concept of romantic irony: an ironic acknowledgment of the fictiveness of one's cognitions and beliefs that is combined with a romantic enthusiasm for creating and embracing such fictive constructs. The influence of romanticism on Stevens's work is well-documented,[9] but this *Adagia* statement adds another layer to Stevens's indebtedness to romanticism:[10] his recurring theme of fiction and fiction-making mirrors the romantic ironist's construction of new forms and new myths as products of creative imagination, where one beholds, simultaneously, a fiction that is not fictive and the fiction that is.

Generally, "Esthétique du Mal" and "Notes toward a Supreme Fiction" are often seen as the best expressions of the theses of Stevens's concept of fiction. In the specific context of Stevens's elegiac works that propose the concept of loss as a fictive construct, "The Owl in the Sarcophagus" occupies a similar status as the poem in which he constructs the guiding fiction; in this poem, fiction becomes the vessel upon which to pin vacated ideals. "The Owl in the Sarcophagus" is in many ways a departure from Stevens's earlier, more epitaphic elegies such as "The Emperor of Ice-Cream" or "The Death of a Soldier," in that it is a longer, more sustained allegorical narrative resembling a type of mythology itself. To be sure, some elements of those earlier elegies survive in "The Owl in the Sarcophagus."[11] The anti-elegiac skepticism of compensatory consolation found in "The Owl in the Sarcophagus" is present in poems like "The Death of a Soldier" and "The Men That Are Falling," as the brunt of the lines like "Death is absolute and without memorial" (*CPP* 81) or "death is stone / This man loved earth, not heaven, enough to die" (*CPP* 174) demonstrates.[12] Also, mock-elegies such as "Cortège for Rosenbloom" and "The Worm at Heaven's Gate" exemplify Stevens's attacks on funeral practices and elegiac consolation.[13] One may claim that Stevens's elegiac sensibilities remain fundamentally ambivalent, in the sense that their embrace of consolatory philosophy is almost always undercut by the cognition of disconsolation.[14] That is not surprising, given his professed creed that "poetry is a form of melancholia,"[15] as well as the close affinity between melancholia and anti-consolatory elegies. The self-consciously constructed fiction of "The Owl in the Sarcophagus," however, is a new element in his work; the poem becomes the fiction-intertext that guides and governs Stevens's later works.

Another element that is new in "The Owl in the Sarcophagus" also follows what Anne Mellor counts as a critical element of romantic irony: fictions and self-conceptions bear with them the seeds of their own destruction, since those are forms or structures that simultaneously create and de-create themselves.[16] It is in this respect that the consolatory fiction of elegies becomes analogous to what D. W. Winnicott calls a transitional object. In Winnicott's theory, infants utilize "transitional objects" as in-between objects that straddle their own world and the world outside of themselves; they then destroy those objects in their developmental process of reality-making. Similarly, consolatory fictions become transitional philosophies, which the elegists create and then continuously reexamine in the process of their cognitive reality-making after their cognitive world is disturbed and complicated by the disappearance of what used to be. "The Owl in the Sarcophagus" reveals three of the critical aspects of Stevens's conceptualization of fiction and consolation: first, the poem uncovers that the concept of loss is itself a construct; second, the concept of loss is created to conceal "lost loss," which manifests itself precisely in this obfuscation; and lastly, the poem recognizes its elegiac fiction as a transitional philosophy that is meant to be created and destroyed in its poetics of the ongoing. Elegiac fictions of loss are meant to keep being made and remade, recreated and re-destroyed, leaving no trace of clear starting or stopping, just as, for the self, there is no starting or stopping.[17] That is the fundamental fiction that Stevens's later elegies keep propounding and de-creating.

Although the elegiac sensibilities of Wallace Stevens's poetry have received much critical attention, his oeuvre includes only a handful of formal elegies.[18] Generally classified as a formal elegy, "The Owl in the Sarcophagus" may be best described as an anti-elegy or self-elegy; the poem, without any mention or hint of the death of the person who occasioned the poem, allegorizes the speaker's descent into a vision of death, in which the speaker realizes the fiction of elegy and universalizes it as the "mythology of modern death."[19] Critics have noted anti-elegiac trends in modern elegy, which often emerge as an assault on elegiac conventions or as a denial of loss and grief.[20] Anti-elegies refuse to embrace the loss-compensation model of understanding elegiac consolation, derived most notably from Sigmund Freud's "Mourning and Melancholia": the mourner receives consolation from a redemptive transformation of the lost object into a compensatory, substitutive form.[21] In the case of an anti-elegiac poem like "The Owl in the Sarcophagus"—one that hardly mentions the deceased, one that foregrounds the poet-speaker's own vision of death, and one that communicates the futility of consolation with its pervasive sense of loss—the same questions persist: what consolation does such an elegy bring about or intend to bring about, if any? And if the poem is more about fictions of mourning than about any consolation it brings, is it even useful to consider such a poem an elegy?

My hypothesis is that "The Owl in the Sarcophagus" brings about a different type of consolation than that of conventional elegies through its insistence on constructing a fiction of loss: paradoxically, Stevens's elegies generate their consolations through their emphasis on how fictive those philosophical constructs are. In investigating this consolatory potential of "The Owl in the Sarcophagus," one must reexamine two common assumptions regarding elegy and the nature of its consolation: that an elegy generally entails a specific object-loss as its occasion; and that the nature of elegiac consolation is primarily located in some form of compensatory gains, whether in the form of religious or poetic afterlife or a newfound sense of community. When we reappraise these assumptions, we find that elegies often communicate the unplaceable nature of the feeling of sorrow they attempt to express, in addition to, or sometimes in place of, the feeling of sorrow arising from a specific loss. The unplaceability diffuses the sense of dispossession, and from this diffusion emerges lost loss: a feeling that a specific loss has lost efficacy and presence. The allegorical impersonality of elegies such as "The Owl in the Sarcophagus" exemplifies not so much the modern skepticism of elegiac convention or the excision of occasional details necessitated by the depths of one's feelings for the dead,[22] but rather the cognition of this unplaceability of the feeling of sorrow, as well as diffidence in claiming one's loss. This inability to trace the pain of loss to a definitive source necessitates a rethinking of the nature of elegiac consolation as, instead, a construct deriving less from a compensation for the lost object than from a creation, through elegy, of the deceased whom one did not feel one could claim to have had or who felt somehow lost to one even while they were alive.[23] D. W. Winnicott's theory of reality-making suggests that an object comes into existence only as it is lost; just as, in Winnicott's case study, the child at first destroys the transitional object in his fantasy in order for the object to come into actual existence, Stevens's elegy shatters a phantom of loss in order to create an object in which an unplaced feeling of loss can find its place.

"The Owl in the Sarcophagus" has been read, despite its impersonal, allegorical presentation, as an elegy for Henry Church. One of the primary differences between this present reading of the poem and previous readings of it is that it proposes less to read the poem as an elegy for a specific individual than to examine the element of its impersonality and allegoresis more closely. In wading through the poem's allegory and unintelligibility from thereon, the present chapter expounds the following theses: that the poem's allegorical obfuscation is a form of lost loss; that, through such unintelligibility, the poem unveils how the notion of loss is a type of fiction; and that the poem attempts to excavate what lies beneath such fictive obfuscation.

Many creditable readings of "The Owl in the Sarcophagus" have been written on the premise that the poem is an elegy for Church.[24] While it is hardly debatable that the loss of Church was likely what triggered Stevens's composition of the poem, the letter that is often referred to as the basis for this reading benefits from a closer examination:

> ["The Owl in the Sarcophagus"] was written in the frame of mind that followed Mr. Church's death. While it is not personal, I had thought of inscribing it somehow, below the title, as, for example, Goodbye H.C., but it was hardly written before I received HORIZON's letter and as it would not have been easy to talk to you about it at the time I omitted the inscription.[25]

The poem was written "in the frame of mind" after Henry Church's death, but at the same time, it was not meant to be "personal," and the equivocation in that sentence—"somehow, below the title, as, for example"—is telling.[26] Regardless of whether or not Stevens actually meant the elegy to be dedicated to Church, however, the poem, even in the apparent presence of a specific object-loss that prompted its composition, conspicuously stays clear of any mention of him; it instead turns the object-loss into a kind of a personal unsaid or even a potential unsayable, in which the feeling of sorrow remains unplaced, unarticulated, or unspecified.

Since unplaced, unexpressed feelings have a way of manifesting themselves as a code or obfuscation, close attention should be paid to the poem's highly allegorical setting, which, if we are to assume a view of the elegy as a personal address, seems, on first glance, like a conundrum:

Two forms move among the dead, high sleep
Who by his highness quiets them, high peace
Upon whose shoulders even the heavens rest,

Two brothers. And a third form, she that says
Good-by in the darkness, speaking quietly there,
To those that cannot say good-by themselves. (I. 1–6)

Composed in six sections, the first section of "The Owl in the Sarcophagus" introduces the three principal figures of this allegory of death: two forms, sleep and peace, and the third form, a female figure. Walter Benjamin theorizes that, for a melancholic mind that perceives the world as one reduced to a state of incomprehension, allegory signifies an act of assignation of subjective meanings in an attempt to reconstruct or restore one's perceptual experience.[27] To rephrase, allegory is a cognitive mechanism of naming the unnamed, which is symptomatic of the hypertrophied subjectivity of melancholia. The allegorical nature of the poem signifies the poem's attempt to conceptualize death, the epitome of the unimaginable; in the words of one critic, "The Owl in the Sarcophagus" becomes an "attempt to contain death within the modern imagination."[28] It is precisely through allegory—its subjective meaning-constructions and restoration of one's cognitive world—that the poem aims to capture the elusive sense of lost loss.

Like the oscillation of the melancholic mind coping with the unimaginable as expressed in Benjamin's theory of allegory, the opening passage of the poem immediately evinces the dialectic between meaning and incomprehension, between the order that contains and the disorder that resists containment; the poem's broken syntax signals unintelligibility, while poetic refrains attempt to give it a frame of order and meaning. The clash between order and disorder manifests itself in the poem's prosody as well; the first two lines start with decapitation, or initial truncation. The truncation creates a sense of poetic irregularity and even highlights it through strong stresses on the first syllables of the lines, while the ends of those lines attempt to reclaim a sense of order through assonantal rhyme, "high sleep" and "high peace."[29] In fact, the incantatory repetition of words—such as "two" and "high"—appears to be the primary organizing principle in the first six lines, for the poem does not establish metrical regularity of iambic pentameter until line 6. The poem's prosodic irregularity reaches its height in line 4, which contains an assortment of spondaic and pyrrhic substitutions, in addition to abrupt caesurae. The metrical brokenness in a line that introduces the pivotal "third form," the most obscure figure among the three allegorical characters, recalls Susan Stewart's claim about the function of an unanticipated caesura, which "is not simply an alternation of a rhythmic pattern, but is as well a gesture of breaking or hesitating that opens the text to the excentric positions of unintelligibility and death."[30] In this manner, the poem vacillates between unintelligibility and the attempted restoration of meanings, out of which the poem's allegory emerges as a kind of stand-in for the inexpressible.

James Longenbach characterizes this allegory as the "geography of the afterlife" and identifies the three figures as "sleep, peace, and the mother of the dead."[31] Among those three, the third figure remains the most cryptic, despite the fact that section I devotes more lines to delineate this figure than it does for the first two:

These forms are visible to the eye that needs,
Needs out of the whole necessity of sight.
This third form speaks, because the ear repeats,

Without a voice, inventions of farewell . . .

And she that in the syllable between life

And death cries quickly, in a flash of voice,
Keep you, keep you, I am gone, oh keep you as
My memory, is the mother of us all,

The earthly mother and the mother of
The dead. Only the thought of those dark three
Is dark, thought of the forms of dark desire.   (I. 7–10, 18–24)

The third figure is the "earthly mother and the mother of / The dead" that makes utterances in "a syllable between life / And death"; her depiction—one of mixture, of life and death, of earthly and nether-worldly—appears more complex than "the mother of the dead," since her role is that of a multitudinous "mother of us all." In order for us to untangle the complexity of this third figure, the first notable feature we discern from the description of these allegorical figures is their familial, archetypal nature.[32] More importantly, the poem indicates that the tenor of the mother allegory—what the mother figure allegorizes—is language; the third form is metonymically linked to language, in that the main action verbs of the third form are "says" and "speaks" (I. 4, 9), and its expressive medium comes in a "syllable," a constituent of language (I. 18).

If the third form, the "mother of us all," is a linguistic function, then its cryptic, contradictory character makes sense, for language too is similarly mixed, ambivalent, and multifarious in its nature. Paul de Man suggests that language, as trope, is always privative and that death is a displaced name for a linguistic predicament.[33] By a reversible logic, language too becomes a displaced name for death, since language, as a system of representation, signals the absence of the represented; it is a presence—a representation, a signifier—that stands for absence—the absence of its referent, or death. In other words, just as language produces representation that indicates the absence of the represented, "mother" gives birth to life that is another name for death: death, after all, is a process that starts at the moment of birth. And in the sense that language gives shape to thoughts that make us human, language is the "mother of us all." Similar to the way in which language includes both the representation and its absence, the third figure encompasses both the living and the dead: in this sense, the third figure becomes the "earthly mother" and the "mother of / The dead." As such, the third figure, the mother figure, becomes an all-encompassing allegorical figure that is aware of its own allegorical nature—a figure of allegory that at once embodies and exposes its own allegorical construction.

In Stevens's poetry, there is always a sense of fragile consolation, of the acute self-awareness of the fiction of whatever consolation it attempts to reach; as fallacious as it may be to believe in fiction, such belief in the fictive nonetheless remains something one cannot live without. In "The Owl in the Sarcophagus," the opening section communicates this awareness of fiction and its necessity through its emphatic repetition of the word "needs": the allegorical forms are "visible to the eye that needs, / Needs out of the whole necessity of sight." The sentiment is akin to that of "necessity is the mother of invention" where fiction is invented out of that necessity, but what is needed here is not only a fiction but also the language that creates the fiction; the assonantal rhyme of "needs" and "repeats" underscores that the "ear" too "repeats" out of necessity, and this necessitated repetition leads to the utterance by the third figure, who is aware of the privative nature of language used in allegory to reconstruct the broken world of the melancholic. The depiction of the speech without a voice recalls the image of the privative realm in which the language resides; Stevens's use of synesthesia in "the ear repeats, / Without a voice" erases the speaker from the repetitive speech, and this repetition without a voice turns into an echo that has lost its speaker or the initial voice—like Nietzsche's shadow inside the cavern.[34] Even as these images are constructed to fill the void, the speaker remains aware of the fact of their fictitiousness: they are "inventions," and those figures are "dark" only because our thoughts of them are dark—our constructions of them make them dark.

In this urgency to conceptualize the elusive notion called death, the allegorist "reifies" an allegory but only to "mock . . . mythological imagination" in the end.[35] In fact, later in section VI, the poem's anti-elegiac turn debunks the very allegorical reconstruction that the poem enacts. But before we investigate the deconstruction of mythology, we need to examine the mythology itself—the speaker's underground journey and the visions of death he encounters there. After the introduction of the three allegorical figures in section I, the poem proceeds to the narration of what has commonly been read as the speaker's underworld descent in section II and narrates his vision of the underworld in sections III to V, before undoing the vision in section VI. In a genre that is as hyperconscious of tradition as elegy, an underground descent is a conventional development, as exemplified by such mythological narratives as Orpheus's descent to Hades to rescue Eurydice.[36] Elegy tends to invoke tradition because tradition signifies continuation; the sense of continuity fostered by literary tradition becomes a substitutive redemption that offsets the disruption of continuity effected by death. As though to sustain this sense of tradition, Stevens portrays the start of the underground journey in section II with primal imagery and archetypal abstraction without details:

There came a day, there was a day—one day
A man walked living among the forms of thought
To see their luster truly as it is

And in harmonious prodigy to be,
A while, conceiving his passage as into a time
That of itself stood still, perennial,

Less time than place, less place than thought of place
And, if of substance, a likeness of the earth,
That by resemblance twanged him through and through,

Releasing an abysmal melody,
A meeting an emerging in the light
A dazzle of remembrance and of sight.   (II. 1–12)

The "forms of thought" seem to refer to the triadic figures of death, which, in the preceding section, are metonymically turned into "thought of the forms of dark desire"; likely for this reason, this place where the "man walked living" has been largely interpreted as the netherworld.[37] At the same time, we can also read this scene as a site of one's interiority: the depth of one's interior selfhood, made of the "forms of thought" that comprise oneself. In other words, we can think of this underworld journey as an allegory that stands for an experience of intense introspection, a melancholic introspection of the hypertrophied subjectivity in response to grief, occasioned by the death of a friend. In these stanzas, Stevens portrays a collapse of the temporal into the spatial into the conceptual—a "perennial" that is less "time than place, less place than thought of place"—whereby the place enters the realm of the timeless like that of Gerard Manley Hopkins's "I wake and feel the fell of dark, not day":[38] a sense of introspection that seems to go on without an end. Furthermore, the entirety of section II is written in one sentence, as though to avoid the closure of a period; it similarly suggests timelessness, stream of consciousness, and an avoidance of determinacy or finality that is a metonymy of death. Then, inside his mind, the speaker sees a meeting between light, remembrance, and sight. In literary tradition, light routinely symbolizes knowledge, and it combines with memory and sight—the "eye" that is the "I"—to make up the interior of a self, a stage on which the self meets the self.

The visions of death in sections III to V proceed in the order of Sleep in section III, Peace in section IV, and the mother figure in section V. In section III, Stevens narrates the first vision, the speaker's encounter with Sleep:

There he saw well the foldings in the height
Of sleep, the whiteness . . .

   . . . Sleep realized
Was the whiteness that is the ultimate intellect,

A diamond jubilance beyond the fire,

That gives its power to the wild-ringed eye.
Then he breathed deeply the deep atmosphere
Of sleep, the accomplished, the fulfilling air.   (III. 1–2, 13–18)

The speaker's vision is that of hypnotic whiteness that is "the ultimate intellect." Stevens's debt to Romantic poets has been thoroughly documented, and in this section, one hears distinct echoes of William Wordsworth.[39] The "wild-ringed eye" recalls not only the image of an owl but also the "wild eyes" of Dorothy in "Tintern Abbey"; the "ultimate intellect" evokes the image of the child in the Intimations Ode as the "best Philosopher" with an "eternal mind."[40] The impulse of the vision in section III is regressive, prompting a rediscovery of one's origin and original wisdom. The Wordsworthian "whiteness" and innocence of childhood constitute the "deep atmosphere" and the "accomplished, the fulfilling air" of one's innate self: the child as the father of the man.[41] In a sense, this regressive vision in section III, in which the speaker finds his ultimate intellect in the depths of his interiority, anticipates the image of the child in section VI; this scene of origin, the primal landscape of whiteness, is the best wisdom that the speaker resorts to in the time of need. The image is, in a sense, a language beyond language; it is a language that leads each of these death phases into a place where words no longer apply and can no longer reach.

If the first vision of sleep is that of one's origin and native purity and whiteness, the second vision—of peace, the "brother of sleep" (IV. 7)—in section IV is that of estrangement, the presence of the unrecognizable, foreign other within the self:

There peace, the godolphin and fellow, estranged, estranged,
Hewn in their middle as the beam of leaves,
The prince of shither-shade and tinsel lights,

Stood flourishing the world . . .

This was peace after death, the brother of sleep,
The inhuman brother so much like, so near,
Yet vested in a foreign absolute,

Adorned with cryptic stones and sliding shines
An immaculate personage in nothingness,
With the whole spirit sparkling in its cloth . . .   (IV. 1–4, 7–12)

Starting with the repetition of the word "estranged," section IV continuously tweaks the familiar into the unfamiliar, by setting one thing next to its antithetical variation. In stanza 3, the fraternal likeness comes to be seen as "inhuman" and "foreign" at the same time; "peace" gets coupled with "death," unveiling the euphemistic meaning of the word "peace" as "death." In stanza 4, the image of "nothingness" is set against the "wholeness" of the spirit as though to suggest that homogeneity or purity of "whole spirit" is another word for "nothingness." Then in stanza 5, an oblique allusion to the figure of a nightingale sets the image of the celebratory, melodious song-bird against the owl, the less heralded nocturnal bird in the poem's title:

Generations of the imagination piled
In the manner of its stitchings, of its thread,
In the weaving round the wonder of its need,

And the first flowers upon it, an alphabet
By which to spell out holy doom and end,
A bee for the remembering of happiness . . . .

This is the figure stationed at our end,
Always, in brilliance, fatal, final, formed
Out of our lives to keep us in our death . . .   (IV. 13–18, 22–24)

The stanza evokes the image of Philomela's tapestry mellifluously through lavish uses of sound devices, including slant rhyme—"thread," "need"—alliteration—"weaving," "wonder"—and assonance—"weaving," "need"—that are framed within an incantatory anaphoric syntax. It reads like a song of a nightingale: the bird Philomela was turned into, and the bird that sings of summer with full-throated ease in Keats's melodious ode. As alluring as the nightingale may be, however, the poem's protagonist is the owl—the bird that "speaks in a hieratic voice and is more a chorister of divine love than a siren singer of sensuality."[42] The poem embodies the other, less celebrated nightbird masquerading as a nightingale, like Aesop's crow and its peacock-like self-presentation: a kind of disfigured Romantic poetry, the melodiousness of which always remains "abysmal" (I. 10). The harmonious music of this poem retains indelible signs of Philomela's severed tongue within it.

The sense of estrangement in section IV manifests not only in its incongruous imagery and disfigured music but also in the brokenness of its sense. Harold Bloom has stated that "The Owl in the Sarcophagus" is "uninterpretable," and passages like stanza 6 seem to corroborate the claim.[43] For a poem that attempts to restore meaning to unintelligibility, there certainly are noticeable numbers of passages that border on pure nonsense, especially if the poem is seen as a representation of an utterance, as in Northrop Frye's view of the lyric as "preeminently the utterance that is overheard."[44] But if one were to be attentive to "aspects of babble, doodle, and riddle" of lyric poetry as Jonathan

Culler suggests,[45] the stanza presents itself as a kind of sound association, in which the mundane—the first flowers, alphabet, and a bee—undergoes a strange deformation and becomes an apocalyptic image of "holy doom and end" (IV. 17). These sound associations, along with the linguistic means of "alphabet," simultaneously spell out a restorative image—one's remembrance of happiness, of a Wordsworthian childhood consisting of learning the alphabet and seeing natural landscapes of flowers and bees—as well as the end of such bucolic bliss. And these two visions—of doom and of happiness—are placed side by side, as if they were a multiple choice, in which one faces either an (A) alphabet to spell out holy doom and end or a (B) bee for the remembering of happiness. In these instances, auditory associations and sound plays—almost as if to suggest that the "a" of the "alphabet" stands for choice A, "b" of the "bee" stands for choice B—might as well become the organizing principle Stevens employs to give shape to the sense of estrangement and its unintelligibility.

This oscillation between meaning and unintelligibility in the language of lyric poetry—the tension between the lyric's proclivity toward becoming both a meaningful, overheard utterance and a puzzling babble—mirrors the same characteristics of the language of mourning; in grief, speech attempts to reach out to others, to gain intelligibility and communicability, while, at the same time, there is also always so much that cannot be said or that remains, and in a sense must remain, a babble. If lyric poetry were an expression of the powerful overflow of emotion, an expression of grief, considered to be one of the acuter kinds of emotion, would provide a stage where characteristics of lyric poetry can be observed in a particularly emphasized or exaggerated form, the way an allegory creates a space where the features of the actual existences it allegorizes are hyperbolized. In this sense, theories of lyric come hand in hand with theories of elegy, in which the former is seen in the latter in a more intense, visible form. If "The Owl in the Sarcophagus" seems "uninterpretable," it is because the poem reveals, in a manner of excess, the seed of uninterpretability—or the feeling of estrangement arising out of the lyric's simultaneous impulse to make sense of what eludes sense and to underscore precisely this elusiveness of sense—that is at the heart of lyric poetry.

After the visions of sleep and peace—sleep's archetypal familiarity and peace's strange, familiar unfamiliarity—section V presents the vision of the third figure:

But she that says good-by losing in self
The sense of self, rosed out of prestiges
Of rose, stood tall in self not symbols, quick

And potent, an influence felt instead of seen.

She spoke with backward gestures of her hand.
She held men closely with discovery,

Almost as speed discovers, in the way
Invisible change discovers what is changed,
In the way what was has ceased to be what is. (V. 1–9)

As discussed earlier, the third figure is the multitudinous "mother of us all," whose selfhood, like Walt Whitman's "Song of Myself," seemingly contains all. The conflation of the self with the other—the inclusion of the other in the self, or the fusion between the two—erases the boundary of selfhood, for a self defines itself through its detection of differences from the other: inside her self where no distinction between the self and the other exists, she loses the "sense of self." The strange coined word "rosed" is itself an expression of inclusiveness: commonly a noun for a flower, the word "rose" is turned into a verb, containing within it both properties of a noun as well as those of a verb, in addition to its resemblances to a past participle of the verb, "rise."

The third figure's multitude, however, differs from that of Whitman's "Song of Myself" in one critical sense: while Whitman's egotism is one of celebration—of expansive inclusion of the elements of the foreign other into one's selfhood—the third figure's solipsism is that of melancholia, an erasure or disappearance of the foreign other in light of one's full immersion in one's subjectivity.[46] The stanza's insistent repetition of the word "self"—"losing in self," "sense of self," "stood tall in self"—is indicative of melancholic self-immersion (V. 1, 2, 3). While the term "melancholia" may refer to a number of various conditions, the critical consensus is that it has a major influence on one's way of seeing, whether it signifies the looking-glass of the "darkness visible," in which everything in sight comes to possess a tinge of darkness,[47] or a less optimistic but more perceptive eye to access the truth.[48] Of particular interest here is the condition of melancholia as "a maximum of consciousness"—an inflation of subjectivity that swells and swallows exteriority.[49] In a sense, the poem's allegorical descent into the depth of one's interiority itself can be seen as the work of elegiac melancholia, in which the lyric-speaker's action turns inward and his subjectivity envelops the whole of the external world. And the all-encompassing "mother of us all" becomes emblematic of this inclusive melancholia, a self-knowing "inner thing" obsessively immersed in its interiority (V. 11)—one who won't give birth, who won't let go of the other inside her, who contains the other when she should be letting out—which possesses what Freud would call a keener eye to the truth.

In the absence of the other—in the self's hypertrophied, solipsistic imprisonment—one loses a sense of oneself, and the self becomes the object of loss. If the consolatory function of elegy is to find, in the face of a disruption in the aftermath of a loss of a life, a sense of presence or continuity in other lives or substitutive forms of lives including that of the poet-speaker, elegiac melancholia and its self-enclosure enact that which it had determinedly set out to counter: the prospect of self-erasure, the lyric-speaker's own dissolution. The first half of section V, therefore, ends with images of privation: its discovery is the fact that "the way what was has ceased to be what is" (V. 9). It is a discovery of loss, of the change and the strange.

Perhaps frightened by the prospect of his own mortality in the depths of his interiority, the poet-speaker attempts a "motion outward" in the latter half of section V:

It was not her look but a knowledge that she had.
She was a self that knew, an inner thing,
Subtler than look's declaiming, although she moved

With a sad splendor, beyond artifice,
Impassioned by the knowledge that she had,
There on the edges of oblivion.

O exhalation, O fling without a sleeve
And motion outward, reddened and resolved
From sight, in the silence that follows her last word—   (V. 10–18)

Breaking out of the repetitive stillness of anaphora in the first half, the second half of section V scurries along, through the predominance of weak stresses in frequent dactylic, anapestic, or pyrrhic substitutions, all of which speed up the movement of the lines. The frenzied pace reaches its height in the apostrophes—"O exhalation, O fling without a sleeve"—which are further hastened onward by the sentence fragments that look for syntactic closure. The apostrophe is also the moment when the poem becomes aware of itself; as William Waters comments on the matter of address to the nonhuman, "All that hailing of abstractions, objects, and people can look like so much empty rhetorical flourishing, address cut off from any possible efficacy."[50] In addition to the self-consciously "poetic" apostrophe, stanza 6 also flaunts poetic diction, peppered with poetic sound devices—alliterations such as "reddened," "resolved" and "sight," "silence," as well as internal half-rhymes like "outward," "word." Stanza 6 becomes a moment of tension in which the poem's self-awareness undoes the fiction it has forged.

But if self-awareness destroys fiction, it also simultaneously restores it; the outward movement of stanza 6 is artificial, but the knowledge of one's own artificiality allows one to act "beyond artifice" (V. 13). The poem's self-awareness mirrors the mother figure's self-awareness, and this self-knowledge—which is itself a motion outward, for a self cannot know or define what a self is without knowing what is not a self—redeems the speaker from his self-dissolution. A "self that knew" her "inner thing" is, in other words, a self that has learned what is not herself. As such, it is precisely through her own self-knowledge that the third figure turns her inward reflection into something that reaches outward, since knowing what is oneself simultaneously makes one aware of what is the Other; in this sense, the "knowledge that she had" of herself in stanza 5 ultimately "impassions" and guides her into the outward movement of stanza 6.

Descending into the depths of oneself to find a core of humanity that one shares with others, or finding the other within the self whereby the move inward becomes the move outward, is the Romantic ideal of intersubjectivity: Whitmanesque interweaving of subjectivities, through projection—"In all people I see myself"—and introjection—"I am large, I contain multitudes."[51] Intersubjectivity is a state of interrelation among subjectivities—unlike the state of self-erasure in hypertrophied solipsism—and in this change of the "inner thing" from a self that is aware of oneself to a self that is aware of what is not oneself and then to a self that regains an outward knowledge, the poem salvages the third figure from the prospect of self-erasure. The consolatory allegory of the three figures reaches its conclusion here: a "motion outward" resolvedly arises from the "silence" that is the figure of death (V. 17, 18). In other words, the deceased may be forever lost, but out of his death, out of the depths of our interiority, the prospect of intersubjective connection between the self and the other emerges. The deceased, then, is not really lost because he lives inside of us for as long as we live. In exchange for the loss of the deceased, we gain a piece of the deceased inside of us, just as Apollo, having lost Daphne, gains a substitutive sign of her in the laurel wreath.

Or so it seems. The dash at the end of the last line of section V overtly indicates that the sentence is not completed; the speaker's thought does not end there. The sentence elides the section break, and the speaker's thought is completed in section VI. What follows the rosy sublime of intersubjectivity is a statement of bathos that undercuts it:

This is the mythology of modern death
And these, in their mufflings, monsters of elegy,
Of their own marvel made, of pity made,

Compounded and compounded, life by life,
These are death's own supremest images,
The pure perfections of parental space . . .   (VI. 1–6)

As Charles Berger points out, "mythology" is not one of Stevens's favored words.[52] Stevens once again returns to the self-awareness that the allegory of the three forms and the visions the speaker encounters in sections III to V are all constructions: a self-taught consolation of heroic renunciations that are mythologized as a discovery of intersubjectivity in the depths of one's interiority. In other words, the promise of intersubjectivity in the allegory of three forms is an illusory fiction. The stanza's lavish uses of alliterations link the word "mythology" to the repetition of the word "made," as if to underscore this awareness of fictiveness—the product of which are the Frankensteinian "monsters" of elegy. The fiction is an invention by the "marvel" of human minds, as well as the "pity" of human hearts—invented, that is, out of necessity, just like the three forms that had become "visible to the eye" because the eye "needs" them "out of the whole necessity of sight" (I. 7, 8). It is a fragile piece of artifice, like a piece of pottery of sorts, delicately made inside the "mufflings" so as to be fired without being exposed to direct flame. As Joan Didion writes, we "interpret what we see, select the most workable of the multiple choices . . . by the imposition of a narrative line upon disparate images, by the 'ideas' with which we have learned to freeze the shifting phantasmagoria which is our actual experience."[53] Allegory, in other words, is a manifestation of human cognitive practice that imposes an arbitrary narrative on unassimilated or inassimilable experiences, such as the loss of the beloved in the case of elegy, and threads together a meaning out of their disparate images; it is a defensive mechanism of human cognition.

But when one is aware of the falsity of the narrative of compensatory consolation, one makes a choice: one could disregard its falsity and force oneself to be consoled by the fictive narrative, or one may abandon the consolatory fiction—a response that can take any number of forms, whether it is disillusionment, skepticism, irony, anger, or rejection of the old and determination to find a new, genuine consolation. This disbelief in compensatory consolation has often been spotlighted as the reason for modern elegists' "transgeneric attack on . . . the psychological propensity of the [elegy] to translate grief into consolation."[54] Seen in this regard, the closing stanza of "The Owl in the Sarcophagus" seems non-consolatory:

The children of a desire that is the will,
Even of death, the beings of the mind
In the light-bound space of the mind, the floreate flare . . .

It is a child that sings itself to sleep,
The mind, among the creatures that it makes,
The people, those by which it lives and dies.   (VI. 7–12)

Instead of basking in the fictive comfort of the "pure perfections of parental space" (VI. 6), the child "sings itself to sleep"; there is no parent, the mythical "mother of us all," or anyone who would lullaby the child into sleep. The ambiguous image is that of solitude. The child is left alone, with the knowledge that the consolatory narrative is a myth but that it is the only thing he is left with.

Stevens's "consolation" seemingly ends in the desolation of the forlorn child: upon the death of a friend, the speaker reconstructs through allegory the disrupted, inassimilable experience of loss. In his allegorical reconstruction, the speaker meets himself and the foreign other in himself. Through his realization that the self contains the self and the other in the depths of its interiority, the speaker arises out of the abyss of his hypertrophied melancholic subjectivity to discover a possibility of reaching redemptive intersubjectivity. Upon realizing the fictitiousness of the allegory and its visions, however, the speaker retreats into himself, left on his own to sing himself to sleep. Critics have often noted that modern elegies tend to enact the work of unresolved "melancholic" mourning, not the "normative" mourning that leads to resolution.[55] Given that the compensatory consolation fails to console the speaker, this poem appears to be no exception to this trend.

The above summary of "The Owl in the Sarcophagus," however, misses a critical undercurrent in the poem: the lack of any occasional details. The poem leaves much unsaid. There are many possible ways to interpret this rather glaring omission for an elegy: it could be a preference for impersonality; it could be a matter of reticence, coming out of the phenomenon of "disappearance of death" in modern society, in which death is hidden away from our view in our everyday social practices.[56] It might be a repression or an intimation of something unspeakable, the kind of feeling we have when we use euphemisms like "passing away" to mean "dying." Or it could be a result of allegoresis, which represents the personal details with impersonal substitutes. And other possibilities abound. But setting aside the authorial intent, which is always a matter of speculation, one may instead examine how the poem is presented and what the poem is made of. The obvious answer is that "The Owl in the Sarcophagus" is constructed as an allegory. Allegory, of course, is a kind of cryptonymy—a code language. And from the poem's discordant imagery, cacophonous voices, and its "babble, doodle and riddle," we deduce the poet-speaker's struggle to express what eludes language, thoughts, and figures of representation—the inadequacy of the language, the unspeakable, the unsayable that lurks within us and yet escapes from us. The allegorical language becomes, in a sense, a makeshift expedient to grope blindly through the incomprehension of the loss.

One may wonder about the obstinate opacity of the poem and hypothesize that its code language—its allegory, which, in Benjamin's dialectic, is symptomatic of melancholia, in that it signifies a melancholic's attempts to reconstruct the system of signification through arbitrary designation of meanings—may also be symptomatic of something else: what Nicolas Abraham and Maria Torok call a "phantom." As discussed in the Introduction, a phantom is a type of sealed-off sorrow in an inaccessible mental grave, which reveals itself through linguistic concealment, often entailing inventions of particular forms of obfuscation, which Abraham and Torok call "cryptonymy."[57] To revisit the cited passage, a phantom "points to ... a memory ... buried *without legal burial place*":

> The memory is of an idyll, experienced with a valued object and yet for some reason unspeakable. It is memory entombed in a fast and secure place, awaiting resurrection. Between the idyllic moment and its subsequent forgetting (we have called the latter preservative repression), there was the metapsychological traumatism of a loss or, more precisely, the "loss" that resulted from a traumatism. This segment of an ever so painfully lived Reality—untellable and therefore inaccessible to the gradual, assimilative work of mourning—causes a genuinely covert shift in the entire psyche. The shift itself is covert, since both the fact that the idyll was real and that it was later lost must be disguised and denied.[58]

The keywords in this passage that are particularly relevant to this poem are "unspeakable," "untellable," "inaccessible," "disguised," and their synonyms. It is certainly common enough for us to describe our pain or loss as somehow beyond expression, as in "I can't describe it in words" or "words can't express my pain." Generally speaking, our feeling of linguistic insufficiency results from the gap between what we want to express and what we end up expressing: the gap between the target of expression and the expression of the target object. And in expressions of loss, we are accustomed to thinking that linguistic expressions are insufficient because, somehow, either the actual pain is quantifiably larger than the linguistic expression of it—despite the fact that we have no way of quantifying actual or linguistic pain—or the empirical pain is qualitatively so different from the linguistic expression of it that the latter cannot match the former—despite the fact that we have no way of measuring this qualitative difference.

But what if the real reason for the seeming insufficiency of linguistic expressions to capture an empirical loss is not simply a matter of the qualitative or quantitative difference between the empirical and the linguistic? That is to say, could it be possible that the insufficiency we think of as linguistic may be, instead, cognitive? Conceivably, linguistic insufficiency results not so much from the limitation of the language itself but rather from our erroneous cognition of the nature of our experience of loss, whereby this error leads us to misdirect our linguistic expression, which ends up capturing a proximate object instead of something else that it is meant to capture. For instance, in the case of the loss of someone, we are accustomed to thinking that the sadness we feel is for the loss of that person who has passed away. But if we consider the person who has passed away to be a kind of a proximate object and think of the sorrow we feel for the loss of that person as what Freud calls a screen memory—or, to be more accurate in this case, a "screen sorrow"—then there would be something else that is the real target of our sorrow, from which the screen sorrow is instituted to safeguard us. In that case, linguistic insufficiency or unintelligibility would be a sign of concealment, an indication that the proximate object of the expressed sorrow—that is, the immediate and readily visible loss of a specific person—is a false screen, and that our mind has not placed our sorrow in the right place, that our mind is struggling in its attempt to place it in a proper place: a sign of sorrow in an unplaced or unplaceable state.

In other words, the opacity of "The Owl in the Sarcophagus" is an indication that the real loss portrayed in the poem may not be so much the loss of Henry Church but rather some other loss that the loss of Church reveals: some other unconscious loss that a loss of a friend rattles the speaker out of his cocoon to confront. For one thing, "The Owl in the Sarcophagus" is a poem of discovery; the poem moves from the witnessing or discovering—the first three sections highlight an unspecified character's act of "seeing" his inner landscape—to the summarizing of the discoveries in the last section. In short, the poem chronicles a journey to discover something, and the fact that one must discover something is itself suggestive enough of the possibility that the poem's real subject, the real loss that the poem wants to capture and express, lies beyond the readily available detail in the poet's biography.

The clues for the readers to discover and identify this real loss behind the "screen loss" may lie in the destination of the speaker's journey: his inner world. The self-reflexivity points to a potential self-mourning, and more than a few critics have noted that self-mourning is ubiquitous in canonical elegies.[59] In that sense, the facile conclusion would be that the real loss one fears or mourns when one experiences someone else's death is the anticipation of one's own death. That, of course, is intuitive enough, but precisely the ease with which we draw such a conclusion should make us skeptical of it.

In order for us to uncover the real loss behind the screen, the passage we must return to is stanzas 3 through 5 in section V, the climax of the introspective journey before the outward escape takes place in stanza 6, and before the bathos undercuts the vision in section VI:

She held men closely with discovery,

Almost as speed discovers, in the way

> Invisible change discovers what is changed,
> In the way what was has ceased to be what is.
>
> It was not her look but a knowledge that she had.
> She was a self that knew, an inner thing,
> Subtler than look's declaiming, although she moved
>
> With a sad splendor, beyond artifice,
> Impassioned by the knowledge that she had,
> There on the edges of oblivion.
>
> O exhalation, O fling without a sleeve . . .   (V. 6–16)

Earlier, I noted a poetic self-consciousness in stanza 6 that pushes the speaker outside of his interiority. The tone shifts from stanza 5 to stanza 6—from the somber, weak-stressed lyric to an apostrophe—and the word that precedes the shift is "oblivion"; the speaker comes to the "edges" of oblivion and then turns back. In the pivotal third stanza, which manifests the speaker's acute awareness of inwardness through the repetition of the sound "in," the poem suggests, through the repetition of the word "discover" and its variant, that a discovery is made.

If stanza 3 acknowledges the fact of discovery, stanza 4 portrays the content of this discovery: what was discovered was "not her look" but a "knowledge that she had." And this knowledge that the poem discovers is of a "self that knew," the "inner thing," one that is characterized by its "sad splendor" and its nature "beyond artifice": a self-knowledge of an introspective self, one that can see through, like the Freudian melancholic's keener eye to the truth, the "sad splendor" of a brutal truth beyond the artificial, self-made, fictive consolation. As previously discussed, elegiac melancholia enacts what it fears the most: in the depth of the self's introspection, the self enters a solipsistic imprisonment, and in this solipsism, without any nonself objects to orient the self, the self loses a sense of self, inducing a state of self-erasure. The expansive melancholic selfhood of the "maximum of consciousness" points to the self's essential solitude, a space where any efforts at introjection—an effort to take in external, nonself objects—would fail, and the solitariness of the self's existence ends up dissolving the self itself. What the "inner thing"—the "self that knew"—reveals is this expanse of selfhood, in which neither the self nor any nonself objects would come into existence.

These clues indicate that the discovery, the brutal truth beyond fictive consolation, is the fact of the self's essential solitude—the essential isolation of the "self that knew" the fact of its solitariness. In this universe where only the self exists, the real loss that the poem mourns for is the illusion of loss—an illusion that one had something and could, and did, lose it, an illusion like that of Apollo who had thought he had Daphne and thought he lost her when she turned into a laurel tree, even if, in reality, Daphne had never been his possession and he could not have "lost" her. As the Stoic philosopher Marcus Aurelius inquires, "How could you lose what you don't have?"[60] That is to say, a claim that we "lost" something presupposes that we previously had it, but in the state of essential solitude that is self-erasure, one encounters no prospect of loss. The disappearance of the prospect of loss is the profoundest loss, against which one guards oneself by creating a fiction that one has lost something—by inventing illusions of loss: the "inventions of farewell."

This—invention of farewell, creation of loss—is the consolation of "The Owl in the Sarcophagus." The consolation of this poem is not compensatory; if nothing is lost, then there is nothing left to be recovered or compensated for. The consolation is that of creation. Stevens once remarked that "the history of belief will show that it has always been in a fiction."[61] Even as the "mythology" of the illusory intersubjective may have proved to be an unpersuasive fiction, this fiction, this creation of loss, is a fiction that, as fallacious as it may be, one cannot live without a belief in.

For the creation of loss is the only way to give existence to the object that the subject is able to relate to. In *Playing and Reality*, D. W. Winnicott remarks on this aspect of destructive creation in the reality-making of object relations as follows:

> he will find that after "subject relates to object" comes "subject destroys object" (as it becomes external); and then may come "*object survives* destruction by the subject." But there may or may not be survival. A new feature thus arrives in the theory of object-relating. The subject says to the object: "I destroyed you," and the object is there to receive the communication. From now on the subject says: "Hullo object!" "I destroyed you." "I love you." "You have value for me because of your survival of my destruction of you." "While I am loving you I am all the time destroying you in (unconscious) *fantasy*." . . . In other words, because of the survival of the object, the subject may now have started to live a life in the world of objects, and so the subject stands to gain immeasurably; but the price has to be paid in acceptance of the ongoing destruction in unconscious fantasy relative to object-relating.[62]

Winnicott adds that this "destruction plays its part in making the reality, placing the object outside the self."[63] Just as the child makes the transition from oneness with the mother to the true object relationship through this destruction, loss is a construct that is a precondition for our relationship to the object-world. The object, hence, comes into being only as it is destroyed. Or, to be more accurate, this destruction places the object outside of the subject's fantasy, and only then can the object actually exist for the subject; while the object stays inside of the subject, it does not exist meaningfully for the subject and become a thing independent of the subject, as an object should. In the case of elegy, the mourned comes to exist only as he or she is lost to the mourner. Having realized the illusory fiction of loss, the subject creates a loss through the act of writing an elegy, and, in that process, comes to know the deceased in ways he or she had not previously known; elegy creates the deceased by enacting his or her destruction.

Read in this regard, the ambiguous image of the lone child singing himself to sleep in the closing stanza becomes not only desolate but also heroic. The "pure perfections of parental space" may be an unpersuasive fiction, but the song the child sings to himself, the song he creates, becomes a fiction that is real (VI. 6). The image of the child in solitude becomes a "sad splendor," like that of the "self that knew" its critical aloneness (V. 13, 11). The child knows its solitary existence, does not resort to the facile mythology of "parental space" or an illusion of the intersubjective communion inside the solipsistic enclosure, and, instead, creates in the void a loss so as to create the lost object.

In its allegory of the three figures, "The Owl in the Sarcophagus" chronicles the mourner's intense introspection that attempts to explore and excavate the real "crypt" underneath the fictive narrative of "loss": the things erased out of our sight, hidden under the fantastic veil of human relations and their losses. Through the three visions of sleep, peace, and mother—one's origin, one's estrangement within the self, and one's motherly, all-encompassing selfhood that contains the self and the other in the self—one discovers that the real "crypt" is the fact of solipsistic imprisonment as a human condition: the solitude in the self and its feeling of emptiness, a state in which loss is effectively lost as one encounters no prospect of loss, where the self is the only thing reflected back in the two mirrors facing one another reflecting further and further into each other with no end. By investigating alongside the poet-speaker's interior journey, we find that what lies beneath the cryptonymy of allegory is the unplaced sorrow that waits to find its place and that the consolation of elegy is not meant to be compensatory but rather creative—that an elegy constitutes an act of bringing into existence that which had not previously existed for us. And it will remain so, insofar as elegies continue to speak in cryptonymies and allegories in ways similar to Stevens's "The Owl in the Sarcophagus," and hide the real object of loss that is the illusory fiction of loss. Elegy's property as a mechanism of creation is precisely the reason we keep writing elegies, despite our keen awareness that a song would never compensate, that it would never "make up" for the void: we do it because it creates something anew. And after this knowledge, the solitude of the child singing to itself becomes an unforgiving reminder of all the cunning passages, contrived corridors, and vain deceptions of the "mythology of modern death" we are led to believe, even as its song adumbrates a path of privation that is the sole presence.[64]

Stevens's later elegies adopt "The Owl in the Sarcophagus" as their intertext, whereby fiction of loss functions as a screen to obfuscate the lost loss. His next major elegy, "To an Old Philosopher in Rome" has often been read as a more conventional elegy than "The Owl in the Sarcophagus,"[65] but if one reads "The Owl in the Sarcophagus" as the exemplary narrative of fictive loss that becomes the intertextual mold upon which Stevens writes his later elegies, an entirely different account of the progression of his oeuvre emerges. "To an Old Philosopher in Rome" was composed some months before the actual death of George Santayana, for whom this elegy is known to have been written. In this regard, the poem is a type of premature or anticipatory elegy, in the tradition of Algernon Charles Swinburne's "Ave atque Vale": the death of the celebrated person, even while he is still alive, is so imminently felt that it prompts mourning. The parallel does not stop there. On the surface, "To an Old Philosopher in Rome" is divergent from Swinburne's "Ave atque Vale," in that the former is primarily a "celebration of the dying Santayana" that carries a tone of a eulogy,[66] whereas the spirit of the latter is decidedly skeptical;[67] the telling rhyme in the latter's concluding stanza, "womb" and "tomb" (192, 193),[68] symbolizes a rejection of the consolatory rebirth-and-renewal motif that is commonly used in pastoral elegies. Nonetheless, Stevens's poem similarly signals the elegist-eulogist's awareness that the eulogy is fictive in its nature and that the proleptic loss, regardless of how powerfully it is felt, is a tenebrous loss that needs to be legitimized. Through this awareness, the poem subverts its panegyric traits and instead betrays the romantic irony that accompanies its elegiac act of fiction-making.

A touch of such subversion is observable from the opening stanza and its images of perspectival diminishment:

On the threshold of heaven, the figures in the street
Become the figures of heaven, the majestic movement
Of men growing small in the distances of space,
Singing, with smaller and still smaller sound,
Unintelligible absolution and an end—   (1–5)

Harold Bloom accounts for this image of diminishment as a "deliberate swerve away from Whitmanian enlargements,"[69] and that is certainly one way of reading the stanza. But the clash between the form and the content makes an alternative reading possible: because of their formal and tonal features, the lines sound too artificially lofty. Especially when combined with a feeling of diminution that the lines convey—such as the emphasis on the words

"Unintelligible" and "end" through a shortened line—the stanza points to the poem's lack of eulogistic conviction. Formally, the stanza has the structure of an alliterative verse, where mid-line caesurae create a majestic balance, but as the alliteration becomes more and more visible—moving from subtle "majestic movement" in line 2 and "small . . . space" in line 3 to line 4 where all stressed words alliterate, culminating in line 5 where all of the words, including unstressed ones, vowel-alliterate—the magnificence of the form comes to seem contrived.

If—like apostrophe, the machination of which has been read as a sign of fiction aware of its own fictive and optative imperative[70]—visible artifices in lyric poetry are seen as indications of a fiction aware of its own artifice, the contrived lyric moment reveals, beneath its superficially sonorous euphony, a subversive realization that whatever moving sentiment the lyricism conveys is an illusion: lyric inflation exposes the poem to be a fictive construct. Adding that to the depiction of how "men" grow "small" relative to the vastness of space called heaven, which is another name for death—and how, as one comes close to one's end, the songs of "absolution" become unintelligible and, by extension, turn into unconsoling gibberish—the stanza carries as its undercurrent an undertone of bathos.[71] That is the crux of the poem: all that is lovely in the poem is contrived, as is a philosopher's self-aware life. But this contrivance is precisely what this poem wants to celebrate: a skeptical belief in creative imagination.[72] As a result, the poem simulates a kind of orchestra, where the violins and lutes of beautification blend with the bass bathos and drowned drums to form a euphonic elegy.

It would be a gross misreading to dismiss the celebratory message of the poem entirely. Stevens's admiration for Santayana is unmistakable, not only, in the poem itself but also in other writings such as "Imagination as Value"; the essay extols Santayana's life as one where "the function of the imagination has had a function similar to its function in any deliberate work of art or letters."[73] Rather, the subversive thrust in "To an Old Philosopher in Rome" suggests that the poem exhibits the double-consciousness of romantic irony, where the warring elements of a lofty panegyric and its subtle sabotages coexist to express an understanding that the poem is constructing a fictive consolation: since Santayana is not dead, the loss has not happened yet, but the dread of its prospect is authentic enough that it has to be given a shape.

"To an Old Philosopher in Rome" is filled with moments of lyricism. While that is one of the reasons why many readers come to view it as a moving poem, the excess of artifice is conspicuous: in addition to apostrophes, alliterations and repetitions stand out, in lines such as "The loftiest syllables among loftiest things" (57), "In choruses and choirs of choruses" (66), and "Total grandeur of a total edifice" (76). One queries why, in the 1950s when the poetic trend was moving toward one of affected naturalness and Stevens's own poems too were shifting toward more conversational modes, "To an Old Philosopher in Rome" stands like a case of lyrical atavism, similar in spirit to that of "Sunday Morning" and its whimsical experiments. That the poem is a formal elegy and formal elegies tend to be more traditionally inclined is one plausible explanation. That a sonorous euphony is an appropriate tone for a tribute to a respected philosopher would qualify as another adequate answer. And the hypothesis proposed here, as yet another possibility, is that the affected lyricism of "To an Old Philosopher in Rome" is an affirmation of the belief laid out in *Adagia*: a belief in a fiction, which one knows to be a fiction.

That makes one wonder what the "fiction" this poem wants to convey is. In "Imagination as Value," Stevens exalts Santayana as an example of lives that "exist by the deliberate choice of those that live them" when most people's "lives are thrust upon them."[74] The reason that those who live by "the deliberate choice" are praised is because they are rarities; the artifice of the poem—its extravagance and its departure from the ordinary—is the formal analogue of Santayana's extraordinary life choices. Santayana is being idolized because the reality is that most of us fall into the category of those whose "lives are thrust upon them," and he embodies a necessary ideal:

        . . . O, half-asleep,
Of the pity that is the memorial of this room,

So that we feel, in this illumined large,
The veritable small, so that each of us
Beholds himself in you, and hears his voice
In yours, master and commiserable man . . .   (34–39)

Following the apostrophe—Stevens has a tendency to use apostrophes to address nonhumans, whether it is the "half-sleep" here or "exhalation" and "fling without a sleeve" in "The Owl in the Sarcophagus," which is indicative of a self-aware sabotaging of apostrophic convention and contrivance—the poem communicates our wants and desires: we want to see ourselves in Santayana, hear our voice in his, because, when we die, we want to be like the man who is deservingly dying in the "total grandeur of a total edifice" (76). The idealized Santayana offers an exemplar of what we want to be when we die and how we want to prepare for our own death.

But just as want is a synonym for lack, desire is an indication of deficiency; we want it because we do not—and perhaps will not—have it. The illumined grandeur of vision is undercut by the veritable smallness of our actual existence. Santayana's example presents a model of "how to": the theme of "how to live, how to shed anxiety or desperation in the urgency with which the states of 'mere being' and death converge."[75] The reason one buys "how to" books is that one does not know "how to" do those things, for the desire to learn how to do something reveals that, in actuality, one does not know how. The smallness of one's actual existence can be remedied or forgotten, even if temporarily, by the grandeur of the ideal; the "how to" books sell because they make us feel as though we can do them or we know how to do them, even if we cannot. Santayana needs to be upheld as an ideal—he needs to remain true to the "dignity and . . . distinction" with which he is portrayed, as well as the "readiness and grace with which he lived up to a classical role"[76]—because the ideal is the fiction we need.

This resistant reading of Stevens's elegiac homage to the respected philosopher derives from the premise that "The Owl in the Sarcophagus" and its motif of the "child singing itself to sleep"—an elegist's making of a fictive consolation with an awareness that it is an artifice—are the intertext that shapes and informs Stevens's later elegiac poems. By using "The Owl in the Sarcophagus" as a key to the cipher of his later works, one gains a fuller understanding of Stevens's effortful search for the willpower to turn fiction into belief. This preoccupation emerges in titles such as "Two Illustrations That the World Is What You Make of It" and "What We See Is What We Think," as well as in Stevens's late conversion to Roman Catholicism, an optative turn to a religion despite his recognition that the belief is a fiction.

This practice of transforming fiction into belief—of believing that the mind, the maker of fictions, is the world itself, even as it operates within the awareness of its fictive and wishful nature—repeatedly surfaces in Stevens's last poems. While that idea itself may not be new, the fiction-making of Stevens's last works masks the real object of loss that the poem seems most reluctant to be cognizant of: that the narrative of loss is itself an illusion to conceal the prospect of the loss of loss; and that the fact of solipsistic imprisonment turns the death of one's own subjectivity into an apocalyptic end, akin to the total obliteration by the flood in Wordsworth's Arab dream. Stevens, however, is more preoccupied with constructing layers of illusory losses than expressing his anxiety over the loss of loss that would surface when those illusions fail; in that sense, the prospect of lost loss is more an undercurrent in Stevens's elegiac poetry than an explicit theme. For a more sustained expressive attempt to capture the anxiety over a loss of loss, we wait for the later twentieth-century poets such as Elizabeth Bishop.[77]

Stevens continues to write poems that insist on the supremacy of the fiction-making imaginative mind to camouflage the prospect of lost loss, whereby the fiction itself simulates the phantom, a signifier of irremediable loss. In the self-summative and self-elegiac "Final Soliloquy of the Interior Paramour," the intense investigations of one's interiority lead to a romantic union between the mind's imagination and the world itself. The central claim of the poem is that the "world imagined is the ultimate good" (3):

Here, now, we forget each other and ourselves.
We feel the obscurity of an order, a whole,
A knowledge, that which arranged the rendezvous,

Within its vital boundary, in the mind.
We say God and the imagination are one . . .
How high that highest candle lights the dark.   (10–15)

The line, "We say God and the imagination are one," has received many critical commentaries as evidence of the ascendancy of imagination.[78] My focus here is the motif of the union between the mind and the world: Stevens adopts the language of love, the most intense moment of adulation where the two merge, forgetting the boundary between the two. The disappearance of the selves—like one that occurs in the fervor of religious devotion—follows the disappearance of the boundary, as one would feel in a perfect union: a meeting of I and You, which, according to Bonnie Costello, can "posit connections that history has restricted" and leads one to "imagine a reality—a future—less fragmented than the one we live in."[79] In this intense love, the moment freezes in the present—"Here, now" or the here and now—creating an effect of timelessness.

This union, however, is being narrated with an intimation of skepticism. Although "here and now" can certainly create a feeling of immediate palpability as well as of timelessness, it can also be rephrased as "now here" or "nowhere": it is a fleeting sensation that borders on nonexistence. Furthermore, this union is arranged by an "order," which can mean a command or imperative. And the imperative is that of the "knowledge" of the fictive and wishful belief. The idea that the mind and the world can be one is, however passionate the union, a wish. Despite this knowledge, the poem ends with a tone of contentment: "being there together is enough" (18). Nonetheless, "enough" is a curious sort of contentment; it is adequate and sufficient for the purpose, even if there are things that remain wanting. Even if the belief that one can will one's mind into an equivalent of the world itself is, in actuality, less a belief than wishful thinking, such tenuous half-belief is "enough," since anything more cannot be hoped for, like a union of illicit lovers who cannot ask for anything more than a fleeting here and now that is nowhere. It is a fiction whose purpose is to obscure, and protect us from, the harsher worldview in which the mind and the imagination have no power and we are left in utter deprivation.

The poem, "The Rock," states in its aphoristic first line: "It is an illusion that we were ever alive" (I. 1).[80] But we construct such illusions because they are necessary. In "To an Old Philosopher in Rome" and "Final Soliloquy of an Interior Paramour," the theme of the fiction aware of its own artifice is an implicit foundation. In "As You Leave the Room," the same theme becomes the point of explicit inquiry.[81] "As You Leave the Room" can be classified as a self-elegy; adopting a gesture similar to Yeats's "The Circus Animals' Desertion," an older poet-speaker in "As You Leave the Room" reviews, as a final glance upon his footprints before his eventual departure, his previous creations, motifs, and the course of his oeuvre up to the present; here, self-repetition replaces self-representation.[82] The poem has generally been characterized as a reworking of an unpublished poem of 1947 titled "First Warmth,"[83] but as a self-elegy, it diverges significantly from "First Warmth."

Employing a structure analogous to the Petrarchan sonnet, in which the octave states the premise or inquiry and the sestet meditates on the subject of the octave, the poem presents in its first nine lines a condition and a question, and then, in the last seven lines, ruminates over the question the first part poses. In the first nine lines, the poem splits the poet-speaker into "you" and "I," constructing an exchange between the two: "*You speak. You say*: Today's character is not / A skeleton out of its cabinet. Nor am I" (1–2). Conventional readings identify "you" as speaking for the poet-speaker's younger life and "I" as his present self,[84] but the phrase "Today's character" remains a curiosity. One may speculate that the poem refers to a survey listing of characters the poet-speaker has employed all the way up to the one he just used today. In that sense, the selves are split less over the temporal gap than the gap between a speaking self and an addressee self: the fissure of self-referentiality. This interpretation gains credence especially because of the following two elements: the italicized emphases on "speak" and "say," which point to the importance of a speaking self; and the negation that casts "I" as the object of the statement about not being a "skeleton out of its cabinet" that "you" speak of.

This negation—that "I" am not a skeleton out of its cabinet—is hard to take at face value. The apparent logic here is the following: because those poems cannot be written by a skeleton, the present poet-speaker cannot be a skeleton. Sometimes, however, repressed thoughts emerge through a negation of them.[85] While Freudian negation is a contested idea,[86] there are two legitimate reasons to think that it productively reveals a facet of this poem: first, a denial would not be needed unless such a thought crosses one's mind; and second, despite the conclusion that those poems are "not what skeletons think about" (6), the poet-speaker then questions himself in the very next line, "I wonder, have I lived a skeleton's life" (7). Given that "a skeleton out of its cabinet" is a likely play on the common expression "a skeleton in the closet," the question, "am I a skeleton," would gain a semi-playful yet self-reproachful, sardonic undertone: am I my own hidden, shameful self? Sardonic humor can often be a symptom of a wayward admission of an unwelcome thought.

The question becomes even more loaded when we consider the poem as a self-elegy of a noted elegist. Elegists, by writing about the dead, form a certain affinity with them; in "Autobiography as De-facement," de Man suggests that the act of making the dead speak and come to life can, by a reversible logic, silence and deaden the living.[87] The act of speaking with and speaking as the dead by writing elegies or elegiac poems can figuratively turn the elegist into a resident of the netherworld, a "countryman of all the bones in the world" (9), who has in fact lived a simulative skeleton's life. The elegiac engagement with all the finessing-out of consolatory or anti-consolatory beliefs and visions, which is an act of fiction-making, can delimit the elegist as "a disbeliever in reality" (8). In other words, when viewed as a self-elegy, "As You Leave the Room" becomes a self-conscious poem about what it means to be an elegist, weaving out fiction-beliefs that seem more like contrivances than the "reality" he disbelieves in.

What constitutes this "reality" is the preoccupation of the second half of the poem:

Now, here, the snow I had forgotten becomes

Part of a major reality, part of
An appreciation of a reality . . .

And yet nothing has been changed except what is
Unreal, as if nothing had been changed at all. (10–12, 15–16)

The poet-speaker situates himself in the fleeting present, a moment in the "here and now," and sees snow that seems like a part of the object-world, which he had forgotten while he was preoccupied with the fiction-making. That the poet-speaker chooses "snow" as a token of reality may be construed as a gesture of defiance against the pastoral tradition, since wintry desolation would be the opposite of the regenerative motif of spring vegetation that is commonly used in elegies. At the same time, the poem conveys plenty of skepticism about this vision of snow becoming a "major reality"; "Now, here" invokes the word "nowhere"—a suspicion that this vision too is an illusory, utopian nonexistence—more strongly than the reverse, "Here, now," in "Final Soliloquy of the Interior Paramour." Furthermore, an indefinite article is used in front of the word "reality," which communicates tentativeness: a sign of misgivings that, perhaps, this "reality" is merely an interpretation or afterimage of the reality rather than the reality itself. Given this lack of conviction, the poet-speaker downgrades an objective "major reality" to a subjective "appreciation of a reality" in the next line, and the sensation of something "I could touch, touch every way" (14) is qualified with a subjunctive "as if" (13).

True to this skepticism, the poet-speaker discovers that "nothing has been changed" despite such vision and an access to a reality of the object-world: nothing except "what is / Unreal" (15–16)—namely, his fictive and subjective interpretations of the objective world of reality. From a phenomenological perspective, a fictive interpretation of an object-reality is all he has; in this sense, the change in what is "unreal" changes everything, even if the object-reality does not actually change. That is the essence of the equivocation in the phrase, "as if nothing had been changed at all": the subjunctive implies a feeling that something has actually changed, in spite of the explicit declaration in the preceding line that nothing has changed. Interpretation inhabits this tenuous territory; it has no power to change the world, but it does change one's way of seeing, which is the only access one has to the world and which, seen in this regard, is an equivalent of the world itself. Nothing changes, yet everything does.

The same principle applies to elegies: elegies, no matter how many times they call the name of the dead,[88] have no power to raise or revive the dead. Regardless of whether they actually existed or only our interpretations of them actually existed, the dead remain unchanged, and the only thing that is changed or can be changed is the way the living regard them. Elegies are written for the living, for they do nothing for the dead. Fictive constructions of loss are the only thing left for the living. And elegists are left to make a mythology out of those creations.

The poem is curiously titled "As You Leave the Room." If, as hypothesized earlier, "you" refers to the speaking self and "I" refers to the spoken self, the title turns "you" around into an addressee. As the poet-speaker's speaking self itself turns into an object and leaves, the poem leaves readers with a sense of wondering: how an objective reality of the bones and stones of the dead themselves adamantly remains unchanging; how one's fiction-belief can change one's subjective world of that reality; and how that amounts to changing everything.

Stevens's later elegies adumbrate how the narrative of "loss" is a fiction constructed to camouflage and shield oneself against the knowledge of its own fictiveness and the prospect of the loss of loss. But as a fiction aware of its own artificiality, it is a fragile artifice that holds within it a seed of its own destruction. Its power becomes manifest when one realizes that it knows it is always on the verge of unraveling: it derives its potency precisely from the fact that it is a transitional philosophy, the destruction of which remakes and renews one's cognitive world in the way Winnicott's transitional object does for an infant. Insofar as survivors are never wholly persuaded by, and thus remain skeptical of, any consolatory philosophies, elegiac poetry has no choice but to be self-aware of its limitations, for it is this honesty that provides a temporary salve and creates an ethical subterfuge:[89] that is the offering of the inconclusiveness of Stevens's "pensive style."[90] While Stevens's elegies convey sufficiently that their narratives are fictions, it is debatable whether or not the poet, the poet-speaker, or the readers "believe in it willingly," as mandated by his "exquisite truth" in *Adagia*. This fragility of artifice, the results of which are our brittle half-beliefs, appears to be the coercive reason that almost obsessively compels the Stevens elegist to create and recreate the fictive narratives in changed and changing forms, as though they are transitional objects in our infantile, unending transitional phase—as though they are alchemical homunculi that keep on failing, in one resurrection after another.

NOTES

1. Wallace Stevens, *Letters of Wallace Stevens*, ed. Holly Stevens (Berkeley: University of California Press, 1966), 820 (abbreviated from here onward as *LWS*).
2. B. J. Legget, *Late Stevens: The Final Fiction* (Baton Rouge: Louisiana State University Press, 2005), xi.
3. Wallace Stevens, "On Receiving the National Book Award for Poetry," in *Wallace Stevens: Collected Poetry and Prose*, ed. Frank Kermode and Joan Richardson (New York: Library of America, 1997), 878 (abbreviated from here onward as *CPP*).
4. Charles M. Murphy, *Wallace Stevens: a Spiritual Poet in a Secular Age* (New York: Paulist Press, 1997), 1: Murphy interprets this search for fiction in the age without master narratives as a "search for God in the secular age in which we live." Alan Filreis also suggests that "Stevens's much-assumed anti-Christianity is really a form of anti-anti-Christianity" ("Review of *Wallace Stevens and the Question of Belief: Metaphysician in the Dark* by David R. Jarraway," *The Wallace Stevens Journal* 17, no. 2 [Fall 1993]: 251). Given the recurring theme of the death of religion in Stevens's oeuvre—evidence ranges from such declarations as "Divinity must live within [oneself]" in the paganistic ideal of "Sunday Morning" and "The heaven of Europe is empty" in "Owl's Clover" to motifs of emptiness such as "empty heaven" in "The Man with the Blue Guitar" and "spirit of the holy temples / Empty and grandiose" in "Like Decorations in a Nigger Cemetery"—it would be restrictive to define Stevens's search as one specifically for a Christian God or a religious god. As Allen Dunn explicates Charles Altieri's claims in *Wallace Stevens and the Demands of Modernity: Toward a Phenomenology of Value* (Ithaca: Cornell University Press, 2013), Stevens's poetry "offers us access to the kinds of values that can withstand interrogation by a secular and skeptical age" (Allen Dunn, "In the Shadow of Central Man: Self-Transcendence and Self-Discovery in Charles Altieri's Reading of Stevens," *The Wallace Stevens Journal* 39, no. 1 [Spring 2015]: 56).
5. Stevens, *CPP*, 22, 23. And "mythology"—as we may glean from Stevens's statement in *Adagia*, "The greatest piece of fiction: Greek mythology"—is a type of fiction for Stevens (Wallace Stevens, *Opus Posthumous* [New York: Knopf, 1957], 178, abbreviated from here onward as *OP*).
6. Stevens, *CPP*, 106.

7. Janet McCann, *Wallace Stevens Revisited: "The Celestial Possible"* (New York: Twayne Publishers, 1995), 93. Remarking on Nietzsche's role in Stevens's philosophical development, Charles Altieri writes the following: "Art is not an escape from the moral but the vehicle by which expression enters into mortal combat with morality to determine what the ultimate models of valuation will become" (Altieri, *Wallace Stevens and the Demands of Modernity*, 23). In a critique of Altieri's work, Barrett Witten argues that art "as a transvaluation of all values is the horizon toward which we should read Stevens' value-creating poetics" ("Poetics and the Question of Value; or, What Is a Philosophically Serious Poet?" *The Wallace Stevens Journal* 39, no. 1 [Spring 2015]: 88). In a recent critical shift toward reading Stevens as a poet of values, Stevens's elegiac poetry may profitably be examined as one arm of his articulation of artistic transvaluation.

8. Stevens, *CPP*, 903. In *Adagia*, there is also a proclamation that poetry "creates a fictitious existence on an exquisite plane" (*OP*, 180).

9. Romanticism "has a special claim on the attention of his readers" and it is what "Stevens himself identifies as his own central tradition" (Joseph Carroll, "Stevens and Romanticism," in *The Cambridge Companion to Wallace Stevens*, ed. John N. Serio [Cambridge: Cambridge University Press, 2007], 101).

10. Critical works that examine Stevens's romantic irony include Anthony Whiting's *The Never-Resting Mind: Wallace Stevens's Romantic Irony* (Ann Arbor: University of Michigan Press, 1996).

11. For instance, Helen Vendler's commentary on "The Emperor of Ice-Cream" as "secrecies of form" that is "always a carrier of meaning" can equally apply to "The Owl in the Sarcophagus" (Helen Vendler, *Wallace Stevens: Words Chosen Out of Desire* [Knoxville: University of Tennessee Press, 1984], 52).

12. In a chapter entitled "Wallace Stevens in a 'Sudden Time,'" Rachel Galvin suggests that Stevens's wartime poetry tends to be self-reflexive (Rachel Galvin, *News of War: Civilian Poetry 1936–1945* [Oxford: Oxford University Press, 2017], 167). Self-reflexivity is one critical element of anti-elegiac skepticism. As seen in Harold Bloom's remarks on "The Death of a Soldier" as "the emergence of the poet's most characteristic voice" (Harold Bloom, *Wallace Stevens: The Poems of Our Climate* [Ithaca: Cornell University Press, 1977], 48), many of the traits of Stevens's later elegies can be traced to these earlier works, including the withholding of "the 'pomp' of religion'" (George S. Lensing, *Making the Poem: Stevens' Approaches* [Baton Rouge: Louisiana State University Press, 2018], 93).

13. Ramazani, *Poetry of Mourning*, 94–97.

14. Even when Stevens invokes pastoral scenes, it is "with perceptibly diminished expectations about the consolations they will offer" (Spargo, *The Ethics of Mourning*, 225).

15. Stevens, *OP*, 160.

16. Anne Mellor, *English Romantic Irony* (Cambridge: Harvard University Press, 1980), 5–6.

17. This phrase was appropriated from Edward Said, *Beginnings* (New York: Basic Books, 1975), 229.

18. Jahan Ramazani counts only two of Stevens's poems, "The Owl in the Sarcophagus" and "To an Old Philosopher in Rome," as "formal elegies" (Ramazani,

Poetry of Mourning, 87), as does Charles Berger ("The Mythology of Modern Death," 166). Berger adds that "Stevens wrote so frequently in the elegiac mode . . . that any attempt to isolate pure elegy in his poetry would be pointless" (Charles Berger, *Forms of Farewell: The Late Poetry of Wallace Stevens* [Madison: University of Wisconsin Press, 1985], 111). Stevens's reputation as an elegist depends less on his formal elegies than the elegiac sensibilities of his oeuvre.

19. Stevens, *CPP*, 374.

20. Ramazani, *Poetry of Mourning*, 1, 3, and Thomas Travisano, *Midcentury Quartet: Bishop, Lowell, Jarrell, Berryman, and the Making of a Postmodern Aesthetic* (Charlottesville: University Press of Virginia, 1999), 245.

21. Sacks, *The English Elegy*, 4–10.

22. Berger, *Forms of Farewell*, 114.

23. Jacques Derrida argues that all our relationships are imbued with a sense of impending loss, a kind of proleptic mourning, stamped with "the signature of *memoirs-from-beyond-the-grave*" and the "remembrance of the future" ("*Fors*: The Anglish Words of Nicolas Abraham and Maria Torok," trans. Barbara Johnson, *The Wolf Man's Magic Word: A Cryptonymy*, ed. Nicolas Abraham and Maria Torok, trans. Nicholas Rand [Minneapolis: University of Minnesota Press, 1986], xxix).

24. Joan Melville, "'Inventions of Farewell': Wallace Stevens' 'The Owl in the Sarcophagus,'" *The Wallace Stevens Journal* 16, no. 1 (1992): 3–21, as well as the Ramazani and Berger texts, among others.

25. Stevens, *LWS*, 566.

26. Critics have noted that Stevens "was prevented by lack of time from inscribing . . . his chosen dedication: 'Goodbye H.C.'" at the time of its publication in *Horizon* (Melville, "'Inventions of Farewell',," 4). The dedication, however, was never added in later editions.

27. In Benjaminian melancholia, the melancholic, who perceives his world as a fallen one reduced to a mass of devalued, meaningless fragments, assigns through allegory arbitrary meanings to those fragments; this subjective assignation of meanings reconstructs the experience of the original world, culminating in the redemptive restoration of the melancholic's cognitive world. This formulation of the Benjaminian template of melancholia derives from *The Origin of German Tragic Drama*, trans. John Osborne (New York: Verso, 1998), 142–235, with the aid of Max Pensky's *Melancholy Dialectics: Walter Benjamin and the Play of Mourning* (Amherst: University of Massachusetts Press, 1993), 36–150.

28. Ronald Sukenick, *Wallace Stevens: Musing the Obscure* (New York: New York University Press, 1967), 224.

29. One of the prominent features in elegy, repetition has been conventionally interpreted as (1) a way to create a sense of continuity through unbroken pattern, (2) a method of reality testing, or (3) an attempt to raise the spirit of the dead from the grave through the act of chanting. For a more detailed discussion of the function of repetition in elegy, see Sacks, 23–26. Although, in this poem, what is repeated is not the name of the dead but rather the names of the allegorical figures of death, Sleep and Peace, Margaret Alexiou's commentary on the particular custom of repeating the name of the dead may be relevant: "one element of the primitive lament which was

never forgotten or ignored ... was the refrain calling the dying man or god by name .... Its function was to raise the spirit of the dead from the grave" (Margaret Alexiou, *The Ritual Lament in Greek Tradition* [Cambridge: Cambridge University Press, 1974], 109). It is as though, by repeating the allegorical names of death, the poem attempts to raise its spirit from the grave of unintelligibility, to turn it into something more familiar and intelligible, and hence more manageable, containable.

30. Susan Stewart, *Poetry and the Fate of the Senses* (Chicago: University of Chicago Press, 2002), 66.

31. James Longenbach, "The World after Poetry: Revelation in Late Stevens," *The Wallace Stevens Journal* 23, no. 2 (Fall 1999): 189.

32. On the theme of ancestral imagery, Joseph Carroll comments that, in "order to create a supreme fiction, Stevens has had to effect an integration of the archetypal, ancestral memory and 'The abstract'" (*Wallace Stevens' Supreme Fiction: A New Romanticism* [Baton Rouge: Louisiana University Press, 1987], 312). Stevens uses the familial naming because it is one template to which the melancholic mind can resort in its attempt to reconstruct its broken world through an allegory. In "Sunday Morning," Stevens writes: "Death is the mother of beauty." Stevens's mother figure can at times be an all-encompassing emblem that espouses expressions and apprehensions of "beauty," consisting of art and nature. Language, as an inclusive medium that captures artistic moments and nature, becomes the tenor of the "mother" allegory.

33. Paul de Man, "Autobiography as De-facement," *Modern Language Notes* 94 (1979): 930.

34. Friedrich Nietzsche, *The Gay Science*, trans. Walter Kaufmann (New York: Vintage Books, 1974), 167: the image refers to the death of God, and Nietzsche asserts that, "given the way of men, there may still be caves for thousands of years in which his shadow will be shown." The "shadow" signifies an absence-presence, a kind of possession in the state of dispossession that is like a privative realm of linguistic predicament. Coincidentally, Milton J. Bates reports that it was a correspondence between Stevens and Henry Church that rekindled Stevens's interest in Nietzsche, who was, for Stevens at the time, "but a dim memory from his earlier reading" (*Wallace Stevens: A Mythology of Self* [Berkeley: University of California Press, 1985], 252–53).

35. Joseph Riddel, *The Clairvoyant Eye: The Poetry and Poetics of Wallace Stevens* (Baton Rouge: Louisiana State University Press, 1965), 240.

36. In *Beyond Consolation*, Melissa Zeiger observes that, since "classical times, elegiac poetry has been shaped or informed by the narrative of Orpheus and Eurydice" (Zeiger, 2).

37. Critics disagree on the identity of the "man" who walks "living among the forms of thought." Harold Bloom suggests that the man refers to Henry Church (Bloom, *The Poems of Our Climate*, 285), while Charles Berger asserts that it is the poet himself (Berger, *Forms of Farewell*, 116). My interpretation is that it is the lyric-speaker who goes to the underworldly interiority of himself.

38. Gerard Manley Hopkins, "Sonnet #44," in *Poems and Prose of Gerard Manley Hopkins* (London: Penguin Books, 1985), lines 2, 6: "What hours, O what black hours we have spent .... / Hours I mean years, mean life."

39. The romantics, Wordsworth especially, are evoked in poems such as "Sunday Morning" (McCann, 7). "The Comedian" traces, like Wordsworth's *Prelude*, the "Growth of a Poet's Mind" (Walton A. Litz, *Introspective Voyager: The Poetic Development of Wallace Stevens* [New York: Oxford University Press, 1972], 120). Aside from Wordsworth, one may also hear echoes of Keats's odes and "The Fall of Hyperion."

40. The quotes are respectively from Wordsworth's "Lines: Composed a Few Miles above Tintern Abbey, on Revisiting the Banks of the Wye during a Tour, July 13, 1798," *The Norton Anthology of English Literature*, line 148, and "Ode: Intimations of Immortality from Recollections of Early Childhood," *The Norton Anthology of English Literature*, lines 110 and 113.

41. Wordsworth, "My Heart Leaps up When I Behold," *The Norton Anthology of English Literature*, line 7.

42. Melville, "'Inventions of Farewell'," 8. The title has also been linked to the elaborate burial rituals of ancient Egypt, in which the writing of the poem enacts the ritual placement of gifts in the sarcophagus to make the deceased's trip through the underworld more comfortable (Veronica Ions, *Egyptian Mythology* [New York: Hamlyn, 1965], 116–18, 127–38). By connecting the owl, the figure of wisdom, with elaborate ancient rites and conventions of death, the title indicates that the poem offers wisdom in the face of death (Melville, "'Inventions of Farewell'," 6).

43. Bloom, *The Poems of Our Climate*, 292.

44. Northrop Frye, *Anatomy of Criticism* (Princeton: Princeton University Press, 1957), 249. The phrase refers to J. S. Mill's famous statement: the voice of the lyric "I" is "overheard" and distinguished "by the poet's utter unconsciousness of a listener" (John Stuart Mill, "What Is Poetry?" in *Essays on Poetry by John Stuart Mill*, ed. F. Parvin Sharpless [Columbia: University of South Carolina Press, 1976], 12).

45. Jonathan Culler, "Changes in the Study of the Lyric," in *Lyric Poetry: Beyond New Criticism*, ed. Chaviva Hošek and Patricia Parker (Ithaca: Cornell University Press, 1985), 43.

46. One may argue that the egotism of Whitman's "Song of Myself" too is that of melancholic solipsism; after all, Whitman is himself a noted elegist who composed such influential elegies as "When Lilacs Last in the Dooryard Bloom'd," in which critics see the ancestry of "The Owl in the Sarcophagus" (Bloom, *The Poems of Our Climate*, 283–84).

47. William Styron, *Darkness Visible: A Memoir of Madness* (New York: Vintage Books, 1992).

48. Freud observes that melancholic patients often have a "keener eye for the truth than others who are not melancholic," which enables them to "come very near to self-knowledge"; see Sigmund Freud, "Mourning and Melancholia," in *General Psychological Theory* (New York: Simon & Schuster, 1991), 167. Melancholia has been theorized as a way of seeing: Julia Kristeva views it as a failure of perception and loss of meaning in her *Black Sun: Depression and Melancholia* (New York: Columbia University Press, 1989), 189. As mentioned earlier, Benjamin defines it as a way of seeing the world through fragmented subjectivity that perceives objects as allegories (Benjamin, *The Origin*, 183).

49. Georges Poulet, "Exploding Poetry: Baudelaire," in *Charles Baudelaire*, ed. Harold Bloom (New York: Chelsea House Publishers, 1987), 70.

50. Waters, *Poetry's Touch*, 2–3.

51. Walt Whitman, *Leaves of Grass* (New York: Vintage, 1992), 206, 246.

52. Berger, "The Mythology of Modern Death," 177.

53. Joan Didion, *The White Album* (Farrar, Straus and Giroux: New York, 1979), 11.

54. Ramazani, *Poetry of Mourning*, 3.

55. Ramazani, *Poetry of Mourning*, 4.

56. Jacobs, "The Dying of Death," 264.

57. Abraham and Torok, *The Shell and the Kernel*, 17, 19.

58. Abraham and Torok, *The Shell and the Kernel*, 140–41.

59. On the frequency of self-mourning in elegies, Ramazani states: "For all their differences, the elegy and the self-elegy cannot be neatly compartmentalized. We have already seen that in Stevens's war elegies the anticipation of [his own] death is a central concern . . . . Moreover, canonical poets had often mourned themselves in elegies while at the same time mourning others: Milton, for example, had turned in 'Lycidas' to glance at his own fated shroud, and in *Adonais* Shelley had ecstatically foreseen his demise" (Ramazani, *Poetry of Mourning*, 119).

60. Marcus Aurelius, *Meditations*, trans. Gregory Hays (New York: The Modern Library, 2002), 21.

61. Stevens, *LWS*, 370.

62. D. W. Winnicott, *Playing and Reality* (New York: Routledge, 1971), 90.

63. Winnicott, *Playing and Reality*, 91.

64. The phrase, the "mythology of modern death," raises the question why Stevens would trouble to qualify the poem's mourning mythology as one of "modern" death, and how a "modern" death would differ from, say, a premodern one. A "modern" death experience can be characterized in a number of ways: secular and scientific, as compared to the more religious one before the advent of modern medicine and hospitals; hidden and closed-off, as compared to the more visible one before the aforesaid phenomenon of the "dying of death"; or in mass and anonymous, as compared to the more personal one prior to the weapons-of-mass-destruction era; and so on. But one modern perspective on death that may be particularly pertinent here is that, in the twentieth-century context since Freud, mourning for death has become a psychological work that involves interpretive activities. For Freud, "mourning is not simply an emotion but the performance of a *Trauerarbeit*, or 'sorrow work': mourning, like interpretation, is an activity" (Alessia Ricciardi, *The Ends of Mourning: Psychoanalysis, Literature, Film* [Stanford: Stanford University Press, 2003], 6). In "The Owl in the Sarcophagus," this interpretive activity of modern mourning, the working-through of the reactive emotions like melancholia, occurs in the form of allegory, for the "literary mode in and by which melancholia manifests itself is allegory" (Olga Taxidou, *Tragedy, Modernity and Mourning* [Edinburgh: Edinburgh University Press, 2004], 91). In other words, the allegoresis of this poem—or, to be more specific, the interpretive "work" that an allegory necessitates—makes this poem a mythologization of a "modern" death experience, for the fact that modernity has

made death an "interpretive" activity. And from his use of the word, "mythology"—which, as mentioned earlier, is not one of Stevens's favored words—we can glean Stevens's ambivalence over this interpretive nature of the work of mourning, as well as over the fictive construct of death that this poem's "mythology" creates: even if this interpretive and constructive work of our mind may help us find a place for the kind of unplaced melancholic sorrow that "The Owl in the Sarcophagus" expresses, that by and of itself hardly feels like a consolation, and yet, that is all we are left with.

65. Berger, *Forms of Farewell*, 134.
66. Bloom, *The Poems of Our Climate*, 360, and Berger, *Forms of Farewell*, 133.
67. Swinburne was skeptical of the English pastoral elegy tradition (Margot Kathleen Louis, *Swinburne and His Gods* [Kingston: McGill-Queen's University Press, 1990], 151, 152).
68. Algernon Charles Swinburne, "Ave atque Vale," in *The Norton Anthology of English Literature*, ed. Stephen Greenblatt (New York: W. W. Norton, 2012), 1537.
69. Bloom, *The Poems of Our Climate*, 361.
70. Jonathan Culler, "Apostrophe," *Diacritics: A Review of Contemporary Criticism* 7, no. 4 (1977 Winter): 65.
71. For Stevens, heaven is one of the "fictive projections of human desires" (William Tate, "Shades of Bliss: Imagining Heaven in Wallace Stevens and Richard Wilbur," *Christianity & Literature* 68, no. 2 [March 2019]: 253).
72. Stevens's ruminative, meta-poetic style is an analogue of Santayana's view of thinking as a virtue unto itself (Kimberly Quiogue Andrews, "Resisting the Intelligence Almost Successfully: Wallace Stevens's 'Academic' Style," *Modernist Cultures* 14, no. 1 [2019]: 59).
73. Stevens, *CPP*, 734. Although Stevens was never formally taught by Santayana while he was enrolled at Harvard University, he owned copies of Santayana's writings, and came to form a friendship with him (Rachel Malkin, "American Philosophy," in *Wallace Stevens in Context*, ed. Glen MacLeod [Cambridge: Cambridge University Press, 2017], 224). Stevens's admiration of philosophers also emerges in the form of poetry-philosophy symbiosis: "one can hear the poet seeking the same credentials as the philosopher for serious thinking, for using abstractions or ideas" (Angela Leighton, "Poetry of Knowing," in *The Philosophy of Poetry*, ed. John Gibson [Oxford: Oxford University Press, 2015], 165).
74. Stevens, *CPP*, 733–34.
75. Lea Baechler, "Pre-Elegiac Affirmation in 'To an Old Philosopher in Rome,'" *The Wallace Stevens Journal* 14, no. 2 (Fall 1990): 145.
76. Edmund Wilson, "Santayana at the Convent of the Blue Nuns," *New Yorker*, April 6, 1946, 64. This Wilson essay, which is an account of a visit to the aged Santayana in Rome, provided the occasion and the context for "To an Old Philosopher in Rome" (Baechler, "Pre-Elegiac Affirmation," 142).
77. Stevens's work "was profoundly transformative for Bishop" (David Jarraway, *Wallace Stevens among Others: Diva-Dames, Deleuze, and American Culture* [Ithaca: McGill-Queen's University Press, 2015], 215).
78. Critics have interpreted this poem as an instance of Stevens's glorifications of the imagination, the notion of the human imagination as God, whether as a

reaffirmation of "the power of the imagination to create the 'supreme fictions,' the fictive constructs that are the world in which we dwell" (Whiting, *The Never-Resting Mind*, 166) or as a sign that Stevens's "faith is a faith in himself" (Edward Kessler, *Images of Wallace Stevens* [New Brunswick: Rutgers University Press, 1972], 86). Other critics have reversed the formula, claiming that "God is the imaginer, the agent and not the object of the imagination" in Stevens's last poems (Leggett, *Late Stevens: The Final Fiction*, 49). The contemporary consensus appears to be that the poem itself is a dramatization of the adage within the poem, "God and the imagination are one" (Milton J. Bates, "Stevens's Letters, Notebooks, and Journals," in *Wallace Stevens in Context*, ed. Glen MacLeod [Cambridge: Cambridge University Press, 2017], 145).

79. Bonnie Costello, *The Plural of Us: Poetry and Community in Auden and Others* (Princeton University Press, 2017), 6.

80. Stevens, *CPP*, 445.

81. Self-referentiality in Stevens's later work has been well-noted, but his mature aesthetics feature abstract meditation itself as a catalyst (Edward Ragg, *Wallace Stevens and the Aesthetics of Abstraction* [Cambridge: Cambridge University Press, 2010], 205).

82. This formulation owes to Marjorie Levinson's discussion of "The Poems of Our Climate" (Marjorie Levinson, *Thinking Through Poetry: Field Reports on Romantic Lyric* [Oxford: Oxford University Press, 2018], 238).

83. John Dolan remarks that the revision "reverses the entire argument of 'First Warmth'" ("'The Warmth I Had Forgotten': Stevens' Revision of 'First Warmth' and the Dramatization of the Interpersonal," *The Wallace Stevens Journal* 21, no. 2 [1997]: 162), while Lee M. Jenkins believes that the first version is superior to the second, claiming that "each revision of 'First Warmth' is also a retreat from the candour of 'First Warmth'" (*Wallace Stevens: Rage for Order* [Portland: Sussex Academic Press, 2000], 128–29).

84. Leggett, *Late Stevens: The Final Fiction*, 139.

85. Sigmund Freud, "Negation," in *General Psychological Theory*, ed. Philip Rieff (New York: Simon & Schuster, 1991), 213–17.

86. Sigmund Freud, "Constructions in Analysis," in *The Standard Edition of the Complete Psychological Works of Sigmund Freud*, Vol. XXIII, ed., trans. James Strachey (London: Hogarth Press, 1964), 257: Freud himself comments on the potential unfalsifiability of the condition, saying that "if the patient agrees with us, then the interpretation is right; but if he contradicts us, that is only a sign of his resistance, which again shows that we are right."

87. De Man, "Autobiography as De-facement," 928.

88. Alexiou, *The Ritual Lament in Greek Tradition*, 109.

89. Stevens's poetics "operates with an aesthetic strategy that, by separating and distancing itself from its social reality, brings forth different potential forms of relationality between poetry and collective life" (Gül Bilge Han, *Wallace Stevens and the Poetics of Modernist Autonomy* [Cambridge: Cambridge University Press, 2019], 5–6), whereby it becomes profitable to examine his elegiac poetry not only through philosophical but also social and ethical dimensions.

90. The phrase "pensive style" is borrowed from Helen Vendler, *On Extended Wings: Wallace Stevens' Longer Poems* (Cambridge: Harvard University Press, 1969), 13–37.

Chapter 2

Sylvia Plath's Poems of 1963
Dysthymia and Subterranean Loss

In *Ambiguous Loss: Learning to Live with Unresolved Grief*, Pauline Boss identifies a phenomenon she names "ambiguous loss" and provides the following description:

> [The] phenomenon has always been the stuff of opera, literature, and the theater. In these genres, losses that remain vague and uncertain are embellished. Homer's Penelope waits for her missing husband; Arthur Miller's father in *All My Sons* insists his son is alive long after a fatal air crash . . . . The very situations that people least understand stir their unconscious. For the one who experiences it, however, the ambiguity of waiting and wondering is anything but romantic. Ambiguous loss is always stressful and often tormenting.[1]

In Boss's formulation, ambiguous loss refers primarily to familial contexts; in any given family, some members may be perceived by others as physically absent but psychologically present—such as in the cases of missing soldiers and kidnapped children—or as physically present but psychologically absent—such as in the cases of Alzheimer's disease or excessive preoccupations that make them emotionally unavailable.[2] Ambiguous loss is particularly pernicious because its lack of clarity complicates the possibility of resolution. Unresolved grief is difficult to problem-solve because one would not yet know whether the loss is final or temporary; one is detained in an indefinite period of indeterminacy, which jeopardizes the possibility of closure. Furthermore, the ambiguity prevents people from reorganizing their life and leaves them in an ongoing state of distress, since the social process of mourning and coping that would be available if there were a clear loss would not be offered to them.[3]

Because ambiguous loss comes with added layers of complications, a normal reaction to it tends to be melancholia, as a type of nonnormative mourning that entails prolonged grief without closure. As is often the case with unresolved mourning, the state of "frozen grief" is due not so much to the internal personality defects of the mourner but rather to the external situation that is outside of the mourner's control.[4] If we are to define trauma as triggered by a breach of trust,[5] ambiguous loss can be regarded as a source of traumatization, in that its absurdity shakes one's confidence in the rationality and justness of the world, which is ill-equipped to provide clarity to the kind of incertitude that ambiguous loss brings about.

It would certainly be tempting to examine Sylvia Plath's poetry through the lens of ambiguous loss in light of the fact that one may find in her biography various kinds and degrees of this type of loss and the sense of melancholia it triggers.[6] A number of poems mourning for the dead father—"Electra on Azalea Path," "Full Fathom Five," "The Colossus," "Daddy," to name a few—paints a portrait of a lyric-speaker spellbound to the shadow of the physically dead but psychologically present father. And if, as Boss suggests, immigration can be a source of incongruence in familial relationships—an emotionally present family member may be physically absent in a country one moves to—the trans-Atlantic migrations by both Plath's parents and by Plath herself in her adulthood can also simulate ambiguous loss; the legacy of this emotional burden may have an intergenerational effect on the family, compounding itself as more ordinary losses inevitably occur.[7] Divorce, too, is another type of ambiguous loss: someone who was a family member is no longer, but is often not entirely erased out of one's familial life, especially when the divorcees have children together. One of Plath's letters to Aurelia Plath on January 2, 1963 points precisely to this predicament: "For goodness sake do tell people I am separated from Ted &, if you feel like it, divorcing him! It is odd to get cards from people like the Aldriches to us both, there's no point in you keeping up any pretense."[8] This ambiguous status is further underscored in another letter: "Ted comes once a week like a kind of a [sic] apocalyptic Santa Claus & when I'm in the country I guess half years & years will go by without him seeing them [children] at all."[9] The key, once again, is incongruence: there is a gap between Plath's own view of her relationships—the letter professes that she considers herself separated and, for all practical purposes, divorced from Ted Hughes—and that of the people around her, who still send her cards addressed to both.[10] The letter also reveals Plath's concern over the impact of this ambiguous loss on her children. It is not a coincidence that these heartaches converge with holiday seasons. Those festive occasions can be especially brutal to people going through this type of relational indeterminacy.

The interest of this chapter, however, diverges from the reading of Plath's poetry through the instances of ambiguous loss in her biography and family relationships. The project of this book is to define and elucidate diverse manifestations of lost loss, which I have proposed as an umbrella term for various ambivalent or unassimilated dispossessions: examples of such include Judith Butler's notion of "ungrievable loss," where the deceased are dishonored and cannot be mourned; Kenneth J. Doka's idea of "disenfranchised loss," where one's grief is not socially sanctioned or understood; as well as Boss's "ambiguous loss," from which the present chapter begins as an avenue into explicating the larger phenomenon of lost loss. Specifically, lost loss is marked by the kind of obstinacy and chronicity associated with a particular sub-category of melancholia: dysthymia. The dysthymic moods of indeterminacy and persistence resemble those that frequently occur in the instances of ambiguous loss, although Boss's formulation does not explicitly link the two phenomena. Dysthymia is often likened to a state of living in the "gray zone," and it is distinguished by its covert nature: although millions of people suffer from it, most people do not know that they are suffering from it.[11] Plath's elegiac poems have frequently been associated with violence and anger,[12] but the present analysis offers a counter-narrative to this assessment: Plath's later poems, particularly the poems of 1963, simulate the mood of quieter dysthymia more so than the eruptive melancholia that her poems have come to be identified with in the reception of her works. In the poems of 1963, no immediate loss is legible and only the faint echoes of amorphous privation are detectable. The presumed loss in these poems has become distant enough that they have lost sight of its origin; dispossessions they seemingly portray are themselves absented or equivocated.

Sylvia Plath's poems of 1963 are generally characterized as a "cycle of death poems" or "poems read as epitaphs."[13] These characterizations partially arise from the occasional self-elegiac tone they employ in their expression of acute desolation; they also derive from readers' knowledge of Plath's suicide that occurred in February of that year. While such biographical reading remains powerful, the poems of 1963, upon closer examination, invite to be read as projecting voices and emotions of less intensity than has been thought. These elegiac poems of 1963 engage not so much with any actual death but rather with an all-engulfing sense of emptiness in which one cannot tell what precisely is being lost. Diverging from Plath's earlier anti-elegies that speak in the voice of traumatic crises, the poems of 1963 function as a mechanism to give name to, as well as find the sources of, the nameless, shifty, vague, uncertain losses of quieter dysthymia.[14] Distancing themselves from the convention-conscious elegies of *The Colossus and Other Poems* and anti-elegiac elegies of much of *Ariel*, the poems of 1963 invent their own coded language to speak and, in so doing, give shape to this profound privation.

The poems of 1963 employ a mode of writing that has been customarily characterized as that "of surrealism,"[15] which resists linear narrative and tends to remain coded, effecting a kind of exclusion of readers.[16] The poems encapsulate the disorienting and fragmentary null language-space of an all-encompassing void, in which the feeling of loss is so pervasive that all things, including the self, seem to be effaced: there is an atmosphere of loss, but one is hard-pressed to distinguish what has been, or is being, lost. Below are two more samples of the ways in which readers have described the interpretive difficulties of these last poems:

> They are poems written out of . . . a state of being in which the speaker . . . has abandoned the sense of audience and cares nothing about—indeed, is hardly aware of—the presence of anyone but herself. [Plath] writes with a hallucinatory, self-contained fervor. She addresses herself to the air, to the walls . . . . There is something utterly monolithic, fixated about the voice that emerges in these poems, a voice unmodulated and asocial . . . . It is as if we are overhearing the rasps of a mind that has found its own habitation and need not measure its distance from . . . other minds.[17]

> . . . the repetitions of mimicry . . . which lead nowhere, that is, which lead solely to the poem they echo.[18]

Aside from the obvious reference to J. S. Mill's model of lyric voice as one of being overheard, the first excerpt attributes the interpretive difficulties of the poems to the speaker's disregard of the readers. The latter excerpt characterizes the disconnection or dislocation, the absence of telos, in the utterance of the language in those poems. Such deadlocking imbroglio prompts us to inquire: do the interpretive difficulties of these poems derive from their exclusion of readers or the lack of linear narrative, or from the possibility that these poems are taking readers to a place they have never become conscious of, a place to which no other poems, not even Plath's poems before 1963, have brought the readers? Like the case of Theodore Roethke's "Elegy for Jane," critical bafflement often surfaces as a sign when a writer attempts to express something for which the language has not yet been formulated. A reexamination of Plath's poems of 1963 uncovers a linguistic and cognitive pioneering similar to that of Roethke's relationally distant elegy. This all-encompassing, profound loss differs from other types of losses, however, in that it derails readers from conventional interpretations; loss of all things, including things like speaker, agent, addressee, the fact of loss, and so on, would disorient and disrupt one's readerly senses and, hence, is prone to appear as a symptom of exclusivity or solipsism, for its expressive tropes are not as readily recognizable.

Part of the reason that the expressive tropes of the poems of 1963 are baffling is that they engage with a different type of loss than is customarily expressed in elegiac poetry. Here, ambiguous loss becomes a critical analogue. In ambiguous loss, the loss often feels as though it is not really one, and this indeterminacy complicates mourning; when the absent seems present and the present seems absent, the resultant confusion freezes the grieving process.[19] The coded, exclusionary language, which critics have observed in Plath's poems of 1963, is one manifestation of the vague privation that defies cognition and, hence, expression.

The above hypothesis becomes more supportable when we examine the progression of Plath's work from its beginning *Colossus* phase. In *The Colossus and Other Poems*, Plath's anti-elegies conform to the standard definition of anti-elegy as the "transgeneric attack" on the customs of traditional elegies that are dependent on their loss-compensation model;[20] that is to say, Plath's anti-elegies of the *Colossus* period operate within the paradigm of the loss-compensation model, in that they generally defy, or lament the failure of, the said model.[21] There are two main features of the *Colossus* poems that are relevant in the present discussion of her anti-elegies: their immersion in the literary tradition;[22] and the presence of specific object-loss. Many of her *Colossus* elegies—such as the collection's title poem, "The Colossus," as well as "Electra on Azalea Path" and "Full Fathom Five"—lament how impossible it is to compensate for the loss of the cherished object, as crystallized by the resigned utterance in the opening line of "The Colossus": "I shall never get you put together entirely."[23] These elegies satisfy both of the two conditions mentioned above: intertextuality and object-loss. And others, whether it is the tradition-conscious "Lorelei" or "The Eye-Mote," or the object-specific "All the Dead Dears," satisfy either one of the two conditions, with sufficiently detectable lament or outrage over the impossibility of recouping the lost object. Even in defiance, the *Colossus* elegies stay within the realm of loss-specific mourning, as defined by Jacques Lacan: "The work of mourning is first of all performed to satisfy the disorder that is produced by the inadequacy of the signifying elements to cope with the hole that has been created in existence, for it is the system of signifiers in their totality which is impeached by the least instance of mourning."[24] The *Colossus* elegies retain a sense of a specific "disorder" and "hole" in one's relational existence, and they chronicle the elegiac speaker's effort to find remedies, which generally ends in a realization of the inadequacy of the signifiers to cope with such a void.

After this *Colossus* phase comes the next phase, which covers most of the *Ariel* poems prior to 1963. Pre-1963 *Ariel* elegies become shiftier in both their allusiveness and their object-specificity, even as they continue to express a similar angst over the powerless, duplicitous consolatory apparatus of loss-compensation. For example, "Daddy"—arguably the most well-known anti-elegy among Plath's oeuvre—presents an object-loss that begins as a father figure and then, in its continuous metaphorical slide, merges into a new "vampire" figure as the speaker acknowledges, "If I've killed one man, I've killed two" (71). In the last stanza, the poem uses four straight emphatic end-rhymes to exclaim that the speaker is "through" trying to recover the lost object, even if such a proclamation proves precisely that she is not through. While the mode of lamentation is similar to the *Colossus* phase, where pre-1963 *Ariel* elegies differ from those of the *Colossus* phase is that the elegies of *Ariel* leave room for multiplicity, blurriness, and equivocation in identifying an object-loss; whereas in "The Colossus" the object-loss remains that of a father even as it dabbles with an allusion to Agamemnon, in "Daddy," the father figure converges into other identities, whether it is a Nazi or a vampire who said he was the father. In another self-elegy, "Lady Lazarus," the speaker not only assumes the identity of a female Lazarus but also conflates the primary object-loss—the things that compose herself—with a Jew in a concentration camp. In "Cut," the lyric-speaker's blood, shed in a kitchen accident where the speaker cuts her thumb instead of an onion, merges with the history of bloodshed to form an elegy for historical losses. The poem catalogs various carnages that took place over the course of the U.S. history as metaphors of the blood pouring from the speaker's thumb. "Little pilgrim" (9) refers to the Puritans, who are the first arrivals from Europe to the New England region of North America; their relations to Native Americans were friendly in some instances and hostile in others, before eventually culminating in the American Indian War. "Redcoats" (20) were worn by the British soldiers who fought against the Patriots during the American Revolutionary War. "Saboteurs" (27) and "Kamikaze man" (28) are World War II references. The list goes on: Ku Klux Klan and lynching, the Cold War, soldiers returning from wars with traumatic brain injuries. These critical events form a storyline of the history of the United States, the collective consciousness of which interacts with and flows from the personal story of the housewife and her bleeding from the kitchen accident.

For all their blurriness, multiplicity, confusion, and conflation, the *Ariel* poems prior to 1963 nonetheless retain some sense of object-loss; they generally function within the loss-compensation paradigm. In poems ranging from "Lady Lazarus" to "Fever 103°," the lyric-speaker takes on various identities, but, in the end, there is usually a speaking "I" to which the poem returns. Likewise, there routinely is some object, whether it is the self, the father, or the blood from a cut thumb, that the poem claims had been lost. The shift from identifiable loss to indeterminate loss, however, begins to surface in poems from this period. Among those, "Parliament Hill Fields" is perhaps the most illustrative.

Written in 1961, "Parliament Hill Fields" begins with a depiction of missing dispossession: "Your absence is inconspicuous; / Nobody can tell what I lack" (1–2). The poem is set in the Hampstead area of north London, and is known to have been occasioned by the miscarriage Plath had suffered little more than a week earlier.[25] Prenatal loss can turn into an ambiguous loss, since social and individual perceptions of fetal personhood have significant variance, presenting challenges for the mourner to process the experience.[26] In some cases, the mourner feels loss but is not certain what she is grieving; in other cases, the mourner may have a well-defined emotional and conceptual framework for what she is grieving but people around her may not share that worldview; or, in different social circumstances, the mourner perceives the loss less intensely than people around her expect her to do.[27] In *Disenfranchised Grief: Recognizing Hidden Sorrow*, Kenneth J. Doka identifies miscarriage as one of the instances in which hidden grief—namely, a type of grief that one has to suppress because it is not validated by the world around us—can occur because of the gap between the subjective valuation of the loss and the social recognition of it.[28] Miscarriage may also become difficult to talk about because child death, which includes miscarriage and stillbirth, generally has a significant psychosocial effect on the mother's identity and sense of self: the more the mother invests herself to become the protector and nurturer of the child, the more stringently their death may be conceived as a failure to fulfill her obligations.[29] Potential harm to self-image ties up one's tongue; the mother opts for silence to circumvent the feeling of shame.

"Parliament Hill Fields" conveys its vague sense of privation against this backdrop. Throughout the poem, there is no explicit mention of miscarriage; there are only oblique suggestions that something is missing—and even the fact of its missing is inconspicuous. As Marjorie Perloff observes, "Parliament Hill Fields" is a poem of absence: an all-engulfing absence, not only of others but also of oneself.[30] The word "absence" is purposefully chosen over "loss"; loss presupposes prior existence, but when one is unsure if something had existed or not, one hesitates to use the word "loss." In this tenuousness, all things seem ephemeral; there is a vague feeling of comprehensive fragility and dissolution, as the "city melts like sugar" (12) and an "ashen smudge" (21) covers up the town. The poet-speaker turns inorganic: "I'm a stone, a stick" (15). Silence dominates this landscape: "silence after silence offers itself" (19). The inefficacy of grief—"I suppose it's pointless to think of you at all" (24)—is doubled in this context: on the first level, there is a sense of futility that derives from the skepticism over elegiac consolation; on the secondary plane, the grief itself feels fruitless when the loss seems undefined and vague, as it often does in the instances of miscarriage.

The unofficial burial of an uncertain dispossession turns ghost-like—a phantom, to use Nicholas Abraham and Maria Torok's terminology: "Ghost of a leaf, ghost of a bird" (28). As the immediacy of the experience etiolates, the loss becomes inaccessible: "Your cry fades like the cry of a gnat. / I lose sight of you on your blind journey" (32–33). When one loses sight of the origin of the traumatic loss, only the faint echoes of amorphous privation are left to be detectable. The loss recedes even further away when the night falls and reminds the speaker that she has another child that she must attend to: the "blue night plants" in "your sister's birthday picture start to glow" (41, 42), signaling to her that this absence that is dissipating cannot eclipse the presence that is already and still there. As the speaker returns to the daily grind and quotidian details of domesticity—"I enter the lit house" (50)—the sense of dispossession that has lost its origin comes to resemble the dysthymic morass of ambiguous loss.

The poems of 1963 inherit precisely this attribute, with a further twist: the speaking "I" of the poems of 1963 increasingly comes to resemble an object undergoing a process of effacement. There remains little of the sense of a specific object-loss. The poems do not so much talk about loss but rather embody it, similar to the way in which an abstract painting expresses something by becoming what it wants to express, rather than showing a specific object-"something" on the canvas. The allusiveness and tradition-consciousness of Plath's earlier elegiac poetry also retreat into the backstage, creating a perception that the poems of 1963 are self-contained and solipsistic, as their voices "lead nowhere" and speak "only to the poem they echo." The sense of any object-loss is itself lost, and all that is left is the prolonged diffusion, even if the poems register enough faint echoes of a sense of dispossession to sound elegiac.

The desolate language-space of the poems of 1963 has left impressions that they express a "strangely elevated and resigned despair" in which "any semblance of struggle has been abandoned."[31] These assessments have prompted psycho-biographical interpretations of the poems of 1963 as "poems . . . written from beyond rage, by someone who no longer blames anyone for her condition and reconciles herself to death"; the implication here is that, when used as the closing of *Ariel*, these poems make Plath's suicide seem inevitable.[32] But if we are to inveigle ourselves into believing Ted Hughes's assertion that the poems of 1963 are ones that Plath "herself, recognizing the different inspirations of these new pieces, regarded . . . as the beginnings of a third book,"[33] it would allow us to bypass the issues of biographical readings, including the controversy over the manipulation of the *Ariel* manuscript by Hughes and the oft-repeated claim that Plath the writer's suicide was the destination of her poetic work.[34] What is crucial in Hughes's aforementioned assessment is that the poems of 1963 can be read as "the beginning of a third book": it is a new direction, a new endeavor, rather than a consignment to one's own demise. In this light, the poems of 1963 constitute not so much a death wish but rather a scholarship on the feeling of ambiguous, nonfinite loss and chronic sorrow, triggered by the loss of one's hopes or ideals related to what a person believes should have been, could have been, or might have been.[35] Chronicity and indeterminacy mark two characteristics of dysthymia; in the 2000 version of the *Diagnostic and Statistical Manual of Mental Disorders*, known as the American Psychiatric Association's *DSM-IV-TR*, dysthymia is distinguished from other types of depression by a length of over two years—the threshold for typical major depression—and its arbitrary criteria.[36] Dysthymia is not a diagnostic term for Plath or for the sentiments expressed by the poems she wrote, but is rather the object that the poems of 1963 study and the condition that they mimic.

Furthermore, the assessment of the poems of 1963 as a start of a third book enables two more changes in our reading of those poems. First, it would unshackle us from the superimposed assumption of "confessionalism" in Plath's work,[37] and would permit us to appreciate its non-confessional elements to a fuller extent. Second, it would also allow us to recognize the steady trajectory of Plath's elegiac poetry: starting with a fixation on a definitive object-loss in *The Colossus*, her elegies then develop into ones with occlusive object-loss in *Ariel*, and finally arrive at the attempts, or experiments, to create a language to express dysthymic, ambiguous double-dispossession in the hypothetical third book. Especially given the publication of the restored edition of *Ariel* in 2004—which is described as following "the arrangement of [Plath's] last manuscript as she left it"[38]—and its exclusion of all of the poems of 1963, as well as a critically observable progression in the modes and motifs of Plath's elegies from *The Colossus*, *Ariel*, to the third book, the possibility of the third book does not appear fanciful.[39]

A closer analysis of the poems of 1963 supports these hypotheses: the poems of 1963 should more profitably be viewed as the beginning of Plath's third book, and there is a progression in her elegiac poetry from the first book to the third book, where her poems shift from a focus on specific object-loss to depictions of loss of loss. It has been argued often enough that Plath's *Ariel* poems resist linear narratives,[40] and the mode of operation in the poems of 1963—as exemplified by "Totem," which, in Plath's own words, is made of "a pile of interconnected images, like a totem pole"—is a nonnarrative collage of images and fragments.[41] The task of a critic is to uncover interconnections among those disparate images: to construct and reconstruct a previously nonexistent story line—a fiction, if you will—from the fragments of images and sounds that are left on the pages, in a manner similar to that of a viewer of an abstract painting imagining a story behind the abstraction, of an archaeologist constructing a historical landscape of a long-lost past, or of a stargazer seeing stars in constellations and conceiving myths. If good criticism reads like a good detective novel, it is because the tasks of literary scholars are to string together disparate elements into a storyline and to provide a useful fiction that carries sufficient credulity of knowledge or understanding.

The first poem of the hypothetical third book, "Sheep in Fog" was initially written in December of 1962; it was then revised on January 28, 1963. Given its exclusion from the restored *Ariel*, however, one can justifiably argue that the poem belongs to the third book. The scene of the poem, as Plath herself explains, is the following: "In this poem, the speaker's horse is proceeding at a slow, cold walk down a hill of macadam to the stable at the bottom. It is December. It is foggy. In the fog there are sheep."[42] The setting is, however, not as important as the shape of the poem: written in tercets, with lines of varied lengths and frequent punctuation. The form is reminiscent of the first poem of *Ariel*, "Morning Song." The comparison between the opening stanzas of the two poems reveals the similarities:

Love set you going like a fat gold watch.
The midwife slapped your footsoles, and your bald cry
Took its place among the elements.   (*CP* 156, 1–3)

The hills step off into whiteness.
People or stars
Regard me sadly, I disappoint them.   (*CP* 262, 1–3)

Both tercets feature curious syntactic parallels: two sentences, one a simple sentence ending in one line and the other a compound sentence covering two lines, although the latter poem omits a coordinating conjunction. The first and the third lines are relatively similar in length, while the middle line is either markedly longer or shorter than the other two. In addition to the similarity of their syntax, both poems portray a scene dominated by one color: gold in the former and white in the latter. Both are pure colors, but the difference between the two is that the former conveys vividness and brilliance, whereas the latter presents an achromatic world.

The lifelessness of this colorless landscape is further underscored by the "morning-mourning" pun, which shows up in both "Morning Song" and "Sheep in Fog." In "Morning Song," the pun is used to hint at the speaker's ambivalence over child-rearing. In "Sheep in Fog," the pun is emphasized with a curious repetition—"All morning the / Morning has been blackening" (8–9). The increasing blackness of the morning introduces the opponent process color, which, in conjunction with the whiteness of line 1, constructs a monotonous, black-and-white landscape. In fact, whether it is the snow in "The Munich Mannequins," the white skull in "Words," the pearl-like skin of the body in "Contusion," or the "blacks" of the moon in "Edge," the poems of 1963 are often colored in black and white.

"Sheep in Fog" presents a world without hue, ashen and languid. Unlike the way "Morning Song" is built around a presence of another human being, "Sheep in Fog" offers a landscape of privation: it is not only colorless but also "Starless and fatherless"—the suffix "less" defines the poem. In particular, "fatherless" is a curious word choice, given how Plath's earlier elegies are preoccupied with the lost father. There is a definite difference between a statement, "one has lost one's father," and the statement, "one is fatherless"; the former indicates a past possession and a subsequent loss of it, while the latter merely describes a state of dispossession, with no conclusive implication of past possession or its subsequent loss. That the poem chooses the word "fatherless" foreshadows a loss of the loss of the father—a loss of the object-loss, which is the feature that differentiates the poems of 1963 from *Ariel* and *Colossus*.

There are enough similarities, and enough differences, between "Morning Song" and "Sheep in Fog" to suggest that the latter may be read as a response of the hypothetical third book to the second book. It is not unusual for a poet to imitate or plagiarize his or her own work; sometimes, the practice has no meaning beyond coincidence, but in this particular instance, this interpretation—that the third book starts polemically against the second book, almost as an act of revising the second book or going beyond where the second book left off—is too tempting to dismiss. The first poem of a book often sets the tone for the entire book. Whereas *Ariel* starts with a presence and then explores the prospect or fact of loss that inevitably follows an object-presence, the hypothetical third book begins with a loss of such loss.

If the first poem of 1963 posits the state of fatherlessness and starlessness, the subsequent poems portray a world that is further absented, with fewer things that one could claim to lose. The poems increasingly move into the state of amorphous privation. In "The Munich Mannequins," the snow is turned into a voiceless entity: "The snow has no voice" (25). Since the dictum of pathetic fallacy suggests that a lyric anthropomorphization of landscape is a projection of the inner world of the speaking self,[43] the snow's dispossession of its voice mirrors the speaker's voiceless state. The loss of one's voice— one of the common identifiers of individuality that is often synonymous with a writer's identity—suggests a condition of self-dissolution, mirrored by the mannequins that have no face or voice that differentiates one from another. The poem expresses this self-dissolution without an enunciating or enunciated "I." And here again, the snow does not lose its voice; rather, it has no voice, where the past possession and its subsequent loss are left unstated and made irrelevant. Cumulatively, the poetic landscape of the hypothetical third book depicts fatherlessness, starlessness, and voicelessness.

Inheriting this privative state, "Paralytic" further effaces sensation, touch, and movement. The presumably paralytic speaker feels no "fingers to grip, no tongue" (3); the tonguelessness is synonymous with the voicelessness of "The Munich Mannequins." The speaker's lungs also turn inorganic like dust bags—like a vacuum cleaner—which are artificially kept functioning by the heart-lung machine;[44] the speaker sarcastically reveres her lungs as "My god the iron lung" (4). It is almost as if the speaker's body is being superseded by machines—the way human fates are seen to be superseded by divine machinations. The speaker is essentially turning bodiless. The penultimate stanza accentuates the self-renunciation process:

I smile, a buddha, all
Wants, desire
Falling from me like rings
Hugging their lights.   (*CP* 267, 33–36)

Disjunctive appositives define the speaker. In line 17, "Dead egg" is what the speaker is likened to. The comparison makes intuitive sense as an image of immobility, although it is poignant that this paralysis is likened to the immutable immobility of a dead egg, as opposed to a live egg, which, while it does not move on its own, will soon be broken open by the birth of a living object. But a "buddha" as a descriptive appositive in line 33 requires a more detailed investigation.

Buddhism has had an intermittent yet persistent presence in the American literary landscape. By some account, its first notable appearance occurred in late nineteenth-century New England, where the confluence of the quietism of New England spirituality and the pantheism of American poetry undergirded New Englanders' embracement of it. The second eruption of American Buddhism came in the 1950s, most prominently in Beat literature and its popularization of Zen.[45] Through it all, the most basic tenet of Buddhism remains to be renunciation, which overlaps, in the American incarnation, with the ethos of transcendentalist spiritual withdrawal, as epitomized by Henry David Thoreau's *Walden*. Renunciation becomes critical because suffering is seen to be caused by the gap between the attachments to or desires for worldly matters and human inability to appease all such cravings. In this context, one's freedom from earthly wants and desires becomes one's salvation. Phrased in this manner, it becomes intuitive that the transplanted American Buddhist teachings strike a similar chord to Dickinsonian stoicism. Emily Dickinson's New England stoicism separates itself from that of rugged American individualism, which, based in part on narrow understanding of Emersonian self-reliance and classical stoicism, manifests in an individual who "learns the limitations of life and, by that, endures and even thrives."[46]

The New England sensibilities of renunciation, as exemplified by Dickinson's line—"missing All, prevented Me / From missing minor Things"—are the cultural ethos in which Plath was raised,[47] and it manifests in her early poems like "Mayflower." "Mayflower" observes how the red haws withstand the assault of snow and winds of black winter, and it testifies that the "best beauty's born of hardihood" in this environment (8). In "Paralytic," too, the best beauty is born of fortitude—perseverance, strong-willed renunciation—however involuntary such renunciation may be. In this state, the speaker, like a buddha, frees herself from wants and desires, which fall off from her "like rings / Hugging their lights" (35–36). By the end of this poem, the inner poetic landscape of the hypothetical third book becomes one of a fatherless, starless, voiceless, motionless, touchless, wantless, and desireless state of being.

This interior scenery accumulates another layer of privation in "Words." The poem has been read in the context of authorship and maternity:[48] a pair that has numerous antecedents, including in the New England Puritan traditions such as Anne Bradstreet's "The Author to Her Book." The disjointed image shows a forest and a woodcutter cutting the wood. Echoes are like phantoms: the absence-presence that exists away from its origin and remains without substance. In the English lyric tradition, traveling off "from the center" inevitably conjures up the echo of W. B. Yeats's "the centre cannot hold" in "The Second Coming": it symbolizes the anticipatory apocalypse of things falling apart. Tree sap makes a partial mirror, and what it wishfully shows is a "white skull / Eaten by weedy greens" (12–13) as the end result of those who are lost in the forest. Definitive finalities can sometimes seem more preferable than the incertitude of ambiguous loss; without closure, the absent stay present.[49] Confusion is excruciating. Words and their interpretive quagmire come to resemble these forests with no clear paths. In these times, one wishes for guidance—"fixed stars" (19)—to re-orient and govern one's life.

After the words turn "riderless" and desiccant in "Words,"[50] "Contusion" portrays how the heart "shuts" and stops (10)—a change from one of the preceding poems, "Mystic," in which the speaker narrates that the heart "has not stopped" yet.[51] The poem is generally read in relation to its dominant metaphors of "waning and cessation,"[52] and it concludes with a funereal image of a sheeted mirror: "The mirror is sheeted" (12).[53] If the fragmentary imagery of "Words" is the forest, "Contusion" sets its stage at the ocean: a night-time seascape, the tide coming and going. Combined with the "color of pearl" (3), the ocean imagery conjures up the echo of Ariel's song in *The Tempest*: "Full fathom five thy father lies; / Of his bones are coral made; / Those are pearls that were his eyes."[54] It is a return to the same theme that Plath engages with in "Full Fathom Five"—except that, this time around, there is no father, no object-loss for which mourning is undertaken. The dead are absent; there is only the ocean that "sucks obsessively" any remnants of the plaintive song (5), and what is left of it is the diffusive echo of dispossessed loss.

"Contusion" is noticeably monosyllabic, especially when compared to Plath's earlier work like "Mayflower." If one were to subscribe to the conventional equation between ornate, Latinate polysyllables and the power of one's intellectual potency, the minimalist monosyllables—accompanied by the successive shortening of line lengths, reminiscent of the performative reticence in Theodore Roethke's "Elegy for Jane"—would suggest a state of its waning. The poem is also notably free of personal deictics, and the body parts come to resemble mere objects; the "body" is not "my" body or "your" body but an unidentified "the body," and the same goes for the "heart" and "mirror." The absence of personal pronouns or possessives in "Contusion" suggests that the poem is freed from any definitive speaker and his or her subjectivity: the objects depicted in it are rendered ownerless. And if we are to build upon the chain of reception that has traditionally interpreted the sheeted mirror as a funereal image, then lifeless, brainless, selfless, and ownerless are the four more additions to the state of increasing privation that characterizes the inner landscape of the poems of 1963.

The final poem, "Edge," is presented in this progressively dispossessory psychic landscape. "Edge" is preceded by "Balloons"; "Balloons" depicts the leftovers of the holiday season that have "lived with" the speaker and her family since Christmas (1), taking up what she exaggeratedly describes as half the space of her apartment. Ordinarily inanimate, the balloons are treated like companion animals—"soul-animals" (3). The sense of joy is palpable: the balloons are likened to cats, fish, peacocks, and contrasted against "dead furniture" (11) like straw mats and other meager objects. This source of delight, however, is fleeting: it ends up being a "red / Shred" (29–30) in the aftermath of an infant's play. The animation of the balloon is purposeful; the balloon is not broken but is rather dead, and its impermanence mirrors the transience of all living things. On transience, Sigmund Freud makes the following remark:

> What spoilt their enjoyment of beauty must have been a revolt in their minds against mourning. The idea that all this beauty was transient was giving these two sensitive minds a foretaste of mourning over its decease; and, since the mind instinctively recoils from anything that is painful, they felt their enjoyment of beauty interfered with by thoughts of its transience.[55]

Freud writes the passage above in the context of failing to convince his poet-friends of the following idea: "Transience value is scarcity value in time. Limitation in the possibility of an enjoyment raises the value of the enjoyment."[56] The reason that this logic—a fleeting thing is valuable precisely because it is scarce, in the economics of supply and demand—fails is that it triggers anticipatory mourning, the pain of which compels people to shun both its transience and its enjoyment. "Balloons" ends with the image of a shredded balloon; since no further commentaries are provided, one is left in the confusion of frozen joy-grief, pondering whether one is supposed to appreciate the joy of transience or to grieve for its evanescence.

"Edge" follows this ambivalence of transience. Susan Van Dyne reports that this poem was initially titled "Nun in Snow" in its draft stage,[57] although the title was ultimately pared down to one word, in keeping with the abstract, minimalist thrust of the rest of the poems of 1963, most of which have a one-word title.[58] From that standpoint, although "Nun in Snow" would certainly refer us back to the motif of self-dissolution in the whiteness of snow in "The Munich Mannequins," such a title would perhaps be too explanatory for a set of poems that are acceleratingly becoming devoid of explanations and authorial imposition of narrative-meaning construction. This poem, which epitomizes a state of privation, is written in a privative, minimalist verse form: couplets. The poem has generally been read as the speaking self's imagining of her own death;[59] this reception owes in no small part to the common assumption that the speaker is a woman and is reflective of the availability of biographical reading, for the fact that the poet died several days thereafter.[60] But even if we are to inherit such a reading and assume that the speaker is the third-person-referenced woman in this poem,[61] the third-person address leaves no remnant of self-reference. The lack of self-referentiality signals the woman's abnegation or renunciation of, or freedom from, her selfhood—a condition that the buddha-appositioned speaker in "Paralytic" embodies. Even though the personal possessive returns in this poem—in contrast to the impersonal, unidentified definite articles of "Contusion" that point to nowhere—there is little of the sense of personal selfhood in "Edge." The poetic psychic landscape retains the self-loss of "Contusion."

The "perfection" of the woman in line 1 certainly recalls the terrible perfection of "The Munich Mannequins" that "cannot have children."[62] In fact, "Edge" brims with images, words, and phrases that have been used, or that point to ones formerly used, in Plath's previous poems, simulating her greatest hits: the "Greek" myth motifs in the *Colossus* phase; the "child," the subject on which many of her oft-anthologized poems, such as "Metaphor," "Morning Song," "You're," "Nick and the Candlestick," and numerous others, are written; the bleeding throat like the one in "Poppies in July"; the moon imagery omnipresent in poems like "The Moon and the Yew Tree," in lines like "The moon sees nothing of this. . . . / And the message of the yew tree is blackness";[63] and the blackness of the moon, which merges with the whiteness of the dead body in "Contusion" and recaptures the monochromatic landscape in "Sheep in Fog."

Recognizing this parading of previously used tropes and images, a reader would be tempted to find a similarity between this poem and one of Yeats's last poems, "The Circus Animals' Desertion." The Yeats poem, however, has a definitive speaking "I" who stakes previous ownership of those "animals"—the characters and themes Yeats uses in his preceding work—and, therefore, the owner has sufficient basis to lament his loss as the circus animals leave the owner-poet behind. On the other hand, Plath's images and motifs float in a null-space without such claim of possession; the poem declares no loss, even as vague, faint reverberations of dispossession are felt and registered as echoes and reechoes. As a result, the poem does not express but rather becomes a lost loss, embodying its embracive melancholy.

It is all too easy to see lines like "We have come so far, it is over" (8) and conclude that "Edge" confirms Plath the writer's suicidal intent or that she had intended this poem to be her last poem like Yeats's "The Circus Animals' Desertion"; for readers looking to unearth her third book, however, a new phase of her poetic work starts here. The narrative of lost loss only begins with this poem, and just as the blackness of the moon suggests that a new moon will begin its calendar from that phase, proceeding to waxing crescent, then waxing gibbous, and eventually full moon—just as the darkness of the night is said to be thickest right before the dawn—"Edge" signifies the verge of a new discovery. Plath's earlier elegies had more to do with a creation of the fiction of loss: *Colossus* poems, including the title poem "The Colossus," narrate an effort to reconstruct a missing object, to forge an illusion that it had existed and has been lost, and a recovery of it must be attempted despite the knowledge that such attempts would never succeed; *Ariel* poems like "Daddy" depict the anti-elegiac frustration with and the recognition of the failure of such recovery attempts. The evolution of Plath's elegies has taken us to a landscape where progressive privation and a resultant effacement of specific losses give shape to the pervasive melancholy of lost loss, which had previously eluded linguistic figurations.

One wonders why the work of a poet who produced only two books of poetry and one novel—two more, if we count the posthumously assembled *Crossing the Water* and *Winter Trees*—has received as much critical attention as it has. Aside from the usual arrays of answers to this question, one hypothesis to account for this phenomenon is to inquire if readers—seeing that the poet could have written more poems and regarding that as a void—construct a narrative of loss to fill that void: a mechanism of fiction-making similar to that of Wallace Stevens's elegiac poetry. Plath's phantomatic third book is itself a lost loss: an imagined loss of a book that never came to be. Readers, forever wondering what kind of book the third book might have turned out to be, keep formulating their readings and extrapolations of her work to cover up the vacuum of that loss. Whether it is John Keats or Emily Brontë, the question of "what could have been?" haunts poets who die young. Curiosities persist: what might the readers be missing, what kind of work might they have produced if they had lived beyond their years? These queries might be more intensely urgent for the readers of the works of writers who commit suicide because of the prevailing view that suicides are preventable. Mourners of a suicide are routinely besieged with ideations of what they could or should have done to prevent suicide; likewise, readers of writers who are lost to suicide are left to wonder what could have or should have been. The mental apparatus fills the gap of the missing presence by creating an imagining of the literary work that may have been produced, and this fantasy complicates the mourning beyond the loss of one particular life. The hypothetical third book is the fiction we build on the foundation of ambiguous loss.

Whether it is the biographical fallacy of how Plath had to write her own death for the reason that "expression and extinction [are] indivisible,"[64] or this present hypothesis of how the poems of 1963 constitute not so much a suicidal musing but rather the start of a never-completed third book that strives to find an expression for an all-engulfing loss of loss, one may note that all these are fictive narratives constructed in place of the void left by the death of the poet, who continues to be inaccessible and who only revisits as readers' imaginations, as unfortunate as it is that the living have the nefarious habit of fantasying the words and thoughts of the dead in their absences.[65] Fiction-making aside, the poems of 1963 reveal a new facet of Plath's elegiac poetry beyond the *Colossus* and much of the *Ariel* phase. Their manifestations of elusive, irresolute dispossession move beyond the melancholia of object-loss and toward the dysthymia of absence mourning; they demonstrate that elegies are aimed to give voice to things that do not yet have a voice, and that words are invented to give shape to things that do not yet exist—things that do not exist but are nonetheless needed. When the word "loss" is constructed, the concept of "possession" also comes into being. In this sense, loss precedes being: in complicated grief, loss predates the presence of the lost object as much as the reverse. Through the narrative of privation, one creates, finds, or accesses the lost object, which comes into existence as a result of the fiction-making compelled by lost loss—the fiction, that is, of dispossession that is meant to subterfuge the notion that important things are always already lost. Elegists continue to construct fictions of loss, for the acute pain that one endures in the finality of acknowledged bereavement can in some sense be more tolerable and somehow more comforting than the vague and pervasive pain one is left with in the indeterminacy of ambiguous loss.

NOTES

1. Boss, *Ambiguous Loss*, 5.
2. Boss, *Ambiguous Loss*, 8–9.
3. Boss, *Ambiguous Loss*, 7–8. Ambiguous loss "is the most stressful loss because its incomprehensibility threatens health and resiliency" (Pauline Boss, *Loss, Trauma, and Resilience: Therapeutic Work with Ambiguous Loss* [New York: W. W. Norton], 2006), 22.
4. Boss, *Ambiguous Loss*, 10.
5. Jenny Edkins, *Trauma and the Memory of Politics* (Cambridge: Cambridge University Press, 2003), 4.
6. Plath's poetry is routinely associated with melancholia both because of the way her poetry displays its symptoms and because of what we know about her biography, such as the fact that Plath carefully read and annotated Freud's "Mourning and Melancholia" (Steven Gould Axelrod, "Plath and Torture: Cultural Contexts for Plath's Imagery of the Holocaust," in *Representing Sylvia Plath*, ed. Sally Bayley and Tracy Brain [Cambridge: Cambridge University Press, 2011], 72). Critics have expressed wariness over biographical approaches to Plath's poetry, suggesting that, while biographical contexts remain fascinating, "the commodity of Plath's life can restrict her poems to the marginal 'extreme' instead of the cultural mainstream" (Marsha Bryant, "Plath, Domesticity, and the Art of Advertising," *College Literature* 29, no. 3 [Summer 2002]: 31). For an overview of recent critical approaches to Plath, see Lisa Narbeshuber, *Confessing Cultures: Politics and the Self in the Poetry of Sylvia Plath* (Victoria: ELS Editions, 2009), xi.
7. Boss, *Ambiguous Loss*, 4.
8. Sylvia Plath, *The Letters of Sylvia Plath, Vol. 2: 1956–1963*, ed. Peter K. Steinberg and Karen V. Kukil (New York: Harper Collins, 2018), 948, underline in the original.
9. Plath, *Letters*, 965.
10. According to Elisabeth Bronfen, the voice of melancholia dominates not only Plath's letters but also her journals as well (Elisabeth Bronfen, *Sylvia Plath* [Oxford: Oxford University Press, 2004], 42).
11. Michael E. Thase and Susan S. Lang, *Beating the Blues: New Approaches to Overcoming Dysthymia and Chronic Mild Depression* (Oxford: Oxford University Press, 2004), 5. Thase and Lang further describe dysthymia as the most under-recognized and undertreated mood disorder, to which mental health experts did not give a name until 1980 (Thase and Lang, *Beating the Blues*, 5). By 2013, however, dysthymia lost its own clinical name, as *The Diagnostic and Statistical Manual of Mental Disorders*, Fifth Edition, subsumed it into "persistent depressive disorder." As stated in the Introduction, the term dysthymia is resurrected here as an emblem of poetic mood, rather than as a clinical diagnosis.
12. Jahan Ramazani, "'Daddy, I Have Had to Kill You': Plath, Rage, and the Modern Elegy," *PMLA* 108, no. 5 (October 1993): 1143.
13. Perloff, *Poetic License*, 187, and Bassnett, *Sylvia Plath*, 136.

14. Plath's later poems "highlight that their speakers have great difficulty in finding reliable names or outward correlatives for their surging affects" (Marta Figlerowicz, *Spaces of Feeling: Affect and Awareness in Modernist Literature* [Ithaca: Cornell University Press, 2017], 36). The argument of this chapter is that one of such unnamable feelings that Plath's 1963 poems attempt to name is the vague, dysthymic deprivation.

15. As compared to the "academic mode" of *The Colossus* (Christina Britzolakis, "*Ariel* and Other Poems," in *The Cambridge Companion to Sylvia Plath*, ed. Jo Gill [Cambridge: Cambridge University Press, 2006], 107).

16. Ann Keniston, *Overheard Voices: Address and Subjectivity in Postmodern American Poetry* (New York: Routledge, 2006), 27.

17. Irving Howe, "The Plath Celebration: A Partial Dissent," in *Sylvia Plath*, ed. Harold Bloom (New York: Chelsea House Publishers, 1989), 13.

18. Louise Glück, "Invitations and Exclusion," in *Proofs and Theories: Essays on Poetry* (New York: Ecco, 1994), 123.

19. Boss, *Ambiguous Loss*, 10–11.

20. Ramazani, *Poetry of Mourning*, 3.

21. Plath's poetry has been seen to reject elegiac conventions in that it has "certain affinities with the gestures of baroque allegory" where the "rites of mourning, instead of being subordinated to the reaffirmation of the symbolic order, tend to predominate and become an end in themselves" (Christina Britzolakis, *Sylvia Plath and the Theatre of Mourning* [New York: Clarendon, 1999], 196). Britzolakis's characterization of Plath's anti-elegy derives from Walter Benjamin's *The Origin of German Tragic Drama*; the melancholy of Plath's anti-elegy is characterized by "its tenacious self-absorption," and it "embraces the dead objects in its contemplation, in order to redeem them" (Benjamin, *The Origin of German Tragic Drama*, 133). This description corresponds to Ramazani's idea of "melancholic mourning" of anti-elegies.

22. The allusiveness of the *Colossus* poems has prompted critics to regard them as being almost "too derivative" (Harold Bloom, "Introduction," in *Sylvia Plath*, ed. Harold Bloom [New York: Chelsea House Publishers, 1989], 1).

23. Sylvia Plath, *The Collected Poems*, ed. Ted Hughes (New York: HarperPerennial, 1992), 129: 1.

24. Jacques Lacan, "Desire, and the Interpretation of Desire in Hamlet," in *Literature and Psychoanalysis: The Question of Reading Otherwise*, ed. Shoshana Felman (Baltimore: Johns Hopkins University Press, 1982), 38.

25. Raymond A. Anselment, "'A Heart Terrifying Sorrow': An Occasional Piece on Poetry of Miscarriage," *Papers on Language & Literature* 33, no. 1 (Winter 1997): 32. Plath's miscarriage reportedly occurred on February 6, 1961 (David Trinidad, "'Two Sweet Ladies': Sexton and Plath's Friendship and Mutual Influence," *The American Poetry Review* 35, no. 6 [November–December 2006]: 27). *The Unabridged Journals of Sylvia Plath* (ed. Karen V. Kukil [New York: Anchor Books, 2000], 531) also mentions Plath's miscarriage in February 1961, in conjunction with her appendectomy in March 1961.

26. The issue of fetal personhood in the contemporary debate over abortion is outside of the scope of this discussion, in part because one's perception of fetal

personhood in miscarriage grief does not align neatly with one's pro-choice or anti-abortion views.

27. Miscarriage has been perceived differently in different eras. Loss-based rhetoric is the norm by which miscarriage is discussed in today's discourse, but that has not always been the case historically; Shannon Withycombe's *Lost: Miscarriage in Nineteenth-Century America* (New Brunswick: Rutgers University Press, 2018) chronicles the cultural shifts in how Americans conceptualized pregnancy and understood miscarriage in periods spanning from the 1820s through the 1910s.

28. Doka, *Disenfranchised Grief*, 125.

29. Patricia Wonch Hill et al., "The Loss of Self: The Effect of Miscarriage, Stillbirth, and Child Death on Maternal Self-Esteem," *Death Studies* 41, no. 4 (2017): 226.

30. Marjorie Perloff, "On the Road to *Ariel*: The 'Transitional' Poetry of Sylvia Plath," *The Iowa Review* 4, no. 2 (Spring 1973): 97. Perloff suggests that Plath's use of nature imagery in this poem may be inspired by R. D. Laing's description of the childhood experience of a mental patient in *The Divided Self* (London: Pelican Books, 1965), 110.

31. Anne Stevenson, *Bitter Fame: A Life of Sylvia Plath* (London: Viking, 1989), 288, and Bassnett, *Sylvia Plath*, 136.

32. Perloff, *Poetic License*, 181.

33. Ted Hughes, "Introduction," in *The Collected Poems of Sylvia Plath* (New York: HarperPerennial, 1992), 15. If Plath's *Ariel* were the combination of "the blood-jet cry of the 'I' and the post-traumatic analysis of the eye" (Helen Vendler, *Last Looks, Last Books: Stevens, Plath, Lowell, Bishop, Merrill* [Princeton: Princeton University Press, 2010], 61), the hypothetical third book may be characterized as highlighting the latter while downplaying the former.

34. Numerous critics—as noted by Jacqueline Rose's *On Not Being Able to Sleep: Psychoanalysis and the Modern World* (Princeton: Princeton University Press, 2003), 49–63—have affirmed the difficulty of escaping biographical readings, of separating the work from the life, in the case of Sylvia Plath. For a catalog of various approaches to reading Plath's work, see also Keniston, *Overheard Voices*, 140.

35. Darcy L. Harris and Eunice Gorman, "Grief from a Broader Perspective: Nonfinite Loss, Ambiguous Loss, and Chronic Sorrow," in *Counting Our Losses: Reflecting on Change, Loss, and Transition in Everyday Life*, ed. Darcy L. Harris (New York: Routledge, 2010), 2.

36. Dan J. Stein et al. ed., "Dysthymic Disorder," in *The American Psychiatric Publishing Textbook of Mood Disorders* (Washington, DC: American Psychiatric Publishing, Inc., 2006), 551.

37. Janet Badia summarizes the receptive origin of the application of the label "confessional poetry" to Plath as follows: "Originating with M. L. Rosenthal's 1959 review of Robert Lowell's *Life Studies*, the label 'confessional poetry' gained popularity in the 1960s as a description of a particular mode of poetic writing, one defined by its hyperpersonal subject matter and perceived transgressions of poetic decorum, and it is in this form that the label is first applied to Sylvia Plath's poetry in the mid-1960s" (Janet Badia, *Sylvia Plath and the Mythology of Women Readers*

[Amherst: University of Massachusetts Press, 2011], 10). Badia further explains the limitation of this mode of reading: "So thrilling is this mode of reading that it can cripple or at least distract readers' critical facilities, rendering them unable to see the deeper meanings of Plath's poetry" (Badia, *Sylvia Plath and the Mythology of Women Readers*, 11).

38. Sylvia Plath, *Ariel: The Restored Edition* (New York: Harper Collins, 2004), xi.

39. The psycho-biographical question of why someone who had just started to write a new book would commit suicide may remain unanswered, but one theory suggests that suicide often seems irrational and spontaneous because it stems from excessive "psychache," which is defined as "the hurt, anguish, or ache that takes hold in the mind"; suicide occurs when the psychache is "deemed unbearable and death is actively sought to stop the unceasing flow of painful consciousness" (Edwin Shneidman, *The Suicidal Mind* [New York: Oxford University Press, 1996], 13). Even when people are not suicidal, they can be inconsistent, as Plath has been described to be (Jacqueline Rose, *The Haunting of Sylvia Plath* [London: Virago, 1991], 10). Also, on the topic of the relation between melancholia and literature, Julia Kristeva chimes in as follows: "if loss, mourning, absence set the imaginary act in motion and permanently fuel it as much as they menace and undermine it, it is also undeniable that the fetish of the work of art is erected in disavowal of this mobilizing affliction. The artist: melancholy's most intimate witness and the most ferocious combatant of the symbolic abdication enveloping him" ("On the Melancholic Imaginary," in *Discourse in Psychoanalysis and Literature*, ed. Shlomith Rimmon-Kenan [London: Routledge, 1987], 105). Kristeva claims that if a poet were to surrender to melancholia, there would be no poetry.

40. These poems replace linear narrative "with the repetitive temporality of trauma" (Britzolakis, "*Ariel* and Other Poems," 118).

41. Plath, *Collected Poems*, 295.

42. Plath, *Collected Poems*, 295.

43. Although many of the poems of 1963 are non-pastoral, Plath's use of pathetic fallacy extends beyond pastoral poems and interpenetrates into other geographic and psychic landscapes (Fiona Sampson, "After Plath: The Legacy of Influence," in *Sylvia Plath in Context*, ed. Tracy Brain [Cambridge: Cambridge University Press, 2019], 353).

44. Laura Perry, "Plath and the Culture of Hygiene," *Sylvia Plath in Context*, ed. Tracy Brain (Cambridge: Cambridge University Press, 2019), 197.

45. Adam Gopnik, "What Meditation Can Do for Us, and What It Can't," *New Yorker*, July 31, 2017, https://www.newyorker.com/magazine/2017/08/07/what-meditation-can-do-for-us-and-what-it-cant.

46. Kenneth S. Sacks, "Stoicism in America," in *The Routledge Handbook of the Stoic Tradition*, ed. John Sellars (New York: Routledge, 2016), 341.

47. Plath's relationship to Dickinson as her literary ancestor, however, was ambivalent and rivalrous, even though Plath at times imitated Dickinson in her early work (Vivian R. Pollak, *Our Emily Dickinsons: American Women Poets and the Intimacies of Difference* [Philadelphia: University of Pennsylvania Press, 2017], 16).

48. Susan Van Dyne, *Revising Life: Sylvia Plath's Ariel Poems* (Chapel Hill: University of North Carolina Press, 1993), 175.

49. Boss, *Ambiguous Loss*, 44.

50. Plath, *Collected Poems*, 270: 16.

51. Plath, *Collected Poems*, 269: 31.

52. Steven Gould Axelrod, "The Poetry of Sylvia Plath," in *The Cambridge Companion to Sylvia Plath*, ed. Jo Gill (Cambridge: Cambridge University Press, 2006), 88.

53. Many critics have written on the function of mirror images in Plath's poems. In particular, Steven Gould Axelrod delves into Plath's interest in *The Golden Bough* by Sir James George Frazer ("The Mirror and the Shadow: Plath's Poetics of Self-Doubt," *Contemporary Literature* 26, no. 3 [Fall 1985]: 286–94), an armchair anthropologist whose works are largely debunked in modern-day anthropology but were "of seminal importance in the forging of the twentieth century literature" (John B. Vickery, *The Literary Impact of the Golden Bough* [Princeton: Princeton University Press, 1973], 135). In the said article, Axelrod cites Frazer's assertion that when a death occurs in a house, there is a "widespread custom of covering up mirrors" to prevent the ghost of the departed from carrying away a mourner's soul, projected outward in the shape of his mirror reflection (James George Frazer, *The Golden Bough: A Study in Magic and Religion*, abridged ed. [New York: Macmillan, 1943], 192).

54. William Shakespeare, *The Tempest*, Act I, Scene II, Ariel's song.

55. Sigmund Freud, "On Transience," in *The Standard Edition of the Complete Psychological Works of Sigmund Freud*, Vol. XIV, ed., trans. James Strachey (London: Hogarth Press, 1957), 306.

56. Freud, "On Transience," 305.

57. Van Dyne, *Revising Life*, 173.

58. The exceptions are "Sheep in Fog" and "The Munich Mannequins," the first two poems of 1963.

59. Perloff, *Poetic License*, 196. Other critics have similarly characterized the poem as "the somber aftermath of the murderous impulse in 'Lady Lazarus' and 'Purdah'" (Heather Clark, *The Grief of Influence: Sylvia Plath and Ted Hughes* [Oxford: Oxford University Press, 2011], 166), or as articulating "the inevitability of death . . . with profound satisfaction" (Carl Rollyson, *American Isis: The Life and Art of Sylvia Plath* [New York: St. Martin's Press, 2013], 226).

60. Heather Clark argues that biographers "have used 'I Thought That I Could Not Be Hurt' to pathologise Plath at the beginning of her life, and 'Edge' to do so at the end" (Heather Clark, "P(l)athography: Plath and Her Biographers," in *Sylvia Plath in Context*, ed. Tracy Brain [Cambridge: Cambridge University Press, 2019], 366), and she offers a sampling of biographical readings in this vein (368).

61. Our understanding of a literary work is dependent, whether as a rebuttal or as a succession, on the pretext and the subtext of its previous interpretations; as one critic puts it, "our current interpretations of . . . texts, whether or not we are aware of it, are, in complex ways, constructed by the chain of receptions through which their continued readability has been effected" (Charles Martindale, *Redeeming the Text: Latin Poetry and the Hermeneutics of Reception* [New York: Cambridge University Press,

1993], 7). While Plath's poems are not "ancient" texts, it is reasonable to assume that the previous chain of receptions has affected our present readings of her work on both conscious and subconscious levels.

62. Plath, *Collected Poems*, 262: 1. In the context of elegy studies, one may read this renunciation of child-conceiving capability as an antithesis to Tennyson's epithalamium consolation in *In Memoriam*. Tennyson's celebration of his sister's wedding functions as a compensatory consolation for the death of Arthur Henry Hallam; the belief that her future child would be seen as the rebirth of Hallam makes up for his loss. The inability to have a child would deny the possibility of this consolatory philosophy.

63. Plath, *Collected Poems*, 173: 27, 28.

64. Charles Newman, "Candor Is the Only Wile: The Art of Sylvia Plath," in *The Art of Sylvia Plath, a Symposium*, ed. Charles Newman (London: Faber & Faber, 1970), 24.

65. It should be noted that there is an ethical issue in fictionalizing a real person (Tracy Brain, "Fictionalizing Sylvia Plath," in *Representing Sylvia Plath*, ed. Sally Bayley and Tracy Brain [Cambridge: Cambridge University Press, 2011], 183–99). The intent and scope of this chapter is to imagine a hypothetical third book; fictionalizing the author is out of its bounds, even if it acknowledges that there is in humans a tendency, without regard to value judgments, to want fictional narratives when there is a feeling of void.

Chapter 3

Elizabeth Bishop's *Geography III*
Un-losing Lost Loss

In a curious similarity to the cases of Wallace Stevens and Sylvia Plath, Elizabeth Bishop's oeuvre includes only a handful of "formal" elegies.[1] Although personal losses are rarely explicitly confronted in Bishop's poems, the sense of constant, low-grade melancholy pervades her work: dysthymia, which, as discussed in the previous chapter, is one manifestation of lost loss. This pervasive feeling of privation in her covertly elegiac, non-elegiac, or anti-elegiac poems is what constitutes her reputation as an elegiac poet. Biographers have remarked on how Bishop's life was filled with losses, and critics have highlighted the reticence and restraint in the descriptive thrust of her work, which is often referred to as "objective poetry."[2] The seeming consensus is that her poetic practice exemplifies sublimation, in which the raw feelings are translated into something of a higher order, and the end result reveals little of the feeling of self-pity or the biographical context; her work is seen to transform "pain" into "art," as epitomized by her frequently anthologized poems "One Art" and, to a lesser extent, "North Haven."[3] Although Bishop's work has long been assumed to be a kind of sublimation, an inquiry into the precise nature of this "sublimation" remains to be undertaken.

The underlying thesis of this chapter is that Bishop's sublimational poetics is rooted in the anxiety of lost loss; if a tragedy remains unrecorded, it will be forgotten and left behind.[4] There are, in her elegiac poetry, dual misgivings over the preservation of dispossessive experience: one's desire to prevent it from being erased out of memory, and one's fear of holding onto the pain of loss. In Bishop's poetry, this conflictual condition results in a creation of a third space, where the experience of loss, in a changed, sublimated form, is preserved as well as distanced and forgotten at the same time. For Bishop, elegies are for neither remembering nor forgetting, but for changing: the act of writing that effects the change operates as a third space between the two poles of remembering and forgetting.

In this endeavor, the function of poetry becomes similar to note-taking: the act of externalizing the memory—such as writing it down in a note—relieves the pressure on the internal memory to retain the item all within one's own memory, and hence facilitates a kind of "safe" forgetting that keeps one from losing the item entirely. As Harald Weinrich points out, "the verb 'forget' is composed of the verb 'get' and the prefix 'for,'" and "one might paraphrase the meaning of 'forget' as 'to get rid (of something).'"[5] The act of writing things down is an externalization of one's memory that allows for forgetting—or "getting rid of the item"—but that, at the same time, resists it by creating a site where that memory can be recalled. Seen in this regard, Bishop's descriptivist poetics points less to her reticence or aversion to overt confessions than to a desire to let go of the experience while still retaining it:[6] her objectivism is a way to avoid losing an experience in its entirety to double forgetting.

The anxiety of lost loss in Bishop's work often manifests itself in the act of externalizing a memory of dispossession, a creation of a space where the experience is neither completely retained nor lost. The sublimation of pain into art occurs as a byproduct of this anxiety-driven externalization. The function of elegiac poetry is not only to exteriorize and exorcise the instance of loss but also to create an ambiguous place where losses are simultaneously expunged and preserved, albeit outside of one's subjectivity. This act of placing one's subjectivity outside of itself in a changed, sublimated form is in essence an act of self-spectralization; this sublimatory transformation turns the self itself into a neither-and-both "third space," either through incorporation, in which a nonself space is made within the self, or through projection, in which a self-space is made within the nonself. In this space, even as the contents—one's past experiences—may remain the same, their containers constantly undergo changes. If Bishop's covertly elegiac, anti-elegiac, or non-elegiac elegies offer us any consolation, it comes not so much from consolatory philosophies but rather from self-spectralization, where one's memories of life experiences undergo continual sublimational changes; these ongoing transformations keep one's thoughts in motion and, by doing so, hold off the stasis of self-assaulting melancholia.

A poem that exemplifies this creation of the "third space" where a loss is both preserved and forgotten is "First Death in Nova Scotia," a poem collected in *Questions of Travel*, which is seen to be a precursor to *Geography III*. Through its emphasis on exteriority, "First Death in Nova Scotia" captures the space between remembering and forgetting. Despite the first-person narrative, the poem constructs more a "picture of the mind at work" than a story;[7] as Eileen John points out, readers "don't learn how Arthur died, we do not hear what it was like to touch his body, and the poem doesn't situate the event in a larger stream of causally related events."[8] Instead of a subjective story line, the poem begins with the description of the external objects at the funeral parlor:

In the cold, cold parlor
my mother laid out Arthur
beneath the chromographs:
Edward, Prince of Wales,
with Princess Alexandra,
and King George with Queen Mary.
Below them on the table
stood a stuffed loon
shot and stuffed by Uncle
Arthur, Arthur's father.   (1–10)

The repetition of words within the same line or across line breaks—such as "cold, cold" in line 1, "stuffed" and "stuffed" in lines 8–9, "Arthur" and "Arthur's" in line 10—creates a syncopated rhythm, which triflingly mimics the apprehensive hesitance in the speaker's voice. But outside of this affective rhythm, there is little that reveals the speaker's emotion.[9] The word, "First," in the title suggests the presence of the speaker's subjectivity; this experience is her "first" encounter with death.[10] Despite that, the stanza itself is remarkably free of first-person subject pronouns; the only first-person pronoun used here is the possessive, in "my mother." The lack of the "I" suggests two possibilities: either the focus is squarely on exteriority and the self becomes irrelevant in this scene, or the passage is so transparently colored by the "I" that it becomes unnecessary or even redundant to use an explicit "I"—the observant "eye" is indistinguishable from the subject "I" to such a degree that the pronoun "I" is needless.

Both of these possibilities apply to "First Death in Nova Scotia." On the one hand, the poem projects a genuine focus on the exterior. Syntactically, Arthur becomes the object of the sentences; as Robert Dale Parker suggests, the poem, by doing so, puts more emphasis on the object than on the subject and highlights that the issue is what gets done to Arthur, not who does it.[11] As Arthur himself becomes objectified, the poem describes in length the royal chromographs and the stuffed loon with what appears to be a digressive attentiveness to the external objects in the parlor. These seemingly irrelevant objects claim the main stage.

On the other hand, the poem's focus on exteriority not only highlights its attention to the objects but also reveals the ways in which those objects function as a correlative of the speaker's subjectivity. Critics have interpreted the poem's descriptive method as a kind of projection, in which the speaker projects herself emotionally into the objects that the child identifies with the cousin;[12] since it is too painful for the speaker to face the reality of her cousin's death, a kind of psychological imperative operates so that the pain can be kept at a distance.[13] There are elements of projection in the poem's descriptive mode. For instance, the stuffed loon becomes a kind of an objective correlative for Arthur in the sense that the lives of both the loon and Arthur were cut short: the loon was "shot and stuffed by Uncle / Arthur" (9–10), and "hadn't said a word" since "Uncle Arthur fired / a bullet into him" (11–12, 13). There is also a parallel between the cleaning and embalming of the deceased's body in preparation for the funeral and the act of stuffing the hunted animal; both acts make the corpse more presentable and viewable. The chromographs of the royal family too are an ironic reminder of what had been severed: the bloodline, the shared family lineage, which is the one thing that makes a royal family what it is.[14] That the first thing the speaker observes after the cold parlor and the body of Arthur is the royal chromograph is suggestive of the speaker's subconscious awareness that the loss of Arthur does not merely signify his death but also a disruption of family lineage.

The speaker's willful description of the surroundings feels like a refusal of the poem to delve into her interiority, but this refusal reveals her interiority precisely by attempting to avoid it. As a result, the exteriority absorbs the weight of the experience, relieving the inner psyche of the child-speaker from this burden. It is all too easy for the child-speaker to "lose" this sorrowful experience of loss to her infanthood incomprehension. Or, inversely, the child-speaker may be overburdened by the weight of this tragedy, which she may not be equipped to process and recognize. After all, this experience is the "first death" for her. C. K. Doreski writes that, for Bishop, childhood is less a matter of what happened and more a concern with perceiving and interpreting occurrences.[15] "First Death in Nova Scotia" creates a space between the occurrence and its interpretation; the child-speaker is neither offering a mere reportage of the occurrence nor engaged in an active interpretation. What is happening in the child-speaker's mind is similar to what Walter Benjamin describes as the creation of "isolated experience" in "On Some Motifs in Baudelaire." According to Benjamin's formulation, experiences that are not assimilated, processed, interpreted, or fully integrated into our consciousness—the "long experience"—remain in us as an isolated experience.[16] Memories of the objects like the stuffed loon and the chromographs are isolated experiences, ones that lie in between the fully interpreted and integrated long experience and discarded or forgotten non-experience: an interface where the occurrence and interpretation, exteriority and interiority, merge.

The poem itself is equivocal about whether or not these objects mean something more than what they are—whether or not they are mere external descriptions or projections of inner emotions. This prevarication triggers the aforementioned critical disagreements over the interpretation of this poem as either an expression of sentimentalism or a pinnacle of emotional restraint. Critical disunity is begotten by poetic indeterminacy. The poem's ambiguous distinction between exteriority and interiority stems from the ambiguous distinction between the speaker's comprehension and incomprehension of little Arthur's death. This oscillation between comprehension and incomprehension is acutely visible in the following stanza:

"Come," said my mother,
"Come and say good-bye
to your little cousin Arthur."
I was lifted up and given
one lily of the valley
to put in Arthur's hand.
Arthur's coffin was
a little frosted cake,
and the red-eyed loon eyed it
from his white, frozen lake. (21–30)

The first three lines portray what Helen Vendler describes as the adult's effort to "conspire in a fantasy of communication still possible, as the child is told, 'say good-bye / to your little cousin Arthur.'"[17] The subsequent seven lines, however, show the child's disengagement from such fantasy. The passive voice—"I was lifted up and given / one lily of the valley"—clarifies that the fantasy of communication belongs to the speaker's mother, imposed upon but not necessarily shared by the child-speaker. If Bishop's speaker is disengaged from this fantasy, the dead himself is likewise disengaged. Arthur remains encased in an incommunicative still object: a casket, "a little frosted cake" that does not participate in this make-believe. The fantasy of communication—an imaginative analogy, of likening the experience of losing someone to that of saying goodbye—could have become for the speaker a way of assimilating this experience, but the poem brings it up only to reject it, keeping the poem in limbo between a comprehension-aiding fiction and its rejection, a state of incomprehension.

The question remains: what are we to make of this focus on the objects? David Kalstone observes that "objects hold radiant interest for [the speaker] precisely because they help her absorb numbing or threatening experiences—the loon in the poem, or the shop window and the blacksmith's in 'In the Village.'"[18] If objects were an aid to one's absorption of one's own experiences, then the objects would become nonselves infused with elements of selfhood, and the self, in turn, would reclaim those self-elements along with the nonselves that contain them: these are the processes of projection and introjection. The poem's focus on exteriority is a mechanism of indirection, whereby the self-elements are found in nonselves and nonselves are found in the self. This indirection creates the in-between territory, a third space, between interpretation and recording, between comprehension and incomprehension, between remembered and forgotten: the in-between space, where the loss is neither retained nor lost.

This third space comes into being as a result of the anxiety over the loss of loss in Bishop's sublimational poetics. An analogy to an unrelated poem helps to illustrate this idea:

With ashen glow, the moon dreams
of becoming full: an engraving
of its dark lost self in the earthshine.
Such multiple mirrorings—

of the sunlight upon the earth upon the moon—
are impossible mournings, their loss
denied by the young crescent's embrace
where the new lives in the old that lives in the new.[19]

The poem, titled "The Old Moon in the New Moon's Arms," alludes to the very phenomenon in its title: the moon in its waxing gibbous phase where the bright crescent, or the new moon, wraps around and figuratively holds in its arms the dim gibbous part, the old moon. In this phenomenon, the loss of the old moon is both blurred and highlighted by the brightness of the new moon; the multiple indirections—of the sunlight reflected back by the earth upon the moon—obfuscate the loss of the "old moon," which is denied and embraced simultaneously by the presence of the "new moon." The Bishop speaker's subjectivity and her focus on objects have a similar relationship: indirections blur the loss as much as they highlight it. And the contradiction of multiple mirrorings, the going back-and-forth within the signification system—in which the old moon at times signifies something that has been lost and at other times something that continues to live, albeit in the new moon's arms—results in inconclusion that itself awaits an assignation of a meaning: an "Echo or mirror seeking of itself" that is "Quietly shining to the quiet Moon," as Samuel Taylor Coleridge would phrase it in "Frost at Midnight."[20]

The focus on the object, its indirection, the in-between space that it creates, and its resultant inconclusion all collude to highlight the color that little Arthur is associated with: white. Creditable readings of "First Death in Nova

Scotia" have discussed the contrast between the primary colors that dominate this poem, red and white. While one may extract various symbolic meanings out of those colors themselves, the most basic and important thing that should be mentioned is what anyone who has ever done any painting would know: white is a color that can be dyed by any color. That is one color that the speaker consistently identifies Arthur with: "Jack Frost had dropped the brush / and left him white, forever" (39–40). Arthur's paraphernalia too is white: Arthur is seen "clutching his tiny lily" (48). And the final image of the poem's psychological landscape is white as well: "the roads deep in snow" (50). If white is the color of blankness that can be dyed in any color—unlike black, the color that cannot be changed or swayed by other colors—then Arthur is an empty vessel that can be filled by any perspective, as if to underline that to be dead is to be dyed, for the dead have no voice. The only voice they have is through the prosopopoeia of the living subject. Arthur's whiteness points to the fact that, in death, he has turned into a locus of transference, of the interpretive activity of the viewer.

For the dead to end up becoming a site of transferential meaning-determinations for the mourners is not a rare phenomenon in elegies. Mourners are said to be enslaved to meaning-assignations; when faced with the death of someone, we often think we can process the experience and move forward if we can find its meanings. Georges Poulet refers to this mechanism as melancholia's "maximization of consciousness":[21] the process of finding and assigning meanings consumes the mental activity of the mourner, and such domination of the thought processes is the symptom of the "maximized consciousness" of melancholia. Meaning-assignation can turn into an onerous search for closure, which sometimes ends with a tiring and a giving up of the effort. The whiteness of Bishop's Arthur—and his readiness to be colored in any color, to be perceived in whatever manner the viewer projects himself or herself—attests to its openness to transferences. The child-speaker's imaginative digression reveals her mental exhaustion, a weariness over the endless search for meanings, as much as her spellbound fascination and a bonding with the past. This complexity of response can only be conveyed by indirection, inconclusion, and in-between space created by the poem's focus on the object. "First Death in Nova Scotia" suggests that this self-spectralization and the construction of the third space between remembering and forgetting constitute a part of the apparatus of Bishop's sublimational poetics; they function as a template with which the poems of *Geography III* portray the theme of loss.

Indirection of loss and the creation of in-between space become a pervasive theme in *Geography III*, Bishop's last book of poetry, which follows *Questions of Travel*. In the words of Anne Colwell, "the poems of *Geography*

III deal with overwhelming loss the way we all deal with the overwhelming light of the sun—they squint, avoid looking directly at it . . . . Paradoxically, but perhaps not surprisingly, this evasion makes the sense of loss both more pervasive and more deeply realized."[22] Just as we detect and view the sunlight only indirectly—through its reflections off objects, windows, and so on—many of Bishop's elegies express their sense of loss through circumvention. As seen in "First Death in Nova Scotia," the result of this obliqueness is the creation of a space of half-remembrance and half-forgetting.

It is a truism that one of the critical functions of elegy is for the bereaved to remember the dead, as is the case with gravestones; remembrance is believed to salvage the dead from oblivion and its totalizing loss. Graves are often made of stone, a conventional metaphor of immutability; elegies and gravestones function as material reminders of the dead. Anthropologically speaking, however, there is another function to gravestones: they also help us forget. By externalizing one's memory onto the stone, one can safely leave things to oblivion.[23] Memorialization—whether it is the edifying of a gravestone or the writing of an elegy—is simultaneously an act of remembering and forgetting, which creates an equivocal space between the two.

This double-function of memorialization has been formulated through historical theorization of memory. Aristotle posited that memory is "like an imprint or drawing in us" of things felt, and that forgetting is a decay of such an imprint.[24] Aristotle's conceptualization of memory is inherited by one of the two conventional theories of forgetting in modern psychology, which argues that the memory trace simply fades or decays, much in the way a signpost that is exposed to sun and rain gradually fades until it becomes illegible.[25] This theory is reinforced by Hermann Ebbinghaus's classic study of memory retention rate, which finds that the amount of memory lost is proportionate to the lapse of time.[26] As Adrian Forty and Susanne Küchler point out, if objects are made to stand for memory, their decay or destruction implies or symbolizes forgetting.[27] In other words, so long as objects symbolize memory, memorialization does not guarantee the preservation of memory. Insofar as decay or destruction is an inevitable fate for an object, remembering and forgetting are both the opposites of one another and inseparable complements to each other—not only because what one remembers will at some point be forgotten but also because, as Heidegger claims, only what has been forgotten can be remembered.[28] Whether by memorializing and elegizing, the symbolization of memory in object forms results in this paradox, containing both a fear of forgetting and a desire to forget.

Bishop's poetry adds another element to this paradox: that of indirection, in which the feelings or moods after one experiences loss are extracted and transplanted into some other objects. Poems in *Geography III*, such as "Crusoe in England," "Poem," and "The Moose," have been read as devices for recovering what is lost by reembodying that life in a new form.[29] This mechanism—of loss and recovery, of remembering and forgetting—is not peculiar to Bishop's elegiac work; conventional elegies customarily profess their intent to remember and preserve the lost object at the same time as bemoaning their inadequacies to do so, for an elegy or memorial is but a displaced effigy of the lost thing that falls short of the thing itself. What differentiates Bishop's elegiac work is the multiplicity of displacement that her indirection creates: the speaker's focus on external objects instead of her inner feelings of loss as in the case of "First Death in Nova Scotia"; or, in the case of "Crusoe in England," the adoption of someone else's story and the transplantation of a feeling of dispossession onto that story, in which the speaker only obliquely laments his loss long after he returns from the uninhabited island. The effect of this indirect approach is analogous to the feeling of seeing a fallen-off scab. A scab is an in-between object: it can simultaneously be a reminder of a fresh wound and a sign of its healing process. Looking at a scab is different from viewing a wound, but it nonetheless fills one's imagination with thoughts of a wound: evasion makes the sense of loss both more pervasive and dispersive.

"Crusoe in England" is a poem of interlocution; its retelling is a kind of translation.[30] The periphrastic design suggests the sense of lost loss, like the old moon in the new moon's arms: a reflection of reflection, losing sight of the original in the process. As Kim Fortuny points out, the poem has generally been read as a thinly veiled meditation on the loss of Bishop's estranged lover, Lota de Macedo Soares;[31] the implication is that Bishop's translational poetics provides a screen that is necessary in expressing personal taboos. The author herself, however, was reportedly horrified by the suggestion that the poem was an autobiographical metaphor for Brazil and Lota.[32] On the motive of writing "Crusoe in England," Bishop's reply was the following:

> I don't know. I reread the book and discovered how really awful *Robinson Crusoe* was, which I hadn't realized . . . . I reread it all in one night. And I had forgotten it was so moral. All that Christianity. So I think I wanted to re-see it with all that left out.[33]

At first glance, the quotation may appear to emphasize Bishop's reaction against the story's immersion in morality and Christianity. This and other pieces of evidence have resulted in the reading of Bishop as a politically and socially engaged poet, and of "Crusoe in England" as a covert literary representation of same-sex relationships,[34] even in spite of the author's denial of such intent. Authorial intent is a matter for speculation; when read by readers who possess biographical knowledge of Bishop's life, the poem can be interpreted as being indirectly about Lota's death, insofar as the practice of reading is a kind of transference. In a loss of loss where an object-loss itself has undergone a disappearance, its indirect expressive traces can lead readers to a range of possible interpretations.

The focus of this present book, however, is the hidden dispossession: how intertextuality can conceal the real loss; how the sense of covert privation emerges in a retelling of a story, of a man who is removed from the site of the remembrance; how the poem functions as a kind of earthshine reflected back as moonlight. The critical part of the previous Bishop quote is the following phrase: "to re-see it with all that left out." "Crusoe in England" is an attempt to salvage things that were "left out." The things "left out" of Defoe's *Robinson Crusoe* are ones that Bishop believes are repressed underneath Defoe's emphasis on Christian preaching and moral victories: the things untold in Defoe's account of Crusoe's triumphant return to his island, which has turned into a prosperous colony. Given that an excavation of repression is an interpretive activity susceptible to the analyst's transference, Bishop is not so much inheriting the spirit of Defoe's Crusoe, but rather transplanting that of her own Crusoe into the story.[35] As Bishop's drafts of "Crusoe in England" reveal, its initial title was "Last Days of Crusoe."[36] The thrust of the title is decidedly self-elegiac, as if the poem is a story about someone who is himself about to be "left out" of this world; it is an impending self-loss that is a type of double-loss. With a foreseeable self-loss looming in the background, the spirit Bishop infuses into her Crusoe is that of someone who is too far removed from the site of loss to be able to articulate his feeling of loss: someone whose feeling of loss is so faint as to be left out of Defoe's original version.

The "left out" objects haunt the poem as metonyms. The poem begins with an account of what has gone missing, as revealed by the double-exposure of a newspaper depiction of a newly discovered island and the speaker's musing on his "old" island that remains "un-rediscovered." This juxtaposition adumbrates the fact that his "old" island continues to be left off the maps, unnamed and unlocated by "books":

A new volcano has erupted,
the papers say, and last week I was reading
where some ship saw an island being born:
at first a breath of steam, ten miles away;
and then a black fleck—basalt, probably—
rose in the mate's binoculars
and caught on the horizon like a fly.
They named it. But my poor old island's still
un-rediscovered, un-renamable.
None of the books has ever got it right.   (1–10)

Line 3 equates being discovered with being born. The principle mirrors George Berkeley's "*Esse est percipi*": to be is to be perceived. One cannot be seen to exist if one is not perceived, or discovered. The flipside of this dictum is that if an object comes to be "born" when it is perceived or discovered, what has not been perceived, discovered, or known would be considered unborn: a nonexistence. In this sense, the island that has remained "un-rediscovered" and "un-renamable" is tantamount to something that was once born but is now missing or dead. By equating discovery with birth, the poem makes a linguistic move to signal the speaker's recognition that things "left out" of our accounts of the world are, in essence, dead.

Crusoe's unrecorded island functions as a metaphor of the poem's object-loss that has gone missing and is perceivable only through its trace. Recollecting such remnants of loss becomes the mission of the poem. True to the elegiac convention, the poem shifts in the second and third stanzas toward a descriptive remembrance of the island. The poem exhibits a singular propensity toward cataloging the details of the island—turtles, lava, beaches, tree snail, berry, among other things—and that has prompted scholars to comment on how the poem "is obsessed with recording and mapping and naming."[37] Proliferation of details is one of the elegiac techniques that became a fixture in the nineteenth century. The representative examples of poems that employ this mode include Alfred Lord Tennyson's *In Memoriam*, a poem that compulsively accumulates the details of personal moments. *In Memoriam* simulates the trend of proliferating furnishings in Victorian funerary practices: like residual memories of pain in the spine, Victorian prototypes are amassed into the spirit of "Crusoe in England" as a type of haunting.

Similar to the way in which the voluminous accretion of personal moments is meant to offset the actual loss of Arthur Henry Hallam in *In Memoriam*, the exhaustive specificity with which Bishop's Crusoe recounts the details of the island in this poem is meant to prevent him from losing the island to inaccurate accounts and eventual oblivion. The speaker's impassioned recounting, however, ironically reveals the threats to his recollective efforts. As suggested by the speaker's proclamation in line 10—"None of the books has ever got it right"—mistaken accounts can easily render his "poor old island" lost and "un-rediscovered" by repressing it under false identifications. Also, the speaker's cataloging effort is at times sabotaged by himself—by his tendency to summarize his findings with phrases like "The island had one kind of everything" (68) or "There was one kind of berry" (76), whereby the summaries suppress the individual objects by subsuming them into a category. The speaker's maniacal desire to "get it right" by collecting and salvaging detailed accounts of the island is rooted in his anxiety over the totalizing loss of his island through mischaracterization, oblivion, or summarization.

In addition to "getting it right," the act of collecting and recollecting details of the past has other functions beyond preservation. In order to explicate the multilayered significance of this conservational effort, one may profitably examine Walter Benjamin's theory of the "collector."[38] Benjamin describes the motive of the collector as follows: the collector "takes up the struggle against dispersion."[39] Dispersion, in the instance of collection, means confusion of the scattering, its meaninglessness, the disorganization void of any "knowledge of [the objects'] origin and their duration in history."[40] If one were to extrapolate the theory of collection and apply it to the act of recollection, dispersion would mean the disorganization of memory bits to incomprehension and their resultant loss to oblivion. That is to say, if we were to liken our memory to the proverbial drawer, dispersion would be a state in which the objects in the drawer were so randomly scattered that we would be unable to find objects we were looking for. The mechanism is similar to the interference theory of forgetting, where people are unable to retrieve a desired memory because other memories interfere and obstruct the path to reach that memory.

To say that the function of collecting and recollecting is to prevent us from losing the object merely reinforces the popular and dominant view of the function of the elegy: to preserve the memory of the dead in order to save it from the totalizing loss of oblivion. Where Benjamin's theory helps is that it elucidates the mechanism of such preservation. For Benjamin, the decisive characteristic of collection is the following:

> [The] object is detached from all its original function in order to enter into the closest conceivable relation to things of the same kind. This relation is the diametric opposite of any utility, and falls into the peculiar category of completeness. What is this "completeness"? It is a grand attempt to overcome the wholly irrational character of the object's mere presence at hand through its integration into a new, expressly devised historical system: the collection. And for the true collector, every single thing in this system becomes an encyclopedia of all knowledge of the epoch, the landscape, the industry, and the owner from which it comes. It is the deepest enchantment of the collector to enclose the particular item within a magic circle, where, as a last shudder runs through it (the shudder of being acquired), it turns to stone. Everything remembered, everything thought, everything conscious becomes socle, frame, pedestal, seal of his possession . . . . Collecting is a form of practical memory, and of all the profane manifestation of "nearness" it is the most binding.[41]

The passage illuminates the object's detachment from its functional relations and its immediate utility. This detachment is the "foundation . . . of that 'disinterested' contemplation by virtue of which the collector attains to an unequaled view of the object—a view that takes in more, and other, than that of the profane owner and which we would do best to compare to the gaze of the great physiognomist."[42] By being taken out of their functional utility, objects are infused with the spirit of a "physiognomist." Through this mechanism, collecting becomes a form of practical memory. By reversible logic, memory takes on a character akin to an act of collection, through its extracting of past events from their original context and rearranging of them into a "new, expressly devised historical system" of personal historical narrative called remembrance.

At the same time as objects are detached from their original context, function, and utility, for the collector, "the world is present, and indeed ordered, in each of his objects."[43] The collected objects become a peculiar half-space where the objects and their worlds are at once defunct and present. Memories, like collected objects, are half-spaces where their contents are at once defunct—in the sense that they are in the past—and present—in the sense that they are still continuously reorganized to produce new meanings in the present arrangements of the subject's universe. That is the mechanism of preservation: storage in a half-space between object-presence and its detachment. Preservation of an object entails its transformation.

Memory is transformative, and this ambivalent cruelty of the preservative mechanism is at the heart of Bishop's Crusoe's "self-pity":

I often gave way to self-pity.
"Do I deserve this? I suppose I must.
I wouldn't be here otherwise. Was there
a moment when I actually chose this?
I don't remember, but there could have been."
What's wrong about self-pity, anyway?
With my legs dangling down familiarly
over a crater's edge, I told myself
"Pity should begin at home." So the more
pity I felt, the more I felt at home.   (55–64)

While it seems rather obvious why Bishop's Crusoe feels self-pity—his loneliness—the phrase, "Pity should begin at home," is curious enough to invite a closer assessment. The preceding stanza gives us a clue to the reasons behind Crusoe's self-pity: after describing the island, the speaker comments, "Beautiful, yes, but not much company" (54). If the fact that the speaker does not have much company is the source of despondency, then the fact of his isolation on this inhabited island must be the reason he pities himself. Judging from the fact that the speaker seems to recall fondly the appearance of Friday—"Just when I thought I couldn't stand it another minute longer, / Friday came" (142–43)—the lack of company and the feeling of isolation appear to be the right answer to the source of his self-pity.

Loneliness, however, is too simplistic an answer for the complexity of Bishop's Crusoe. One possible complication is the "nightmares" in stanza 9 (134). What makes those nightmares so nightmarish is the taxonomy that the speaker would have to compile on each and every uninhabited island, if the uninhabited island actually were to spawn other uninhabited islands as it does in this dream. The linguistic emphasis falls on those lines that depict the act of taxonomy, with filler words like "eventually" and "for ages" (139, 140) and their accompanying caesurae that function as speed-bumps to make readers stop at the culminating apposition: "their flora, / their fauna, their geography" (141). To say that Crusoe would have "had to" live on each and every island is rather strange (138), since there is no one around to force him to carry out the taxonomical task. What prompts the speaker to continue surveying the islands is his collector instinct: the desire to seek completeness, to put together meaningless pieces of the scatter into a meaningful system of properties and relations, and to recapture the social structure constructed from scientific knowledge, akin to that of his familiar European homeland.

What fuels the speaker's collector instinct is the fact that he finds himself surrounded on an inhabited island by foreign objects, which, to him, are devoid of any meaningful system of properties and relations. The trick of displacement is that, by virtue of the fact that the subject has himself been extracted from his original context, all objects in the surroundings come to seem as though they in turn are extracted from their original contexts—and those objects must, therefore, be put back together in the "new, expressly devised historical system" of a collection, during which process a collector, like a mourner, becomes enslaved to meaning-assignation. One method Bishop's Crusoe uses to rearrange the "foreign" objects of the uninhabited island is to turn them into resources for his "island industries" (87) that manufacture products he used to have while he was in England—his original "home" island. The taxonomy continues in the fifth stanza, with the speaker enumerating "one kind of everything" as though the island were his partial Noah's ark (68). The stanza portrays how the speaker turns the island's foreign objects—an unfamiliar dark red berry and a flute with an unfamiliar scale—into things he is able to recognize: a "home-brew" (79) that bears enough resemblance to beer, or a "home-made flute" (82) that bears enough resemblance to a flute. This domestication of foreign objects into things vaguely familiar, objects with a faint feel of "home," is what the collector instinct guides Bishop's Crusoe to do.

In this sense, the poem is not so much an affirmation of creativity emerging from an exile's spinnings,[44] but rather an admission of human frailty, which, when faced with a foreign and disorienting circumstance, prompts the speaker to look for any trace of familiar things that may guide him out of his discomfort.[45] Nonetheless, the "home" Bishop's Crusoe creates with his collecting and domesticating of foreign objects is merely an approximation. Similar to the way in which additional memories interfere with one's efforts to recall previous memories, Crusoe's recollected images of home become corrupted into a simulacrum the longer he is removed from his "home" and the more "home-made" the things he produces on this island become. In this process, the idea of home itself becomes blurry, turning into a kind of autonomized idea which Jacques Derrida calls a "ghost":

> Once the ghost is produced by the incarnation of spirit (the autonomized idea or thought), when this *first* ghost effect has been operated, it is in turn negated, integrated, and incorporated by the very subject of the operation who, claiming the uniqueness of its *own* human body, then becomes, according to Marx as critic of Stirner, the absolute ghost, in fact the ghost of the ghost of the specter-spirit, simulacrum of simulacra without end.[46]

Once the idea of "home" becomes an autonomized ideation in one's exile, it becomes a ghost and then undergoes an endless interiorization and ghost production, whereby a ghost becomes a ghost of a ghost. In exile, one is removed not only from the physical home but also from the idea of home as well. Furthermore, any preservation of it—an attempt to create a collection that approximates the previous system of meaning—only expedites its transformation.

To return to the initial inquiry into the source of the self-pity that Bishop's Crusoe feels, one may interpret it as originating from this recognition of the transformative loss: a loss, in exile, of not only home but also the memory of home, which, through the interferences of time and the false approximations of it one makes in one's exile, erodes into a simulacrum, then endlessly into a simulacrum of simulacra. For this reason, the transformative and dissolutive nature of the preservative mechanism proves to be unkind to us when we seek to sustain objects as we remember them. The dictum of "Pity should begin at home" expresses a sentiment akin to "Home is where the pity is"—a rephrased version of "Home is where the heart is"[47]—and constitutes a philosophy of someone who recognizes this fact of dispossession: any effort to reclaim the lost object will only amplify the sense of loss. This philosophy—the speaker refers to it as the "smallest" (88) of the island industries and the only one toward which he does not feel any "deep affection" (86)—is "miserable" (89) because it provides no consolation. All it does is that in its transference of the object of one's sorrow from one thing—namely, the loss of home in this case—to another—namely, the realization of a totalizing loss, for which one can only pity oneself—it moves one's thoughts forward and keeps the stagnancy of melancholia at bay, the way the pain of a new injury sometimes takes one's mind off the pain of an old one.

If, in "First Death in Nova Scotia," indirection and diffusion of sorrow occur through the object's absorption of one's experience, in "Crusoe in England," the same occurs as a result of numerous layers the poem creates between the locus of its occasioning sorrow and the locus of its present narration. There are spatial and temporal removals between the presently narrating Crusoe, now in England, and the things that he has lost. First, there is the temporal distance: his island, his experiences on the island, and his feeling of homelessness upon being stranded on the island are all in the past tense. Then, there is the spatial remove: Crusoe is no longer on the island, and is on "another island" that "doesn't seem like one" (154, 155). By virtue of these distances, all the objects and memories are extracted from their original contexts, and are collected and stored in changed forms as a Benjaminian collector would do. No object is more symbolic of this phenomenon than the knife Crusoe used while he was on the island, which "reeked of meaning, like a crucifix" (162). Transferred out of its original context and having lost the meaning it once had, the knife is placed in a newly expressed system of meaning—a museum:

The local museum's asked me to
leave everything to them:
the flute, the knife, the shrivelled shoes,
my shedding goatskin trousers
(moths have got in the fur),
the parasol that took me such a time
remembering the way the ribs should go.
It still will work but, folded up,
looks like a plucked and skinny fowl.
How can anyone want such things?   (171–80)

The flute, the knife, the shoes, the goatskin trousers—those have all turned into objects that have been divorced from their utility. This recognition prompts the question, "How can anyone want such things?"[48] Much in the same way Crusoe first records and names foreign objects on the uninhabited island like a collector, the things he used while he was on the island are now being collected like foreign objects. The ironic musing of "How can anyone want such things?" arises as much from the realization that Crusoe himself, along with his belongings, has now turned into part of a collection: strange and useless. This knowledge—that his past selves, his past experiences, of which the knife that "won't look at" him anymore is symbolic (168),[49] can also be lost from their original circumstances and need to be rearranged into a new system of meaning if they are to be salvaged from a totalizing loss—is terrifying enough that it has to be deflected with irony. These multiple layers of removes—from the time when the objects were originally put to use, from the places where they were being used, and from the meanings and utility that they used to have—diffuse and accentuate the sense of dispossession.

In the end, "Crusoe in England" presents itself as an elegy for things that are left out of one's time, records, consciousnesses, or stories—things that have lost their original meanings and circumstances, things that have disappeared into oblivion, or things whose truths have been overwritten by fictions or falsities. Crusoe's "un-rediscovered" island is emblematic of this expunged loss. "Crusoe in England" reveals the anxiety over the loss of loss as an underlying impulse in Bishop's elegiac poems. This unease compels poetic creations that simultaneously retain and release the lost objects, through their adoption of a "collector" character as well as their ambivalence over such a character, along with deliberations about the "miserable philosophy" that it represents. This anxiety-driven collection is a constitutive characteristic of Bishop's elegiac sublimation.

Bishop's sublimational poetics is anchored by the creation of in-between space and the function of a collector, which are motivated by the anxiety of losing loss. "Poem" and the rest of *Geography III* poems inherit these impulses; these poems also undertake the act of note-taking, whereby losses are recorded in changed and estranged forms outside of one's subjectivity. Like the preceding poems, "Poem" posits a similar premise of removal and distance: that is, the distance between the pictorial character of the painting and its linguistic portrayal by the ekphrasis, between the speaker and the speaker's uncle whom she never met, between art copying life and life itself, and between "life and the memory of it," as Bishop writes in one of the lines (53).[50] "Poem" begins as an ekphrasis, translating the painting's visual representation into a verbal form of the poem and illuminating, in the process, the distance and difference between the two:

About the size of an old-style dollar bill,
American or Canadian,
mostly the same whites, gray greens, and steel grays
—this little painting (a sketch for a larger one?)
has never earned any money in its life.
Useless and free, it has spent seventy years
as a minor family relic
handed along collaterally to owners
who looked at it sometimes, or didn't bother to.   (1–9)

In removing the painting from its original context and rearranging it in a new system of a verbal construct, "Poem" takes on the character of a collector, who possesses a keen understanding of the transformative nature of the preservative mechanism of collection. What becomes apparent from the passage is the worthlessness of this painting: "Useless and free." A touch of irony is hard to miss. Similar to Crusoe's musing—"How can anyone want such things?"—"Poem" is concerned with the use of the useless. It is an effort to salvage this painting from a totalizing loss of oblivion, which, if not for the poem giving it a voice, would be the fate of this painting.

This irony originates in the painting's seeming incongruence between appearance and substance: the painting's resemblance, in size, to a dollar bill and its lack of monetary value, as indicated by the statement that it "has never earned any money in its life" (5). In one of her interviews, Bishop further underscores how worthless this painting really is:

> "An uncle of mine. Uncle George. My grandmother owned four of his paintings . . . . I wrote a new poem about this. It is called 'Poem' and has to do with one of his pictures. I had already written about him once before."
> "In 'Large Bad Picture,' you mean?"
> "Yes."
> "Was he a good painter?"
> "He was a very bad painter."[51]

Since the artwork's survival generally hinges in no small part on its artistic merit, this painting—a middling painting by a "very bad painter"—could easily have been lost to obscurity, and it almost was, since it was only casually, collaterally handed along to owners who "didn't bother to" look at it most of the time; not being perceived is akin to nonexistence. The painting survives by virtue of the poem, having undergone the process of destruction that a translation of an object into a different medium would entail. The incongruence between the "bad" painting and the good poem that salvages it adds another layer of irony. "Poem" is similar to "Crusoe in England," in that it too is an elegy for things that were "left out"—of record, of memory, of art history, of things extracted out of their utility. "Poem" is an elegy for useless things. One minor difference is that "Poem" starts out comically, and its faint feeling of dispossession is made facetious by the discrepancy between the solemnity of the elegiac undertone and the frivolity of the object-loss.

The uselessness of the painting is underscored by the rhetorical redundancy: line 5—the painting "has never earned any money in its life"—and the beginning of line 6—"Useless and free"—essentially repeats the same content. There is, however, another layer of meaning to this redundancy. On one level, the word "free" means that the painting has no monetary value. But on another level, the fact that the painting has no monetary value or no utility also gives it a certain freedom, in the sense that things that are "free" of value are also "free" to be used in ways that are not originally intended, for those objects either fulfill no intended utility to begin with or have been extricated from it. Canonical paintings—which are considered to be valuable and not "useless and free"—would come with inherited meanings that poets writing ekphrases cannot entirely disregard; an ekphrasis on a famous painting like "Landscape with the Fall of Icarus" by Pieter Breughel would inevitably be read under the overtone of W. H. Auden's "Musée des Beaux Arts" for the fact that language inherits the chain of reception, retaining echoes of past works that have been integrated as a part of the literary tradition. An unknown painting, however, stipulates no such limitations. Like the little Arthur in "First Death in Nova Scotia" whose whiteness can be dyed in any color, the useless painting becomes a blank canvas; the poem transforms it into a site of transferential meaning-assignations and extrapolations, where the author of the ekphrasis is free to create new and unintended meanings.

It is precisely through this freedom that "Poem" becomes something more than an elegy for the painting as a representative of forgotten things; it also becomes an elegy for the speaker's great-uncle, whom she never knew. As an elegy for someone she previously did not know—an elegy of an imagined loss, with some similarities to Roethke's "Elegy for Jane"—the poem first forges a connection between the speaker and the deceased, and then recognizes its loss:

I never knew him. We both knew this place,
apparently, this literal small backwater,
looked at it long enough to memorize it,
our years apart. How strange. And it's still loved,
or its memory is (it must have changed a lot).
Our visions coincided—"visions" is
too serious a word—our looks, two looks:
art "copying from life" and life itself,
life and the memory of it so compressed
they've turned into each other. Which is which?   (45–54)

"Poem" has sometimes been read as "a sudden recognition . . . [of] the strangeness and intimacy of meeting the spirit of place in this 'minor family relic,'"[52] but it seems to me that what the poem recognizes is not so much the meeting with a vague "spirit of place" but rather an encounter, through the shared "look" at the same locale, with the spirit of someone the speaker had not previously known. The poem initially denies any previous link between the speaker and her great-uncle—"I never knew him"—and then takes out the negation in the second sentence to forge a connection: "We both knew this place" (45). The relationship is constructed where it had not existed before, by virtue of the shared word—the word "knew" is used in both sentences—to describe the shared landscape, a landscape the two had looked at, albeit in separate times and through separate eyes. If the pain of loss in "Crusoe in England" is like that of phantom pain—like a pain in a lost limb, it is a pain in the emotional space within himself that he has lost, which he only recognizes in the erosion of the memories and keepsakes of his experiences on the uninhabited island—the lamentation of loss in this poem is an almost celebratory one, in which the speaker recognizes a newly formed connection. This creation, alongside the recognition of its simultaneous loss, results in the mixture of muted joy and sorrow.

In the introductory chapter, I examine Roethke's "Elegy for Jane" as a poem about a type of lost loss, in which one did not know the deceased well and was deprived of an opportunity to lose him or her. While Sandra Gilbert's *Inventions of Farewell* classifies "Elegy for Jane" as a poem of friendship by placing it in the section entitled "Mourning the Deaths of Friends,"[53] it speaks more to the fact that the language to express this type of dispossessed loss is sorely lacking in the current elegiac discourse and that the difficulty of categorizing this variety of elegy stems from this inadequacy. Elegies for people whom we hardly knew and who were not famous function outside of both the loss-compensation paradigm of classical elegies and the melancholic mourning paradigm of modern elegies. Bishop's "Poem" focuses less on the lamentation over the loss of an opportunity to know the uncle well enough to "lose" him than on the visionary experience that borders on wonderment over the discovery of such loss; the tone of the poem is more celebratory and less sorrowful than that of Roethke's "Elegy for Jane." Nonetheless, it participates in a similar project: a reclamation or salvaging of a "lost loss" that would otherwise be unavailable to us had the poem not given it an elegiac form.

The visionary experience in "Poem" results from self-spectralization, a turning of the self into the other and its reverse: creation of a half-space between the two. The poem dissects this vision as a coinciding of "two looks," in which the two individuals meet at the intersection between "life and the memory of it."[54] The two people's experience is divided into two elements, life and its memory, which then meld into one another to the point where they cannot be distinguished from each other, where we would not know "which is which." Life and memory are inseparable—memory is part of what makes up our life, or so we think—but upon a closer look, we divide them into two, reorganize them, and assemble them back into a synthesis; this motion of thoughts staves off, however fleetingly, the stasis of self-assaulting melancholia, and this cognitive motion that disturbs the stillness of the maximized consciousness is what anchors the sublimatory poetics of Bishop's elegiac work.

Other poems of *Geography III* also operate through this apparatus of cognitive reorganization; they tend to leave the lost object unnamed and to address it only obliquely in some translated form or as a concept rather than an actual presence. In "In the Waiting Room," the sense of looming loss—of innocence, of lives in the war outside—is diluted by the inchoate cognition of a child-speaker who is starting to, though does not quite, understand the world she is in. "The Moose" has been described by critics as an "elegy for place," rather than for "the" or "a" place or the moose, and "The End of March" is read as a poem for the end of life,[55] where the "end" becomes a symbolic one that is oxymoronically entangled with the end of the death-like winter months. In all these poems, the feeling of loss is faintly recorded despite the lack of any specific object-loss, like a kite string without a kite in "The End of March": "the ghost . . . / A kite string?—But no kite" (22–23). In "Objects & Apparitions," phantoms are preserved in the form of translation. As tenuous as the sense of loss may be in these poems, those amorphous losses need to be recorded and collected, if one hopes to stave off the prospect of lost loss.

A similar dynamic is at work in Bishop's most studied elegiac work, "One Art." One may argue that "One Art" is more explicitly about the theme of loss than any other poems in *Geography III*. While its theme is explicit, the target of its lament is as opaque as any. The speaker of "One Art" enumerates various things she has lost, but the focus is less on them than on her wish to turn the fact of loss into an art form. This indirection is reminiscent of "Crusoe in England." Bishop's Crusoe obsessively collects and recollects the objects that will be lost, but his lamentation is less concerned with those objects than with the unawareness of things that have not been collected or recorded, of things inevitably effaced, transformed, and sublimated by elegiac remembrance. Also, like "Poem," "One Art" places itself in the in-between space of irony, the incongruence between its tonal lightness—"the joking voice" (16)—and the weightiness of the dirge. While "One Art" remains the crown jewel of Bishop's oeuvre, it exists in the context of other poems that precede and follow it in *Geography III*.

One may wonder if the lost objects named in "One Art"—lost door keys, the hour badly spent, places, names, the mother's watch, loved houses, two cities—are the traces of losses that have been lost to incomprehension, whether to repression and oblivion in "First Death in Nova Scotia," to fiction in "Crusoe in England," or to losses of opportunities to build a connection in "Poem." Much has already been written about "One Art,"[56] and my only contribution here is to add one more layer of complexity to the phrase in the final line, "*Write* it!" If, as suggested by the earlier discussion of "First Death in Nova Scotia," the act of writing things down creates a third space between remembering and forgetting, then the transformation effected by writing anchors Bishop's sublimational poetics. By "writing," the poem means here the acts of self-spectralization and of collection, which reorganize the expired, lost objects into new containers: it embodies the poetics of the ongoing, which is not a moving-on but an ambivalent moving-forward. The past does not change, and it is not easy to assuage one's sorrow. But just as the old wine is transferred into a new wineskin and the old wine gradually absorbs the smell and the texture of the new wineskin to undergo a subtle transformation, this poetics of the ongoing blunts the stasis of melancholia.

The underlying thesis of Bishop's poems in *Geography III* and their predecessors in *Questions of Travel* suggests that, if objects are to be inevitably lost, then at least one could, and one would want to, preserve the fact of their losses, the concept of loss, or even just the vague traces of losses, as part of an endeavor to "un-lose" the loss. These facts, concepts, and traces surface as external objects infused with self-meanings in "First Death in Nova Scotia," as a collection of meaningless and useless things in "Crusoe in England" and "Poem," as the *National Geographic* story about cannibalism in "In the Waiting Room," and as a fantasy of a dream house in "The End of March." And in "One Art," losses are molded into the form of art.

Elegy is an act of putting into a new meaning system an object whose original meanings and original forms have expired. Therefore, an elegist—one who details and recollects the lost experience or object—takes on a character akin to that of a collector extracting an object out of its original form or circumstance and rearranging it in another. Changes of forms or contexts do not console—the laurel wreath did not stop Apollo from lamenting the loss of Daphne—but the motion of thoughts that they create can, at times, help assuage, even temporarily, the pain of self-pity. From beyond the layers of multiple removes, the anxiety over losing the loss, alongside the resultant impulse to "un-lose" loss, continues to haunt. This conflicting desire to retain the lost object but to facilitate the moving-on defines Bishop's sublimational poetics.

NOTES

1. It has been noted that Bishop never felt comfortable as an overt elegist (Jonathan Ellis, *Art and Memory in the Work of Elizabeth Bishop* [Burlington: Ashgate, 2006], 49). The exact number of her published elegies depends on how one defines the term, but the critical consensus is that there is a relative scarcity of overt elegies in her oeuvre, particularly among works published in her lifetime. Poems such as "Cootchie," "Anaphora," "The Burglar of Babylon," "First Death in Nova Scotia," and "North Haven" qualify as elegies. Others, such as "Aubade: an elegy," were never judged complete. There is also a proposed book-length poem called *Elegy*, which her 1977 application for a Guggenheim fellowship describes as being "partly written," but it was never finished (Brett C. Millier, *Elizabeth Bishop: Life and the Memory of It* [Berkeley: University of California Press, 1993],

538). The present author's archival research at Vassar College confirms a copy of Bishop's Guggenheim fellowship application ("Statement of Plans," in *Elizabeth Bishop Papers*, Archives and Special Collections Library, Vassar College Libraries, Box 40.7). There are notes in Box 64.20 that appear to be evidence of a rudimentary planning of this project, and a snippet of it reads as follows: "The ELEGY poem— make it in sections, some anecdotal, somelyrical [sic] / different length – never more than two short pages." As a side note, this absence of Bishop's elegiac work may itself be considered a form of lost loss—poems about loss lost to self-censorship, or lost to an archival labyrinth. The compilation of Bishop's uncollected poems, drafts, and fragments, *Edgar Allan Poe & the Juke-Box*, edited by Alice Quinn, contains traces of an elegiac project around the 1950s; Charles Berger identifies "For M.B.S., buried in Nova Scotia," "Where are the dolls who loved me so . . . ," "A Short, Slow Life," and "Syllables" as potentially publishable poems that might have provided further proof of Bishop's mastery in the realms of strict, heartbreaking elegiac ethos (Charles Berger, "Bishop's Buried Elegies," in *Elizabeth Bishop in the Twenty-First Century*, ed. Angus Cleghorn et al. [Charlottesville: University of Virginia Press, 2012], 43). Overall, the fact that these poems went unpublished reinforces evidence of Bishop's discomfort with elegies in spite of the plaintive thrust in her work, and cements her standing as an elegiac poet with few formal elegies—a suggestive symptom of lurking lost loss and a characteristic that she shares with other poets studied in this book.

2. Thomas Travisano, *Elizabeth Bishop: Her Artistic Development* (Charlottesville: University Press of Virginia, 1988), 7. Colm Tóibín also remarks on Bishop's reticence and restraint: for Bishop, "language was . . . a way to restrain experience . . . . Our time on earth did not give us cause or need to say anything more than was necessary" (Colm Tóibín, *On Elizabeth Bishop* [Princeton: Princeton University Press, 2015], 2).

3. On the artistic achievement of "North Haven," Eleanor Cook details the elegiac traditions and allusions behind the poem, the working of which is captured in line 20, *"repeat, repeat, repeat; revise, revise, revise"* (Eleanor Cook, *Elizabeth Bishop at Work* [Cambridge: Harvard University Press, 2016], 255).

4. Cook, *Elizabeth Bishop at Work*, 240. The theme of forgetting is central in poems like "One Art," which grows out of Emily Dickinson's concept of an art of forgetting, as formulated in "Knows how to forget!"

5. Harald Weinrich, *Lethe: The Art and Critique of Forgetting*, trans. Steven Rendall (Ithaca: Cornell University Press, 1997), 1.

6. Bishop's distaste for overt confession is well-known, as represented by her oft-quoted critique of confessional poetry: "You just wish they'd keep some of those things to themselves" (Elizabeth Bishop, *The Collected Prose* [New York: Farrar, Straus and Giroux, 1984], xix).

7. Helen Vendler, *The Music of What Happens: Poems, Poets, Critics* (Cambridge: Belknap Press, 1988), 296.

8. Eileen John, "Poetry and Cognition," in *A Sense of the World: Essays on Fiction, Narrative, and Knowledge*, ed. John Gibson (New York: Routledge, 2007), 226.

9. Aside from the affective syncopation, critics have pointed to other poetic devices that create a sense of "near-sentimentalism" (Anne Stevenson, *Elizabeth Bishop* [New York: Twayne Publishers, 1966], 48). For instance, the trimeter of the poem is seen to add a dirge-like weight to the lines (Bonnie Costello, *Elizabeth Bishop: Questions of Mastery* [Cambridge: Harvard University Press, 1991], 195). Considering that trimeters have been historically used for light verse, such as in Middle English poetry, the effect of the trimeter here includes not only a dirge-like gravity but also a certain lighthearted incomprehension of the child who has not yet come to a fuller and firmer grasp of the concept, and the weight, of human life or death.

10. Emmanuel Levinas writes that the "death of the other" is the "first death": "The death of the Other affects me in my very identity as a responsible I" (Emmanuel Levinas, *Dieu, la mort et le temps* [Paris: Grasset, 1993], 21, 31, quoted in Derrida, *The Work of Mourning*, 204–5). One reading of the Levinas quote may be to interpret it as giving credence to the reading that any elegy is a potential self-elegy. But on a closer look, if we interpret it to mean that deaths we witness constitute our own first "deaths" that will continue until the "final" death that is our own, it reinforces Derrida's claim that it is only "in us" that the dead may speak, and that it is only by speaking of or as the dead that we can keep them alive (Pascale-Anne Brault and Michael Naas, "Editor's Introduction," in Jacque Derrida, *The Work of Mourning* [Chicago: University of Chicago Press, 2001], 9). For Derrida, keeping the dead "alive, within oneself" becomes "the best sign of fidelity" (Derrida, *The Work of Mourning*, 36). The death of the other pains not only in and of itself but also in the sense that it marks a death of a part of oneself where the other had existed through introjection; it signals a disintegration of the wholeness of the previous self and necessitates a cognitive reconstruction.

11. Robert Dale Parker, *The Unbeliever: The Poetry of Elizabeth Bishop* (Urbana: University of Illinois Press, 1988), 103.

12. Travisano, *Elizabeth Bishop*, 171.

13. Charles Tomlinson, "Elizabeth Bishop's New Book," review of *Questions of Travel*, by Elizabeth Bishop, *Shenandoah* 17 (Winter 1966): 88–91. The poem has also been characterized as Bishop's exploration of the "silence as a carrier of trauma" (Linda Anderson, *Elizabeth Bishop: Lines of Connection* [Edinburgh: Edinburgh University Press, 2013], 134).

14. The fact that little Arthur has the same first name as Uncle Arthur is suggestive of the namegiver's own self-consciousness of his bloodline, his desire to maintain the family cohesion by giving his own name to his son. As a biographical side note, Bishop's uncle was in fact named Arthur (Martha Carlson-Bradley, "Lowell's 'My Last Afternoon with Uncle Devereux Winslow': The Model for Bishop's 'First Death in Nova Scotia,'" *Concerning Poetry* 19 [1986]: 129).

15. C. K. Doreski, *Elizabeth Bishop: The Restraints of Language* (New York: Oxford University Press, 1993), 97.

16. Benjamin, "On Some Motifs in Baudelaire," 315–21.

17. Helen Vendler, "Domestication, Domesticity, and the Otherworldly," in *Elizabeth Bishop*, ed. Harold Bloom (New York: Chelsea House, 1985), 86.

18. David Kalstone, *Becoming a Poet: Elizabeth Bishop with Marianne Moore and Robert Lowell* (New York: Farrar, Straus and Giroux, 1989), 220.
19. "The Old Moon in the New Moon's Arms," *Georgetown Review* 10, no. 1 (Spring 2009): 198, lines 1–8.
20. Samuel Taylor Coleridge, "Frost at Midnight," in *The Norton Anthology of English Literature*, Ninth Edition, Vol. 2, ed. Stephen Greenblatt (New York: W. W. Norton, 2012), lines 22, 75.
21. Poulet, "Exploding Poetry: Baudelaire," 70.
22. Anne Colwell, *Inscrutable Houses: Metaphors of the Body in the Poems of Elizabeth Bishop* (Tuscaloosa: University of Alabama Press, 1997), 171.
23. Michizou Toida, *The Structure of Forgetting* (Tokyo: Chikuma Shobou, 1984), 176, 180.
24. Aristotle, "De Memoria et Reminiscentia," in *Aristotle on Memory*, trans. R. Sorabji (Providence: Brown University Press, 1972), 51.
25. Alan D. Baddeley, *Essentials of Human Memory* (Hove: Psychology Press, 1999), 119.
26. Alan D. Baddeley, *The Psychology of Memory* (New York: Basic Books, Inc., 1976), 8.
27. Adrian Forty and Susanne Küchler, ed., *The Art of Forgetting* (Oxford: Berg, 1999), 4.
28. "Just as expecting is possible only on the basis of awaiting, remembering is possible only on that of forgetting, and not vice versa" (Martin Heidegger, *Being and Time*, trans. John Macquarrie and Edward Robinson [London: SCM Press, 1962], 388–89).
29. Colwell, *Inscrutable Houses*, 202.
30. Bishop herself at times defined poetic creation as an act of translation, as in the following quotation: "It's true that many poets don't like the fact that they have to translate everything into words" (Marilyn May Lombardi, *The Body and the Song: Elizabeth Bishop's Poetics* [Carbondale: Southern Illinois University Press, 1995], 140). Similarly, adopting others' voices or letting the other speak in her poems is one of the basic features of Bishop's poems (Mariana Machova, *Elizabeth Bishop and Translation* [Lanham: Lexington Books, 2017], 17).
31. Kim Fortuny, *Elizabeth Bishop: The Art of Travel* (Boulder: University Press of Colorado, 2003), 110. Also, Susan McCabe, *Elizabeth Bishop: Her Poetics of Loss* (University Park: Pennsylvania State University Press, 1994), 199; Lorrie Goldensohn, *Elizabeth Bishop: The Biography of a Poetry* (New York: Columbia University Press, 1992), 67–69; Gary Fountain and Peter Brazeau, *Remembering Elizabeth Bishop: An Oral Biography* (Amherst: University of Massachusetts Press, 1994), 265. In *Elizabeth Bishop: A Miracle for Breakfast*, Megan Marshall also confirms that, had Lota lived to one more March birthday, the couple would have spent seventeen years together, which mirrors the final lines of the poem, "Friday, my dear Friday, died of measles / seventeen years ago come March" (Marshall, *Elizabeth Bishop: A Miracle for Breakfast*, 226).
32. Fountain and Brazeau, *Elizabeth Bishop*, 333. Fountain and Brazeau further point out that "Bishop would not have been comfortable with a biographical study of

this sort. She . . . had a ferocious sense of privacy" (Fountain and Brazeau, *Elizabeth Bishop*, xi). Bonnie Costello also remarks on Bishop's discomfort with biographical studies: "Her poems do not so much veil or transmute the personal as expose the categories of the 'personal' and 'impersonal' to scrutiny" (Bonnie Costello, "Bishop's Impersonal Personal," *American Literary History* 15, no. 2 [July 2003]: 334). Costello further argues that "it is a mistake to read the literary allusions and borrowings" of "Crusoe in England" as "a mere mask of autobiography" (Bonnie Costello, "Bishop and the Poetic Tradition," in *The Cambridge Companion to Elizabeth Bishop*, ed. Angus Cleghorn and Jonathan Ellis [Cambridge: Cambridge University Press, 2014], 83). While it is true that new documents and manuscripts have been released as a result of Bishop's will that entrusts to others key decisions about the handling of her posthumous material (Angus Cleghorn et al., *Elizabeth Bishop in the Twenty-First Century* [Charlottesville: University of Virginia Press, 2012], 2), that information signals Bishop's preference that biographical studies of her work be pursued after her death.

33. Lloyd Schwartz and Sybil P. Estess, ed., *Elizabeth Bishop and Her Art* (Ann Arbor: University of Michigan Press, 1983), 319.

34. Fortuny, *Elizabeth Bishop*, 110. Also, the intertextuality of the poem has been seen as a screen that permits Bishop to address her personal struggle with the public taboo of homosexuality (Joanne Feit Diehl, *Elizabeth Bishop and Marianne Moore: The Psychodynamics of Creativity* [Princeton: Princeton University Press, 1993], 91–110).

35. Crusoe's anachronistic attempt to quote the lines in Wordsworth's "I wandered lonely as a cloud"—*Robinson Crusoe* was published in 1719, while "I wandered lonely as a cloud" was published in 1807—was questioned in *The New Yorker*, and it has been read as a sign that Bishop was nudging the reader that the speaker of "Crusoe in England" is not the "real" Robinson Crusoe (Lloyd Schwartz, "Back to Boston: *Geography III* and Other Late Poems," in *The Cambridge Companion to Elizabeth Bishop*, ed. Angus Cleghorn and Jonathan Ellis [Cambridge: Cambridge University Press, 2014], 144).

36. *Elizabeth Bishop Papers*, Archives and Special Collections Library, Vassar College Libraries. Box 58.16.

37. Sally Bishop Shigley, *Dazzling Dialectics: Elizabeth Bishop's Resonating Feminist Reality* (New York: Peter Lang, 1997), 144.

38. Beyond the superficial resemblance of the words, "collecting" and "recollecting" have similar functions in that they both perform an assemblage of scattered elements, whether in physical or psychic arrangements. Walter Benjamin equates "collector" with "allegorist"—"in every collector hides an allegorist, and in every allegorist a collector" (Walter Benjamin, *The Arcades Project*, trans. Howard Eiland [Cambridge: Belknap Press, 1999], 211)—and allegoresis, an act of putting together fragments in a meaningful manner, anchors the restoration of one's melancholic, fragmented universe into a whole.

39. Benjamin, *The Arcades Project*, 211.

40. Benjamin, *The Arcades Project*, 211.

41. Benjamin, *The Arcades Project*, 204–5.

42. Benjamin, *The Arcades Project*, 207.
43. Benjamin, *The Arcades Project*, 207.
44. Susan McCabe, "Bishop's 'Crusoe in England,'" *Explicator* 48, no. 1 (Fall 1989): 59.
45. That is a decidedly different persona from that of Defoe's imperialistic, moralistic, always positive and wish-fulfilling Robinson Crusoe, as suggested by the comparison between Bishop's and Defoe's Crusoes in Steven Hamelman, "Bishop's 'Crusoe in England,'" *Explicator* 51, no. 1 (Fall 1992): 50–53.
46. Jacques Derrida, *Specters of Marx: The State of the Debt, the Work of Mourning, and the New International*, trans. Peggy Kamuf (New York: Routledge, 1994), 127.
47. The phrase may also refer to the saying, "Charity begins at home." In that case, too, the irony remains that pity, like charity, should first be directed to one's own immediate surroundings and then disseminated to others.
48. As the drafts of "Crusoe in England" reveal, the line "How can anyone want such things?" was added over the course of the revision of the poem (*Elizabeth Bishop Papers*, Archives and Special Collections Library, Vassar College Libraries, Box 58.16). It suggests that the initial belief in the power of remembrance was tempered by a reservation over the transformative mechanism of recollection.
49. If we are to return to Berkeley's "to be is to be perceived," the knife's imperception of Crusoe feels as though Crusoe no longer exists.
50. The materiality of an art form offers a "kind of connecting mechanism for mind and world and for the sensations of physical and emotional touch" (Peggy Samuels, "Bishop and Visual Art," in *The Cambridge Companion to Elizabeth Bishop*, ed. Angus Cleghorn and Jonathan Ellis [Cambridge: Cambridge University Press, 2014], 181). This depiction is suggestive of the in-between space that Bishop's elegiac poems create and occupy.
51. George Monteiro, ed., *Conversations with Elizabeth Bishop* (Jackson: University Press of Mississippi, 1996), 64–65.
52. Jamie McKendrick, "Bishop's Birds," in *Elizabeth Bishop: Poet of the Periphery*, ed. Linda Anderson and Jo Shapcott (Newcastle: Bloodaxe Books, 2002), 140.
53. Gilbert, *Inventions of Farewell*, 288.
54. Details—as slight as elms and geese in the case of "Poem"—invest memory with totemic significance (Barbara Page, "Home, Wherever That May Be: Poems and Prose of Brazil," in *The Cambridge Companion to Elizabeth Bishop*, ed. Angus Cleghorn and Jonathan Ellis [Cambridge: Cambridge University Press, 2014], 140), and "First Death in Nova Scotia," "Crusoe in England," and "Poem" are all detail-reliant poems.
55. Parker, *The Unbeliever*, 121, 127. "The End of March" has also been read as a poem of hermitage and solitude; Bishop conceptualized "The End of March" as her version of W. B. Yeats's "The Lake Isle of Innisfree," which in turn was inspired by Henry David Thoreau's removal to Walden (Marshall, *Elizabeth Bishop: A Miracle for Breakfast*, 263), whereby renunciation becomes symbolic of a displaced sense of loss.

56. A sampling of recent critical reading of "One Art" includes the following: the poem has been read as "the nearest thing to a naked poem she ever published" (Barbara Page, "Elizabeth Bishop: Stops, Starts and Dream Divagations," in *Elizabeth Bishop: Poet of the Periphery*, ed. Linda Anderson and Jo Shapcott [Newcastle: Bloodaxe, 2002], 22); as even-keeled words on the concept of loss (Naomi Beckwith, "Necessary Fluster," *Poetry* 200, no. 3 [June 2012]: 266); as an instance of deviation from Bishop's preference for happy endings (Jonathan Sircy, "Bishop's 'One Art,'" *Explicator* 63, no. 4 [Summer 2005]: 241); as an effort "to explore and enhance the relationship between thought and feeling" through its form, villanelle (Vidyan Ravinthiran, *Elizabeth Bishop's Prosaic* [Lewisburg: Bucknell University Press, 2015], 200); and as a contemplation about "loss without compensation" (Cook, *Elizabeth Bishop at Work*, 239).

Chapter 4

Sharon Olds's *The Dead and the Living*
Distant Loss and Ethical Empathy

In *Distant Suffering: Morality, Media and Politics*, Luc Boltanski introduces a concept called "distant suffering," which he explains in the following passage:

> To summarise, on the one hand there is an unfortunate who suffers and on the other a spectator who views the suffering without undergoing the same fate and without being directly exposed to the same misfortune. To adopt an acceptable attitude, the spectator cannot remain indifferent nor draw a solitary enjoyment from the spectacle. However, he cannot always intervene directly; he cannot always go into action . . . . The further the spectator is from the unfortunate the more the disjunction between their situations seems to be insurmountable and in consequence action becomes more problematic.[1]

Distant suffering refers to the objective hardship of people—the "unfortunate" in the above passage—which is seen from the perspective of someone, a "spectator," who does not experience the same pain and who is situated at a far enough distance to preclude intervention. The challenging aspect of this circumstance is what Boltanski calls "disjunction," which occurs between the safety of the spectator and the precarity of the unfortunate. When compounded by obstacles to action, the asymmetry becomes problematic: as Susan Sontag observes in *Regarding the Pain of Others*, compassion is an unstable emotion that withers when left untranslated into action.[2] The situation lends itself to the proverbial spectator's dilemma: a condition in which one's powerlessness to do anything about a misfortune makes one's compassion seem hypocritical—and one's viewing of the other's suffering perverse. Consequently, for the spectator, apathy often becomes a more desirable alternative. In this predicament, is committing oneself to the cause of helping others through speech, even if it only amounts to speaking to somebody else about what one has seen of the news on the television, sufficiently moral?[3] Would it become more acceptable as a concerned individual if one were to go on tweeting or creating and sending memes to a number of followers who, in turn, circulate those messages? Or are these actions yet another reincarnation of the egoistic ideal of self-realization,[4] an opportunity to cultivate oneself through absorption in one's own pity at the spectacle of someone else's suffering?[5]

Those questions are all worthy inquiries, but the focus of this chapter—"distant loss" and the question of ethical empathy—develops and diverges from them; whereas distant suffering is an observed phenomenon that sufferers experience, distant loss is a subjective feeling of dispossession, emptiness, or discomfort that the spectator feels within himself or herself upon witnessing distant suffering, whether or not he or she is fully cognizant of it. The exact nature of the emotions evoked by distant loss can be variegated: for some, it is a profound sense of grief and indignation that prompts them to search for redress and actionable solutions, such as engaging in activism or finding proper organizations to make donations to; for others, it is a feeling of discomfort, palpable enough to stir their psyches when they encounter the phenomena on TV or other media, but faint enough that it allows them to go on with everyday life; and yet others may remain unaffected or apathetic on the conscious level, secure enough in the surfeit belief in their environs that those misfortunes would not happen to them, even as a subterranean sense of disturbance may register and lurk at the unconscious level. The concept of distant loss is also necessitated by the fact that, in most industrial and postindustrial societies, the cultural norms of mourning limit the acts of grieving to the deaths of family members or other intimates;[6] the acuteness of grief is expected to correspond to the proximity of the relations. At the farther end of human relationships, the idea that one has "lost" the distant other becomes contested. My contention is that, in ways that are significant or insignificant, distant loss affects the spectator. Certain segments of the spectators are drawn to compassion not only because it is a socially acceptable attitude but also because they possess a degree of sensitivity to the emotional effect of distant loss. Lost loss triggers the desire to "un-lose" the loss; as seen in the previous chapter, Elizabeth Bishop's speaker is moved to recuperate the relic of the great-uncle she does not know in "Poem." Likewise, distant loss—which I classify as a type of lost loss, in that the designation of "loss" is frequently deprived from the spectator in its occurrences—compels spectators to take ownership of its suffering, even if they are not experiencing it themselves.

As trauma studies continue to evolve, one of the consensuses that has emerged in recent decades is that trauma is not only a psychological phenomenon entailing unconscious emotions that leave traces of an otherwise unavailable reality or truth,[7] but also a socially engineered creation that is born out of the discomfort experienced at the core of an individual's or society's sense of identity.[8] When examined as a social theory, trauma is fundamentally a result of what Jenny Edkins calls a betrayal of trust.[9] Humans are incredibly resilient; "bad" experiences are not sufficient to cause trauma. Whether it is a case of a neglected child, where abuse involves betrayal by the person the child should most be able to trust, or a case of a conscript sent to an unjust war, whom the state breaks faith with and deceives,[10] it is this breach of trust that turns a horrific experience into traumatism.

Even when the intensity of pain may or may not rise to the level of traumatism, distant loss has a disquieting effect on the spectator because it chips away at precisely the same root: trust. Oftentimes, the spectator has as much at stake in the stability of the community as the sufferer does. Questions persist as to how far one's sense of community extends: would it be limited to one's neighborhood, people sharing one's nationality as a type of imagined community,[11] the whole international community, the animal kingdom, or all living things? Regardless, other people's suffering becomes evidence of the potential vulnerability of one's society. The origin of this mechanism—that we feel a sense of discomfort when we witness another community member's suffering as a potential threat to our own place in that community—has a number of partial explanations: social conditioning, whereby, as mentioned in the previously referenced Boltanski passage, compassion becomes the socially acceptable attitude; sympathy, as a naturally occurring emotion, in the mode of Adam Smith's *Theory of Moral Sentiments*; and availability heuristics, where the probability of an occurrence is judged by associative distance.[12] Although its conclusion is more nuanced and less definitive than has been portrayed in the popular media, a 2010 psychological study reports that viewers of vivid violent media gave higher estimates of the prevalence of crime in the real world than the control group, suggesting that watching other people being subjected to violence impacts the viewers' social reality beliefs.[13] The anguish of the sufferer is communicative albeit in an attenuated manner, in that it plants in the mind of the spectator a seed of distrust in the overall security of the environs.

Reasonable skepticism exists as to whether one can be genuinely affected by the suffering of distant others.[14] The answer put forth by the "Public" sequence of the first section in Sharon Olds's *The Dead and the Living*, "Poems for the Dead," is, however, affirmative. As Russell Brickey observes in his 2016 book-length study of Olds, this group of poems represents the communal dangers of both humanity and nature and, by doing so, argues for empathy.[15] As ekphrastic representations of brutality and disasters, these poems specifically explore questions of empathy toward remote sufferings that trigger the feeling of distant loss. The spectator has a vested interest in distant suffering; it originates from the possibility of the betrayal of trust—whether in the safety of the community or in the belief in the goodness of the world. As this self-interest sublimates itself, however, one is also moved to a humanitarian concern for the other's well-being. What is at stake is the question of the ethics of empathy—what kind of empathy is possible and ethical, when one is a mere spectator for whom temporal or spatial distance disallows any possible pursuit of recourse or intervention?—and the mechanism by which distant loss engenders helpful, constructive, nonexploitative empathy.

Epicurus once proclaimed, "Death . . . is nothing to us, seeing that, when we are, death is not come, and, when death is come, we are not."[16] Generally, life and death are thought of as either opposites or a part of the continuum where they are nonetheless not simultaneously present. Art, however, can create a curious phenomenon in which its artistic life can coexist at the same time with the death of its subject; survival is bound up with the artwork's ability to preserve both the artist and the model, since, to paraphrase Shakespeare, as long as the artwork lives and audiences exist, it gives life to those represented in it.[17] That is to say, the lives of those portrayed in art can continue to be "present"—in the sense that things that happen in a book are always retold in the present tense—even as their real-life models might be long "past," creating a condition that may be referred to as afterlife or "life in death."

In *The Dead and the Living*, Sharon Olds introduces a series of poems that portray this "life in death," where pictorial or photographed lives of those presumed dead are preserved in the form of ekphrasis. *The Dead and the Living* is divided into two parts, "Part I, Poems for the Dead" and "Part II, Poems for the Living." The first part is further subdivided into "Public" and "Private." In the Public section of "Part I, Poems for the Dead," Olds collects instances of photographic witnessing of historical disasters and atrocities that have taken place all around the world—in China, Russia, Eurasia, Africa, South America, and North America. A fuller index of what each poem in the series portrays would read as follows: "Ideographs" depicts the executions of Chinese revolutionaries in 1905; "Photograph of the Girl" concerns the Russian drought and famine in 1921, also known as the Povolzhye famine, which is estimated to have claimed the lives of about five million people; "Race Riot, Tulsa, 1921" refers to the titled event, the race riot that took place in Tulsa, Oklahoma, in 1921, one of the worst incidents of racial violence in the history of the United States; the subject of "Portrait of a Child" is the Armenian genocide perpetrated by the Ottoman Empire, which is dated around 1915; "Nevsky Prospekt" references the period of instability between the February and October Russian Revolutions in 1917, which led to the dismantlement of the Tsarist autocracy and the emergence of the Soviet Union; "The Death of Marilyn Monroe" is perhaps the best known incident for a U.S. readership, the probable suicide of the actor in 1962; "The Issues" is dated 1978, and it falls on the late phase of the Rhodesian Bush War; "Aesthetics of the Shah" takes place in the backdrop of the Iranian Revolution in 1978–1979, which involved the overthrow of the monarchy with an Islamic republic; and "Things That Are Worse Than Death" brings us to Chile in the 1970s and 1980s and the atrocities of the Pinochet dictatorship.

The poems in the Public section of *The Dead and the Living* are written from the perspective of an interested but uninvolved news reader, rather than from that of an activist, participant, or direct witness. The theses of the previous chapters of this book stipulate that the deaths of temporally, geographically, or relationally distant people can turn into a type of lost loss: those include people who had not meaningfully "existed" for us before we learn about their deaths, as well as people for whom we might not have sufficient grounds to claim rights to mourn, as we would otherwise with family members and close friends. As such, Olds's poems present us with the following questions: what kind of emotions do these ekphrastic renditions of sufferings evoke in readers? And what kind of possibilities for empathy do these poems generate, when losses are indirect—in the sense that they are mediated through photography and poetry—and distant—in a geographical and historical sense?

Olds's ekphrases juxtapose the actual death of the photographed subject with his or her artistic life, while resisting the universalizing aestheticization of the subject. "Photograph of the Girl" is perhaps the best exemplification of her ekphrastic strategy. A seminal piece in this collection that is based on a photograph of a girl who died in the Russian drought and famine of 1921, "Photograph of the Girl" is marked by the description of the girl's physicality, which, even when it undergoes emaciation, preserves the identity of a girl who is on the verge of reaching womanhood. With a particular focus on gendering images, the poem highlights the effort to assert the photographed subject's individualized identity, and in that process, the vague feeling of discomforting identification one initially feels when looking at photographs of disasters and sufferings in some historically or geographically distant locale sharpens its focus and develops into a form of empathy. Gender imagery, as employed in *The Dead and the Living*, produces a representation of the dead that enables viewers to feel as though the deceased subjects continue to assert their living identity, and that is one anchor that triggers readerly empathy in cases of indirect, distant loss mediated through multiple artistic expressions in the form of ekphrasis.

As a first step toward exploring the possibility of empathy in the instance of ekphrastic distant loss, it will prove instructive to survey the nature of photography as art by examining some of the canonical texts on the subject. In one strand of critical theory, photography has frequently been associated with the sense of death, inauthenticity, and deindividuation. In *Camera Lucida*, Roland Barthes comments on a photograph of a young man condemned to death:

> I observe with horror an anterior future of which death is the stake. By giving me an absolute past of the pose (aorist), the photograph tells me death in the future. What *pricks* me is the discovery of this equivalence. In front of the photograph of my mother as a child, I tell myself: she is going to die: I shudder, like Winnicott's psychotic patient, *over a catastrophe which has already occurred*. Whether or not the subject is already dead, every photograph is this catastrophe.[18]

In this passage, Barthes talks about the elusiveness of the photographed subject: an inability to find his true likeness in the photo and the experience of seeing death in the living figure of him. The same premonition of death extends to photographs of other people, even while they are still alive; that prompts Barthes to conclude that "every photograph is this catastrophe." In "The Work of Art in the Age of Its Technological Reproducibility," Walter Benjamin remarks on the loss of authenticity, or aura, in photography. Because of its reproducibility, photography removes its subjects from the specific context of their being, and in that process, it denudes the art of its tradition, history, and uniqueness of existence, which he calls "aura":

> In even the most perfect reproduction, *one* thing is lacking: the here and now of the work of art—its unique existence in a particular place. It is this unique existence—and nothing else—that bears the mark of the history to which the work has been subject.[19]

And Susan Sontag, most notably in *On Photography* and *Regarding the Pain of Others*, cautions us on the deindividuating effect of photography; her overarching claim is that concerned photography has done as much to deaden our conscience as to arouse it. Below are some of the memorable words from her *New Yorker* article in 2002, "Looking at War":

> Making suffering loom larger, by globalizing it, may spur people to feel they ought to "care" more. It also invites them to feel that the sufferings and misfortunes are too vast, too irrevocable, too epic to be much changed by any local, political intervention.[20]

Together, these theories constitute a panoramic view of photography as a medium of impersonality, with deindividuation and inauthenticity as keywords: it is a venue where universalization goes hand in hand with the loss of the particularized subject, triggered by deindividuation that creates inauthenticity. In Barthes, it occurs because the photograph is a catastrophe, in that one can never find the actual likeness of the photographed subject in it; instead, one finds anticipation of death. In Benjamin, reproducibility removes photography from history and context, which makes it a manipulatable medium and dilutes the aura of the photographed subject. And in Sontag, universalizing—or "globalizing," which, in this context, is synonymous with deindividuating—tendencies of the photograph strip the photographed subject of what makes the subject who he or she is. To photograph people is to violate them, by seeing them as they never see themselves, by having knowledge of them they can never have; it turns people into objects that can be symbolically possessed.[21] In short, a photograph is a medium in which the photographed subject becomes as lost as it is retained in the process of its still preservation.

The objective here is not so much to endorse or criticize these views of photography—because these theories have been influential, scholars have long debated various aspects of them[22]—but rather to analyze the poems in *The Dead and the Living* as instances of the curious coexistence of life and death that occurs despite this deindividuating, inauthenticizing mechanism of photography. The first poem of part I of *The Dead and the Living*, "Ideographs" makes this conflict explicit. The epigraph dates and situates the ekphrasis: "*a photograph of China, 1905.*"[23] In the photograph, two men are being tortured, awaiting execution. The scaffolds are the size of a person, and one of those two men fixed onto one of the scaffolds is effectively dehumanized: he is "asleep" (6)—unconscious—as his arms are nailed to the wooden boards that are shaped like a Chinese character that denotes a person. In essence, he has physically become one with his execution stage, while his personhood is subsumed into the logogram. The other man—despite, or perhaps because of, the fact that he is pinned to a more complexly shaped, tortuously cruel scaffold—has his eyes open, looking directly at the viewer. The poem imagines him speaking to us: "*Save me, there is still time*" (29). This imagination of voice emanates from our perception of his self-assertion, his will to survive in spite of his imminent death.

Whereas the two men about to be executed in "Ideographs" struggle and oscillate between the state of individuation and deindividuation, "Photograph of the Girl" displays itself as a representative case of the "life in death" phenomenon, in which the featured subject withstands the pressure of photographic annihilation through a particular form of identity assertion. "Photograph of the Girl," published in 1984, is descriptive; it is mainly composed of the images of one girl from the 1921 famine in Russia. Like the photograph of the condemned young man in Barthes's *Camera Lucida*, "Photograph of the Girl" also describes a girl who is about to die in the not-so-distant future. The most notable feature of this poem is that its gaze is on the evidence of the girl's life, rather than her death. In this poem, only the caption suggests her impending death, and little else does: "The caption says / she is going to starve to death that winter / with millions of others" (12–14).[24] This interlocution—"The caption says"—makes it seem as though the speaker of the poem is not convinced, or is not able to find evidence, of the girl's looming death anywhere in the photograph itself, outside of the words of the caption. The caption's universalizing—that she would die with "millions of others"—also casts doubt on whether this specific individual would actually die in the famine or not: did the photographer or the caption-writer actually confirm this particular photographed girl's death? By pointing to these mediations, Olds's speaker signals wishful skepticism: the girl's death may perhaps be a presumption on the part of the caption-writer. The viewers of the photograph continue to see her alive, and at the end of the poem, they are left without firm evidence that she did in fact die because of the famine.

This skepticism stems not so much from the belief that photography and its commemorative and substitutive function are a defense against death but rather from the poem's particularization of the girl in the photograph.[25] The girl in the photograph is referred to with a definite article: "the girl." Even if the girl remains unnamed, she is given dignity as a definite, particularized individual, rather than one of the deindividuated many, as in "a girl." In contrast, the title of the poem refers to the photograph as a concept noun; the photograph is not specified, or even made into an indefinite singular, but is turned into a conceptual object. That may be a function of the fact that this particular photograph has not been reliably identified and may not have actually existed,[26] but this antithetical treatment of the photograph and the girl—one is rendered abstract and the other is made concrete—is strange enough to draw readerly attention.

Individuation of the girl is driven by another noteworthy aspect of the poem: its emphasis on her gender and sexual identity. Side by side with drought, heat, and hunger, the poem portrays her biological maturation—puberty, ovaries, and her first eggs released from them:

> Each day she grows thinner, and her bones
> grow longer, porous. The caption says
> she is going to starve to death that winter
> with millions of others. Deep in her body
> the ovaries let out her first eggs,
> golden as drops of grain.   (11–16)

The reproductive organ is an odd target to focus on in a description of a famine victim. Menstruation can stop in times of starvation, but the imagery functions as a resistance to that reality, as biological fertility extends to and merges with the sight of agricultural fertility: "golden as drops of grain." This resistance takes a form of particularization of identity, which is achieved through the poetic descriptions of the girl's physicality; body parts are meticulously described, such as in the depiction of her bony features and the radius of her arm.

Another curious feature of the poem is the statement in line 10: "She cannot be not beautiful" (10). Conspicuous for its double-negative, this statement reads, on the one hand, as though to communicate an assumption that, extrapolating from her appearance in the starved state, the girl's normal, non-starved appearance would be that of a beautiful girl; on the other hand, it also suggests this poem's effort to extract the truth of this girl. John Keats declares in "Ode on a Grecian Urn": "Beauty is truth, truth beauty." In this passage, beauty does not necessarily mean that the girl is physically attractive; what it proposes is that her beauty lies in her truthfulness to her existence. The word beauty has several implications: first, as a sign of her gender identity, a criterion of judgment often more stringently applied to women than to men; second, the beauty of her will to live, her aforesaid resistance to her condition; and third, as visibly extractable evidence of the girl's truth, her true state as a living being.

Furthermore, line 8 focuses on the "layers of clothes" worn by this girl in the midst of a heat wave. Wearing multiple layers of clothing is a social act of what one may regard as "doing gender," a concept first formulated by Candace West and Don Zimmerman.[27] If the puberty imagery is suggestive of the girl's biological identity, this clothing imagery solidifies her gender identity as it arises at the interactional level of social expectations. Traditional gender imagery is purposefully employed, but more to dignify than to oppress. In a normative social setting, doing gender can be "a new trap house understanding of gender" where noncompliance with the prescribed gender code can become punishable as social deviance.[28] But in this drought—a condition in which the girl is so emaciated that she is hard-pressed to assert her gender identity—doing gender becomes an act of resistance: the girl is not about to be a nameless victim stripped of identity attributes, as disaster casualties tend to be. Combining these features—the attention to body parts, the statement about beauty, and the attempt to do gender—this poem delineates by focusing on the photographed girl's physical, biological, social existence her gender identity as an act of will.

The strange "life in death" in "Photograph of the Girl" is achieved by this focus on identity, which is sustained through particularized attention to the photographed girl's gender. While there is a plethora of theories on identity, one pillar of its conceptual foundations is that identity is a product of history; as John Locke expostulates, one's personal identity "extends itself beyond present existence to what is past . . . whereby it becomes concerned and accountable, owns and imputes to itself past actions, just upon the same ground, and for the same reason that it does the present."[29] History is precisely what this poem reconstructs: 1921, Russia, drought, famine, the presumed age of the girl herself. If obfuscation of history and context leads to inauthenticity as Benjamin suggests, this ekphrasis restores, albeit as a poetic reconstruction, the historical dimension: namely, the personal and social histories behind this photograph. With the addition of this diachronic element, the photographed girl is brought to life as an individual in this artwork through her biological operation and social attribution—as "the" girl in the photograph. That is not to say, however, that she is entirely free of universalization; there are, after all, millions of others who died alongside her in that impending winter as the caption reminds us, and much of the deeper biographical information about this girl continues to be inaccessible. Critical readers have advocated caution, noting that "the poem ends ambiguously."[30] A totalizing triumph of individuality over deindividuation is not quite what this poem offers, with its characteristic resistance to closure.[31] But even as other starvation victims loom large in the background, the photographed girl remains solitary in this ekphrasis, as a sole subject that captures readerly attention. Her body is hers alone; she is not an idea, but a palpable form. In this sense, the photographed girl continues to be an individual even in the pressure of universalization, and she is alive in the artwork, even if she is dead in actuality.

With regard to the pain of others, humanitarianism entails several triggers of tension, one of which occurs between an abstract universalism and a narrow communitarianism.[32] Because humanitarianism originates from reactions to individual instances of suffering but has a broader scope and objective—of helping everyone, rather than just one individual—it traverses the distinction between the universal and the individual in ways that can at times be deleterious to the latter. This tension surfaces in variegated forms, and one manifestation converges with the universalizing, deindividuating force of photography: in the name of promoting social change and rescuing a large number of people, individuals with distinct identities are effaced and turned into ideas of sufferers. In a sense, this erasure of the individual through idealization is what "Race Riot, Tulsa, 1921" warns of. Until the poem zooms in on a single victim in line 8, it depicts crowds: the throngs of "white shirts of white men" (1) and the "dark glowing skin of the women and / men going to jail" (5–6). Individuals are subsumed into group identities or—more pointedly—the color of their skin. Of all the people captured in this photograph, only this single victim gains any semblance of humanity; the sun darkens his face "more and more toward the color of the human" (15). It is an irony that this victim appears to be dead, as though to suggest that the only way to evade group subsumption and to regain one's humanity is through death.

Against this mechanism of individual erasure, Olds's intervention in *The Dead and the Living* presents itself as a third path: universalist particularism, expressed in the form of the identity assertion of unspecified individuals. This enterprise of the ekphrastic identity assertion of "life in death" continues in "Nevsky Prospekt." The title indicates that the photographed location is the main street in the city of St. Petersburg, Russia. The subtitle suggests that the photograph was taken in July, 1917: the transitional period between the February and October revolutions, after the old regime was replaced in the initial revolution by the provisional government, which was removed by the Bolshevik government in the latter revolution. The target of this poem's sympathy is sufficiently evident from the sarcasm of the closing line: "*This is more important than your life*" (19). History books may indicate that these revolutions are important events, but Olds's poem deems the lives of people depicted in this photo to be more important than the revolutions. One could argue that "Nevsky Prospekt" and many of the other poems in the "public" section of *The Dead and the Living* are—if one must remain faithful to one's aesthetic assessment of the poetic work—adjudicated to be less artistically accomplished than "Photograph of the Girl." Regardless, all poems in this sequence have a shared goal: the restoration of the individual. "Nevsky Prospekt" too maintains its allegiance to this project of restorative fiction: while acknowledging the limits of spectatorial effort, the poem underscores the attributes of the individual within the constraints of what can be redeemed from a photograph.

This redemptive effort, however, is met with various obstacles. In the first two lines, the poem acknowledges, "It's an old photo, very black and / very white" (1–2). Distance between the event and the viewer is made apparent, in terms of time—"old"—and the medium—"photo." The black-and-white photo—emphasized as "very black and / very white"—creates even more distance, as something symbolic of age and as something divergent from the color vision through which the majority of people regard the world. These chasms become an impediment to the identity assertion of the victims in the photograph and the empathy that is engendered from it.

The trope to overcome these impediments largely aligns with that of "Photograph of the Girl": the gendering images of a woman lifting up "her heavy skirt as she runs" (3) and an old woman "in massive black" turning and looking behind her (6–7), among others. But "Nevsky Prospekt" adds something extra: a model of empathy that goes beyond mere identification. In *Empathy: Its Nature and Uses*, Robert L. Katz modifies Theodor Reik's classic theory in *Listening with the Third Ear* and proposes a theory of empathy that develops in four stages: identification, incorporation, reverberation, and detachment.[33] In this model, the first three stages explore various levels of intersubjective entanglement between the empathizer and the empathized, ending with detachment that pulls away the empathizer's subjective involvement. The defining feature of this model is the paradoxical dynamics of engagement and disengagement: one is at once emotionally engaged with and also sufficiently disengaged from the target of one's empathy, presumably as a measure to retain fuller cognition of one another's boundary integrity. Originating from clinical practice, Reik's model proposes empathy less as a sentiment than as an attitudinal stance that, like romantic irony, amalgamates conflicting demands. "Nevsky Prospekt" analyzes what is at the heart of this paradox:

The wide grey stone square
is dotted with fallen inky shapes
and dropped white hats. Everything else is
heaving away like a sea from the noise we
feel in the silence of the photograph
the way the deaf see sound . . .   (12–17)

All things, except for the men, women, and children depicted in the photograph, recede like an ocean tide, and all that is left is the "noise we / feel in the silence of the photograph": the feelings evoked in the viewers by the photograph. Since photographs do not speak, the "noise" that the spectators feel from the silent photograph is an imagined construct of synesthesia. This imaginary noise is likened to "the way the deaf see sound." Naturally, deaf people would have a hard time hearing, but the poem transforms the auditory into the visual in their mind's eye. The engagement–disengagement paradox of empathy arises from this inaccessibility. The process of empathy is at once an acknowledgment of this inaccessibility and an imagination, understood as a fictive construct, of what we know to be inaccessible. In the detachment phase of the Reik model, empathy is engendered specifically from the respect for the other's inviolability and the acknowledgment of the limits of the spectator's subjectivity that stems from it.

The Dead and the Living is not blindly approbative of all types of empathy, however; the poems evince the awareness of the pitfalls and risks of compassion. In "The Death of Marilyn Monroe," Olds paints a poignant picture of vicarious traumatization. Vicarious traumatization refers to a specific type of counter-transference in which professionals involved in the care of trauma survivors are themselves affected by their patients' traumatization. The application of this concept, while initially aimed toward psychotherapists, encompasses other types of professionals including healthcare providers and first responders.[34] "The Death of Marilyn Monroe" relates the impact of the actress's death on the ambulance workers: how "their lives took / a turn" (15–16). As with the previous poems in the sequence, the physicality of the victim becomes the focus: her "cold / body" (1–2), her breasts "flattened by / gravity" (7–8), and her "caught / strand of hair" (5–6). In turn, the corporeity triggers the workers' empathic engagement with the deceased, which is evidenced by their efforts to make her presentable by trying to close her mouth, eyes, and so on. The poem declares that, as a result of this encounter, these workers have fundamentally been transformed: "These men were never the same" (11). Symptoms described in the ensuing stanzas reveal a quintessential case of secondary trauma: namely, a feeling of powerlessness, depression, ideations of death, and the impact of those emotions on the family. In this poem, the target of the reader's empathy is not so much Marilyn Monroe—whose corporal existence impacts the paramedics but who is otherwise largely depicted as a vessel of people's projected emotions, just as she was while she was alive—but rather these ambulance workers. It is a commentary on responsible empathic engagement: removed from the immediacy of experience, spectators are capable of diagnosing the scene panoramically, discerning both primary and secondary traumas. As tertiary participants, readers—and the omniscient speaker who speaks for the readers—become the identifiers of compassion fatigue.

Part of the struggle of *The Dead and the Living* derives from the question of ethics: how can a spectator, removed spatially and temporally from the scene of disasters, sensibly and ethically inject himself or herself in the depictions of the suffering of other people without violating their autonomy and subjectivity? The first six poems of the Public sequence of the volume feature no first-person speaker; the poems are largely composed from an omniscient perspective with a focus on description. The role of this spectatorship culminates in "The Death of Marilyn Monroe": the advantage of, and responsibility of, tertiary involvement is the ability to oversee both primary and secondary traumatizations—namely, to retain the capacity to be empathic toward both the sufferer and the helpers who suffer in the process. The trend changes, however, toward the later portions of the sequence, as the initially invisible speaker becomes more critically involved. In "The Issues," Olds portrays a scene from the Rhodesian Bush War; the subtitle indicates that the photograph is from 1978. In this poem, the speaking "I" appears for the first time in this sequence, paving a way for a fuller intersubjective engagement that culminates in the final poem of the section, "Things That Are Worse Than Death." The Public sequence begins with "Ideographs," which deploys a speaker who describes the photographs but steadfastly remains in the background, and it ends with "Things That Are Worse Than Death," in which the speaker takes on an active role, imagining herself in the position of the Chilean family who are tortured in front of each other.

The sudden surfacing of the first-person pronouns in "The Issues" suggests that the lyric-speaker is beginning to insert her own subjectivity, rather than remaining on the sideline: it is the proverbial moment of an armchair viewer of a disaster reaching for the phone to dial the donation hotline. Involvement nonetheless heightens the demarcation between the speaker's subjectivity and that of the victims, owing to the engagement-detachment paradox of empathic structure. It is this separation that enables the speaker to guard against one of the pitfalls that compromises the ethics of empathy: usurpation. Usurpation is a type of objectification, in that it infringes on the integrity of another human being's autonomy, inviolability, agency, and subjectivity; it often manifests itself as an act of putting one's words into someone else's mouth or using another person's experience as a service to further one's own perspectives, interests, or agendas. And this pitfall of usurpation is what the "I" speaker in "The Issues" seems to be wary of.

One of the distinguishing marks of "The Issues" is the repeated first-person action: "I can see" (2), "I see" (7), "I see" (11). The repetitions ascertain that the scene depicted here is subjective—mediated and circumscribed by the speaker's vision. At the same time, by enunciating the separation between the sufferer's and the speaker's fields of vision, the speaker refrains from making assumptions beyond what she sees with her own eyes. The emergence of the speaking "I" voice signals multiple breakthroughs. In its empathic engagement, the poem successfully extricates the victims' subjective experience from the speaker's; that, in turn, allows the speaker to recover and retain her own recognition of her selfhood and visions, reconfirming her awareness that she too is an individual who is different and separate from the victims. Olds's speaker wants to respond to the victims as individuals with an internal cohesion that must be respected and, to borrow the language of clinical psychotherapy, not "as an object in a climate of empathic understanding."[35]

Although the Reik-Katz model of empathy may move prescriptively from identification, incorporation, reverberation, to detachment, Olds's model is not as neatly compartmentalized: while the "I" voice gestures toward a move away from immersion in the photographed subject's subjectivity, it also does not enact total detachment. Olds's speaker observes the scene of the suffering but avoids speculating on the interiority of the victims; this attitude resembles the behavior of a clinician who objectively and professionally tries to make sense of patients' situations. But at the same time, the voice also turns into a crude outburst of a frustrated witness that is hardly like one of a clinician—"Don't talk to me about / politics. I've got eyes, man" (14–15). Keeping a precarious balance on the attachment-detachment threshold, Olds's lyric-speaker walks the tightrope to avoid exploitative usurpation and to strive toward ethical empathy by engaging with the photographed subjects intersubjectively, which entails circumventing speculative imaginations but listening to the imaginative "noise" from the photographs.

The final poem of the sequence, "Things That Are Worse Than Death" is dedicated to Margaret Randall, an activist writer who has lived and traveled extensively abroad, including in Central America. The poem begins ostensibly as a conversation between the speaker and the "you" addressee, presumably an incarnate of Randall: "You are speaking of Chile, / of the woman who was arrested" (1–2).[36] The quotation of the Randall character describing how the guards relish the torturing—"'as they like to do'" (6)—conveys indignation. And the refrain of the title phrase—"Things that are worse than death" (7, 11)—underscores the unimaginability of the horror: what has befallen the Chilean victims is more injurious than the unfathomable.

An identification phase similar to that of "The Issues" begins in line 8, but in this poem, it moves quickly to incorporation: "I can see myself taking my son's ash-blond hair in my fingers" (8). The speaker's subjectivity then reverberates to form an idea of a previously unfelt horror: "Things that are worse than death: / this new idea enters my life" (11–12). The empathic engagement of "Things That Are Worse Than Death" is driven by these two refrains: the evocative words of the Randall character, "'as they like to do'"; and the epitome of the unimaginable, "Things that are worse than death." Transformation occurs in the speaker, but this inner change contains parallels to that of the secondary traumatization experienced by the paramedics in "The Death of Marilyn Monroe." It is a curious mixture of compassion, abashment, a kind of sheepishness—"nothing I have experienced was worse than death" (17)—as well as detachment, and concession. Although the Chilean victim's suffering and the Olds speaker's lived experience are distinctly different, this distance would not result in apathy or preclude compassion, even if her tertiary participation as a listener to the horror were less direct and more dilute than the Randall character's involvement or investment in Central America.

The project of the Public sequence of part I of *The Dead and the Living*, as it regards the poems in which the photographs depict the dead subjects while they were still alive, is the subjectivation of those victims. This subjectivation emerges from the lyric focus on the identity of the victims; as best as one can gather as a viewer of the news in a faraway land, Olds scrupulously collects details, in a manner that one critic characterizes as "modified naturalism."[37] Those details enliven the photographed subjects and sustain their life in death, allowing them to assert their own living identity, against the pressure of universalization and against erasure by death. Often, what gives life to the details that Olds collects in these poems is the gendering imagery: the multilayered clothing, skirts, ovaries, the first eggs, and beauty. These images, while sometimes oppressive in a gender-normative society, turn affirmative in the otherwise nameless, estranged photographic subjects in times of crisis, for they create a sense of artificial authenticity: it is a kind of authenticity that we understand to be imaginary, but we are willing to suspend our skepticism of it despite our full awareness that it is a fictional creation.

In all, the Public sequence of *The Dead and the Living* poems delineates a descriptive, rather than prescriptive, vision of responsible spectatorship: an engagement-detachment model of empathy. In this state, one is simultaneously involved and removed as a clear-eyed tertiary-level participant safeguarded from primary and secondary traumatization. When one finds oneself at the optimal range of engagement and disengagement, this in-between space of participation enables one to thwart the cognitive habit of objectifying the other by recognizing the sufferer's individual identity. In *The Dead and the Living*, the identity assertion in the ekphrastic "life in death" has three critical implications. First, this shaking of the boundary between life and death can lead the living viewers to question their own status as a living being: if the dead can be alive, even if only in an art form, can the living also be dead? If the dead can be represented as alive in art, our death may also be captured in it, and this reversibility reveals the profound loss, as hypothesized by Barthes's *Camera Lucida* as well as Paul de Man's theory of prosopopoeia, in which the living can be "struck dumb," frozen in the anticipatory occurrence of their own death.[38] From as early as the Roman period, writers have frequently regarded their literary subjects' survival—as well as their own survival as a writer—as being bound up with the durability of the artistic product. In addition to the previously discussed Shakespearean proclamation in Sonnet 18, Romantic poets in particular are known for this culture of posterity,[39] which is defined by the desire to live in the afterlife of an artwork. The threat to the survival of books is literally and figuratively a nightmare, as seen in the dream of the Arab Sage in William Wordsworth's *The Prelude*, an episode that portrays a deluge and its destruction of books as a palpable embodiment of this threat. For writers disposed to this life after death, writing their own epitaphs becomes a requisite action, whether it is W. B. Yeats's later poems or John Berryman's "opus posthumous" sequence of *The Dream Songs*. There is a sense of discomfort in seeing a dead person alive in a photograph. The sentiment does not merely arise out of nostalgic reminiscence by the bereaved; it makes us discover death in our own living existence.

The second implication is a derivation of the first; plainly and reductively speaking, the simplest and most straightforward feelings that we tend to have when we see a photograph of someone who we know is dead are varying degrees of sadness and identification—the feeling of "what if it happens to me?" These feelings stem from this shaking of the boundary effected by art forms; a curious system of anticipatory identification is triggered in the living, as the living and the dead become connected through this reversibility, where the dead can be given a representation as a live subject while the living authors can write their own eulogy in anticipation of their own death. In addition to stirring our doubt about our own existence, these photographs also create a tenebrous bond of identification between the dead and the living.

The third implication of this identity assertion of the dead as living in a poem is that it creates a new possibility for the ethics of photography. Sontag's criticism of universalization, Benjamin's opining of the loss of aura, and Barthes's confessed discomfort with not finding the true likeness in the photos of his deceased mother despite the objective similitude—these all come from the same root: ambivalence about universalizing and individualizing, where reproducibility takes the photographed subject further away from the origin. While universalizing is inevitable in many ways, a portraiture that accentuates identity assertion, as is done in Olds's ekphrasis, creates sufficient waverings that bring the photographed subject closer to her origin. The in-between mental space created by this oscillation—between universalizing and individualizing, between violation and inviolability of the photographed subject, between usurpation and respect, and between objectification and subjectivation—allows for a more ethical identification with the subject, in that it gives the spectator a pause, a moment of hesitance, which helps the spectator recognize the subject's humanity. This hesitance softens the "violence" of photography, allowing the subject to retain his or her imaginary authenticity. Olds's poems point to the possibility that ekphrases present an interpretative site that is conducive to the photographed subject's identity assertion. The degree of ambivalence and hesitation that ekphrases demand from their reader becomes the seed of a more ethical form of empathy.

The present chapter has liberally used the term "ethical empathy" so far without sufficiently defining what it entails. The notion of ethical empathy develops from, and offers a counter-discourse to, currently dominant assumptions about empathy. A preliminary definition of ethical empathy would be that it is a type of empathy that is self-aware—of the balance between engagement and detachment so as to avoid usurpation and exploitation of the sufferers, as well as of the deontological obligations that the empathizers must be mindful of, whether as an active interventionist or as a passive spectator with no recourse to action. What it means is that empathy would be mobilized for higher purposes, instead of being weaponized against out-groups, the vulnerable, and the precarious. The higher purposes stipulate that one must forecast the implications of sympathetic alliance in order to avoid deleterious consequences.[40]

One of the foundational premises of the conventional idea of empathy, which the present notion of ethical empathy calls into question, originates from Adam Smith's *Theory of Moral Sentiments*. According to Smith's theory, empathy is largely an automatic process of the human mind:

> The mob, when they are gazing at a dancer on the slack rope, naturally writhe and twist and balance their own bodies, as they see him do, and as they feel that they themselves must do if in his situation.[41]

Smith's formulation stipulates that empathy is similar to reflex in that it occurs in humans without awareness, as spectators do when they watch a tightrope walker in the air. The passage suggests that it involves a certain type of identification: "as they feel that they themselves must do if in his situation." In plain English, one might be tempted to say that empathy is about "putting oneself in someone else's shoes." According to Smith, this process of identification between the viewer and the sufferer occurs naturally and unconsciously.

Recent psychological studies have noted, however, that this feeling of empathy is not always automatic—nor is it necessarily desirable that it be.[42] Perceivers commonly fail to empathize with out-group targets, and sometimes even enjoy out-group members' suffering.[43] Furthermore, the famed phenomenon of "diffusion of responsibility" has shown that empathy often diminishes even in response to seemingly irrelevant contextual shifts, such as when multiple observers, as compared to a single observer, witness a target's suffering, as suggested by the case of Kitty Genovese;[44] the concept has been deployed as a legal defense in various war crime trials as well, including the Nuremberg trials of the Nazis as well as those of the defendants accused in the My Lai massacre. In addition to such failures of empathy involving perpetrators or onlookers of atrocities, conventional wisdom from various fields indicates that clinicians, caregivers, and others in professions that demand a certain level of emotional involvement with clients or patients are advised to withdraw empathy in some contexts. In specified circumstances, empathy drains, and makes people vulnerable.

An experiment conducted by S. Mark Pancer in 1979 at the University of Saskatchewan suggests that people shut down empathy when it is expedient to do so. In this experiment, a table was set up in a busy tunnel between the library and the arts building at the University of Saskatchewan campus. The researchers secretly measured the distance people kept from the table while walking past it. Two features of the situation were manipulated. The first was whether or not the table had a box requesting charitable donations placed on it. The second was who was stationed at the table: no one, an undergraduate, or an undergraduate sitting in a wheelchair. Both the request to donate and the presence of a handicapped person were considered triggers to empathy. The end result was that, instead of approaching these triggers, people avoided them: they were found walking a wider arc around the table in the presence of either of the triggers and keeping the greatest distance in the face of both the handicapped student and donation box.[45] Aside from the well-known phenomenon of "collapse of compassion"—a theory that stipulates that, as needs for help increase and become overwhelming, the degree of compassion people feel ironically tends to decrease[46]—what this experiment suggests is that there is a switch that turns off our empathic capacity: in this instance, it was an unwelcome nudging to donate to charity, in the form that people may have found coercive.

By reversible logic, however, if we are able to turn off our empathy, we may also be capable of activating it for higher purposes. Testing the human capacity to choose to be empathic seems to be the enterprise of *The Dead and the Living*, particularly in the Public sequence of Poems for the Dead. All of the poems in this section are narrated from the point of view of an ordinary American reader, describing things that happened somewhere faraway, in some distant enough past, or to some unfamiliar enough people whom the hypothetical reader would likely regard as out-group members. People that readers might classify as "not one of us" are not a natural or automatic target of empathy. While these poems have received tepid critical attention as merely anthologizing "approved causes,"[47] the recent debacle of political correctness and the return of incivility in the public arena indicate that it is a strenuous task to uphold the principle of compassion and decency, even for, or especially for, humanitarianism when it involves a nationally, racially, or culturally distant Other. To recap the list of poems collected in this sequence, along with their locations and time periods, it would read as follows: "Ideographs," in China, 1905; "Photograph of the Girl," in Russia, 1921; "Race Riot, Tulsa, 1921," in Tulsa, Oklahoma, 1921; "Portrait of a Child," in Armenia, 1910s to 1920s; "Nevsky Prospekt," in Russia, 1917; "The Death of Marilyn Monroe," in USA, 1962; "The Issues," in Rhodesia, 1978; "Aesthetics of the Shah," in Iran, 1978–1979; and "Things That Are Worse Than Death," in Chile, 1970s and 1980s. Among these, "The Death of Marilyn Monroe" is somewhat of an outlier, in that it occurred in the United States about twenty years or so prior to the publication of *The Dead and the Living*; one might, however, be able to make a case that celebrities live lives that are sufficiently distant from ordinary people's that they become easy targets for projective identification but remain difficult to empathize with.[48] "Race Riot, Tulsa, 1921" is the only other poem that is situated within North America, but the incident occurred over half a century ago; it often goes untaught in public education today, and involves a historically oppressed group. Other than those two, the locales of the poems are all somewhere foreign and remote for a median American reader, geographically and chronologically.

Collectively, the larger question of the Public poems of *The Dead and the Living* may be summarized as the following: How can ordinary people, sitting comfortably on the living room couch, responsibly choose to empathize with geographically and chronologically "foreign" people, in a way that is not usurpatory or exploitative, through an indirect medium of photography, one fraught with ethical conundrums? Olds's reluctance to discuss her personal life is well-documented,[49] but based on available information, she had not gone abroad to witness or participate personally in the resistance in El

Salvador, Chile, Russia, or elsewhere; she did not work as an overseas correspondent or volunteer for partisan armies abroad, unlike some of her contemporaries who became poet-witnesses or poet-activists, such as Carolyn Forché or Margaret Randall. The hypothetical speaker of this sequence is a figuration of an ordinary spectator, sufficiently distanced and safeguarded from the catastrophes seen through the second-hand accounts of the photographs and the news media. How do we respond, as human beings, to fellow human beings who suffer from our own communal inhumanity, and how do we speak and act upon what we have seen and heard but not directly experienced?

The Dead and the Living suggests that the unsettling discomfort that we feel when we see photographs like those captured in its poems can be the rumblings of ethical empathy. According to the theories of photography surveyed earlier, photographs can be an exploitative, appropriative form of media that robs the photographed subject of its individuality. As such, photographs of people's suffering sometimes make spectators feel as though they are being coerced into being empathic, and that creates unease. In 2015, the photograph of a drowned three-year old Syrian boy lying on the beach provided a galvanizing image that swayed many citizens and political leaders in Europe to admit refugees into their countries. At the same time, numerous accounts of how this photograph was forged—unsubstantiated allegations that the boy's body was moved to a more optimal location for a photo opportunity—surfaced, alongside accusations that sensationalistic images obstruct more rational policy talks about immigration. While many of the claims of fakery or calls for isolationism in the name of rationality are in no small part driven by xenophobia, one must also not overlook the emergence, in some corners of a number of people's psyches, of the genuine hesitation about turning the suffering of a small child into a tool to coerce people into taking empathic actions. Depictions of refugees often polarize into fantasies of identification or absolute othering,[50] but this dynamic is counterproductive: a moment of pause or hesitation induced by the engagement-detachment dilemma of ethical empathy is one potential avenue of transcending such divarication. This hesitance, as resulting from a clash between profound sorrow and resistance toward it—between the inclination to empathize with other people's suffering and the reluctance to exploit or usurp it for the sake of self-actualization or promotion of one's cause[51]—holds within it the germ of an ethical form of empathy: empathy that is self-aware. One building block of this ethical empathy, particularly in the cases of distant or distanced loss of strangers from the remote past or places captured by photographs, is artificial authenticity: the ekphrasis is authentic enough to trigger readers' compassion while the knowledge of its artificiality obstructs instinctive identification. This paradoxical authenticity burgeons forth from the identity portrayal of the dead, the halfway space of their life in death, gendering imagery, and power of detail, as exemplified by "Photograph of the Girl" and other Public poems of *The Dead and the Living*.

NOTES

1. Luc Boltanski, *Distant Suffering: Morality, Media and Politics*, trans. Graham D. Burchell (Cambridge: Cambridge University Press, 1999), 114.
2. Susan Sontag, *Regarding the Pain of Others* (New York: Picador, 2003), 101.
3. Boltanski, *Distant Suffering*, xv.
4. Charles Taylor, *Sources of the Self: The Making of the Modern Identity* (Cambridge: Harvard University Press, 1989), 516–21.
5. Boltanski, *Distant Suffering*, xiv.
6. Kenneth J. Doka, "Disenfranchised Grief and Trauma," in *Handbook of Traumatic Loss: A Guide to Theory and Practice*, ed. Neil Thompson et al. (New York: Routledge, 2017), 378.
7. Cathy Caruth, *Unclaimed Experience: Trauma, Narrative, and History* (Baltimore: Johns Hopkins University Press, 1995), 3–4.
8. Jeffrey C. Alexander, *Trauma: A Social Theory* (Cambridge: Polity Press, 2012), 15–19.
9. Edkins, *Trauma and the Memory of Politics*, 4.
10. Edkins, *Trauma and the Memory of Politics*, 4.
11. Benedict Anderson, *Imagined Communities: Reflections on the Origin and Spread of Nationalism* (London: Verso, 1991), 6–7.
12. Amos Tversky and Daniel Kahneman, "Availability: A Heuristic for Judging Frequency and Probability," in *Judgment under Uncertainty: Heuristics and Biases*, ed. Daniel Kahneman et al. (Cambridge: Cambridge University Press, 1982), 163.
13. Karen Riddle, "Always on My Mind: Exploring How Frequent, Recent, and Vivid Television Portrayals Are Used in the Formation of Social Reality Judgments," *Media Psychology* 13, no. 2 (2010): 155–79.
14. Sontag argues that images of suffering can evoke a range of responses other than empathy; those include prurient interest, religious transfiguration of pain to sacrifice to exaltation, and a sense of delight (*Regarding the Pain of Others*, 95–99). Sontag quotes from Edmund Burke's *A Philosophical Enquiry into the Origin of Our Ideas of the Sublime and Beautiful*: "I am convinced we have a degree of delight, and that no small one, in the real misfortunes and pains of others" (*Regarding the Pain of Others*, 97).
15. Brickey, *Understanding Sharon Olds*, 112.
16. Epicurus, "Letter to Menoeceus," in *Stoic and Epicurean*, trans. Robert Drew Hicks (New York: C. Scribner's Sons, 1910), 169.
17. Shakespeare, "Sonnet #18," 1929, lines 13–14.
18. Roland Barthes, *Camera Lucida: Reflections on Photography*, trans. Richard Howard (New York: Hill and Wang, 1982), 96, emphasis in the original.
19. Walter Benjamin, "The Work of Art in the Age of Its Technological Reproducibility," in *Walter Benjamin: The Selected Writings*, Vol. 4, ed. Howard Eiland and Michael W. Jennings, trans. Edmund Jephcott et al. (Cambridge: Belknap, 2003), 253.

20. Susan Sontag, "Looking at War," *New Yorker*, December 9, 2002, https://www.newyorker.com/magazine/2002/12/09/looking-at-war.

21. Susan Sontag, *On Photography* (New York: RosettaBooks, 2005), 10.

22. A sample critique on Sontag's *On Photography* reads as follows: "The more significant problem with which Sontag is concerned may be that, in her view, the Western world has become aggressively materialist, sexually brutal, and morally corrupt. This may be true, but the author's intense urge to say so and have the reader agree prompts her to make statements that are unsupported and perhaps unsupportable" (Harvey Green, "Review of *On Photography* by Susan Sontag," *Winterthur Portfolio* 14, no. 2 [Summer, 1979]: 210).

23. Sharon Olds, *The Dead and the Living* (New York: Knopf, 1984), 5.

24. Olds, *The Dead and the Living*, 6.

25. In *What Is Cinema?*, André Bazin unveils the fundamental drive of photography as akin to the practice of embalming the dead; its aim is "survival" in the form of "the continued existence of the corporeal body," which provides "a defense against the passage of time . . . , for death is but the victory of time" (André Bazin, *What Is Cinema?* Vol. 1, trans. Hugh Gray [Berkeley: University of California Press, 2005], 9). In effect, Bazin's theory of photography "assigns photography an elegiac identity or capacity" (Josh Ellenbogen, "On Photographic Elegy," in *The Oxford Handbook of the Elegy*, ed. Karen Weisman [Oxford: Oxford University Press, 2010], 684). Building from this premise, I contend that Olds's "Photograph of the Girl" goes beyond the project of elegiac commemoration.

26. In *Understanding Sharon Olds*, Brickey suggests that the photograph that inspired this ekphrasis could be any of a number of photographs taken during the dreadful Povolzhye famine (Brickey, *Understanding Sharon Olds*, 114).

27. Candace West and Don H. Zimmerman, "Doing Gender," *Gender & Society* 1, no. 2 (1987): 125–51.

28. Candace West and Don H. Zimmerman, "Accounting for Doing Gender," *Gender & Society* 23, no. 1 (2009): 112–22.

29. John Locke, *The Locke Reader: Selections from the Works of John Locke with a General Introduction and Commentary*, ed. John W. Yolton (Cambridge: Cambridge University Press, 1977), 184.

30. Cheryl Walker, *Masks Outrageous and Austere: Culture, Psyche, and Persona in Modern Women Poets* (Bloomington: Indiana University Press, 1991), 201.

31. The "resistance to closure, to authoritative tones and statements, and to simulations of a unified argument or a confident, consistent voice" is one of the defining characteristics of the developed styles of many contemporary American poems (Stephen Burt, "American Poetry at the End of the Millennium," in *The Cambridge History of American Poetry*, ed. Alfred Bendixen and Stephen Burt [Cambridge: Cambridge University Press, 2014], 1144).

32. Boltanski, *Distant Suffering*, xiii.

33. Arthur J. Clark, *Empathy in Counseling and Psychotherapy: Perspectives and Practices* (New York: Routledge, 2014), 100.

34. Siddharth Ashvin Shah, "Mental Health Emergencies and Post-traumatic Stress Disorder," in *Emergency Public Health: Preparedness and Response*, ed. Girish

Bobby Kapur and Jeffrey P. Smith (Sudbury: Jones & Bartlett Learning, 2011), 493–516.

35. Clark, *Empathy in Counseling and Psychotherapy*, 101.

36. In *Motherhood and War: International Perspectives*, Tracy Crowe Morey and Cristina Santos discuss oral interviews collected by Margaret Randall in Nicaragua, as well as those collected by Cherie Zalaquett in Chile (Tracy Crowe Morey and Cristina Santos, "*Las Madres Guerreras*: Testimonial Writing on Militant Motherhood in Latin America," in *Motherhood and War: International Perspectives*, ed. Dana Cooper and Claire Phelan [New York: Palgrave, 2014], 62).

37. Carolyn Wright, "Review of *The Dead and the Living*," *Iowa Review* 15, no. 1 (1985): 160.

38. de Man, "Autobiography as De-facement," 928.

39. Andrew Bennett, *Romantic Poets and the Culture of Posterity* (Cambridge: Cambridge University Press, 1999), 1–2. Also, Samantha Matthews describes the perspective of readers in the Romantic period and their sensibility as one that "interpreted the book as the embodied medium of the dead poet's spirit" (Samantha Matthews, *Poetical Remains: Poets' Graves, Bodies, and Books in the Nineteenth Century* [New York: Oxford University Press, 2004], 4).

40. For example, Arlie Russell Hochschild explores the "deep story" of Louisiana bayou country residents and the mechanism through which they "close the border to human sympathy" toward people they view as "line cutters"—minorities, women, immigrants, refugees, the brown pelican as the symbolic victim of chemical pollution such as the 2010 BP oil spill, among others—based on their belief that their in-group cohorts are suffering as much as, or if not more than, those out-group members and that their plights are being ignored (Arlie Russell Hochschild, *Strangers in Their Own Land: Anger and Mourning on the American Right* [New York: New Press, 2016], 135–52). In the present definition of ethical empathy, a type of compassion toward in-group members that facilitates misrepresentation or vilification of out-groups would not count as ethical empathy, since it is neither consequentially sound—exclusion and antagonization are problematic because, if Olds's ekphrases are any indication, the suffering of those viewed as belonging to out-groups will in the end destabilize the whole community—nor deontologically acceptable, with respect to values such as equity and egalitarianism.

41. Adam Smith, *The Theory of Moral Sentiments*, ed. Knud Haakonssen (Cambridge: Cambridge University Press, 2002), 12.

42. Jamil Zaki, "Empathy: A Motivated Account," *Psychological Bulletin* 140, no. 6 (2014): 1608–47.

43. Mina Cikara and Jay J. Van Bavel, "The Neuroscience of Intergroup Relations: An Integrative Review," *Perspectives on Psychological Science* 9, no. 3 (2014): 245–74.

44. John M. Darley and Bibb Latane, "Bystander Intervention in Emergencies: Diffusion of Responsibility," *Journal of Personality and Social Psychology* 8, no. 4 (1968): 377–83.

45. S. Mark Pancer et al., "Conflict and Avoidance in the Helping Situation," *Journal of Personality and Social Psychology* 37, no. 8 (1979): 1406–11. Also

discussed in Jamil Zaki, "Empathy as a Choice," *Scientific American*, July 29, 2013, https://blogs.scientificamerican.com/moral-universe/empathy-as-a-choice/.

46. Daryl C. Cameron and B. Keith Payne, "Escaping Affect: How Motivated Emotion Regulation Creates Insensitivity to Mass Suffering," *Journal of Personality and Social Psychology* 100, no. 1 (2011): 1.

47. Gregerson, *Negative Capability*, 37.

48. Studies have shown that fans identify with celebrities and that fan attachments are often part of the normal course of adult development in the areas of identity, intimacy, and generativity (Gayle S. Stever, "Fan Behavior and Lifespan Development Theory: Explaining Para-social and Social Attachment to Celebrities," *Journal of Adult Development* 18, no. 1 [March 2011]: 1–7). Marilyn Monroe may be a peculiar case, however; Monroe has been characterized as "a virtual allegory of the performer's alienation from the face and body that are nominally the instrument of her fame"; she was seen more as a vessel than as an individual with a full-fledged interiority (Leo Braudy, *The Frenzy of Renown: Fame & Its History* [Oxford: Oxford University Press, 1986], 580).

49. Brickey, *Understanding Sharon Olds*, 1.

50. Angela Naimou, "Double Vision: Refugee Crises and the Afterimages of Endless War," *College Literature* 43, no. 1 (Winter 2016): 228.

51. In *What is a Child?: Popular Images of Childhood*, Patricia Holland describes the mechanism of problematic sympathy, particularly with images of suffering children: "Paradoxically, while we are moved by the image of a sorrowful child, we also welcome it, for it can arouse pleasurable emotions of tenderness, which in themselves confirm adult power" (Patricia Holland, *What is a Child?: Popular Images of Childhood* [London: Virago, 1992], 148).

Chapter 5

Post-9/11 Elegiac Poetry
The Unsaid

After a catastrophic event, two competing impulses customarily surface: a desire to record and preserve it in the form of art, and a repulsion toward—and compulsion to suppress—such efforts. In the aftermath of 9/11, too, this phenomenon occurred: a profusion of artistic responses to the event arose, and a critical repudiation of them ensued. Practitioners of the latter would cite Theodor Adorno's dictum that there can be no poetry after Auschwitz; readers are keenly sensitive to artistic exploitations of tragic events. In response, those sympathetic to the former would espouse Czesław Miłosz's statement in *The Witness of Poetry*: "Whoever invokes genocide, starvation, or the physical suffering of our fellow men in order to attack poems or paintings practices demagoguery."[1] Non-expressivity becomes collusive with the silencing of the suffering. A curious ethical space is born between expressivity and its disavowal.

When there are two antithetical impulses, such opposition is often resolved by the synthesis of those forces: expressivity continues, but it entails an omission of the most vehemently disavowed elements. Taboos—the unsaid and the unsayable—are formed through this process, and losses are diverted and made into inaccessible "lost loss." As one instance of this mechanism, some of the seminal "falling man" poems, including Wisława Szymborska's "Photograph from September 11," have been criticized but also canonized by the readerly public. The shared trait among those "falling man" poems is that they leave something unsaid, namely, the aftermath of the fall. Once the unsaid is formed, subsequent expressions begin to function under the veil of artistic prevarication, occluding the essence of what has been lost. The initial spate of explicit elegies mourning 9/11 comes to be replaced by poems of equivocation. And these oblique elegiacs of 9/11, exemplified by such poems as Louise Glück's "October," give voice to the afterimage of 9/11 at the same time as effacing it, as though to suggest that this poetics of unsaying is where wounded readers could come to peace with a tragedy of this magnitude.

The events of 9/11 triggered an outpouring of poetry. On September 23, *The New York Times* reported that poetry "suddenly appeared all over: haiku on sidewalks, quatrains on church walls, epics scrawled across sidewalks in chalk."[2] In an oft-cited anecdote, a fire chief issued a statement in response to the emergence of poetry everywhere: "Thank you for the food and the blankets and the flowers but please—no more poetry."[3] As another instance of the poetic overflow, over 25,000 poems written in immediate response to 9/11 were published on poems.com alone; three years later, the number of poems there had more than doubled.[4] Laurence Goldstein's 2009 report on the response of American poets to 9/11 observes that, alongside poetry writing, there was a surge of poetry reading in the weeks and months following the attacks.[5] Ulrich Baer corroborates that public poetry writing and reading became popular in New York immediately after 9/11.[6] On September 25, *The Baltimore Sun* asked four Maryland poets to share the verses that had haunted them since September 11, 2001; those included Emily Dickinson's #341, "After great pain, a formal feeling comes—," May Swenson's "Too Big for Words," a poem about the Challenger tragedy, and William Stafford's "Objector."[7] W. H. Auden's "September 1, 1939" and W. B. Yeats's "Easter, 1916" were among the poems much circulated on the Internet, even as they elicited critical responses from contemporary poets as "inappropriate."[8] The former was often seen as irrelevant because of its tone, and the latter's memorable line, "A terrible beauty is born," prompted some visceral rejection, for its potential implication of aestheticizing the terror, deaths, and destructions in the events of 9/11. Even the unfavorable reactions testify to the ubiquity of poems post-9/11.

Multiple observers have offered their explanations for this profusion of poetry: poetry can be sublimatory and transformative, and it offers a language of healing to those who are in need. In "Poetic Responses to 9/11 and Adrienne Rich's *The School Among the Ruins*," Lin Knutson argues that people were moved to write poetry because of "poetry's ability to convert suffering into imagery and to incorporate a wide range of responses to the event, from the harsh and uncompromising, to the language of faith, to the tripping and self-serving."[9] In the report cited earlier, Goldstein characterizes the purpose of poetic responses to 9/11 as follows: "to witness the condition of anguish people were undergoing and, yes, to provide hope that those events would not constitute some indelible reality that would darken the post-9/11 climate for decades, or forever."[10] In Don DeLillo's novel *Falling Man*, one of the characters muses about the therapeutic options available to her fellow survivors: "People read poems. People I know, they read poetry to ease the

shock and pain, give them a kind of space, something beautiful in language
. . . to bring comfort or composure."[11] Poetry, with its relative brevity, may
be considered less taxing on minds that have been ravaged and occupied by
the forces of traumatic events.

To be sure, there are critics who do not find redemptive elements in the
poetic form itself: in *Future-Founding Poetry*, Sascha Pöhlmann puts it
bluntly that poetry was quickest to react after 9/11 not because of any "inherent qualities that make poetry the appropriate form of art with which to
address such events, but rather because its production times are much shorter
than those of fiction, drama, sculpture, or painting."[12] Since there are plenty
of poems that take decades to write—to cite one example, Elizabeth Bishop
took twenty years to write the poem "The Moose," and that is hardly an
outlier—this assessment of the brevity of production times is debatable. But
even if one grants that argument, one might also advocate that, for the walking wounded, the promptness of the rescue is itself part of the salve. In one
way or the other, poetry came to be seen as an embodiment of comfort, composure, beauty, and fellow feelings that those in pain could look to as support.

The connection between language and healing goes back a long time.
In Plato's *Phaedrus*, the Egyptian god offers King Thamus writing as a
"remedy"—"*pharmakon*"—that can help memory. In Greek thinking, the
analogy exists between medical treatments for the body and writing as a
medicine for the soul; if the former aims to cure the body, the latter strives
to provide words that heal the soul and lessen its suffering. According to
Martha Nussbaum, Democritus turned this analogy between medicine and
writing into one between medicine and philosophy;[13] words heal, in the form
of thought and philosophy. Pedro Lain Entralgo claims that philosophical discourse was thought to have a healing effect on the psyche by bringing one's
mind to the state of temperance.[14] Temperance is crucial in a culture where
moderation is thought to be the cornerstone of good life. Aristotle's idea of
"catharsis" has its mirror image in the medical act of purging.

The modern-day conception of language as a healing mechanism, particularly with regard to the link between poetry and therapy, coincides with the
rise of the movement that M. L. Rosenthal began to refer to as "confessional
poetry" in an essay entitled "Poetry as Confession." Many of the major practitioners of confessional poetry—Robert Lowell, Sylvia Plath, Anne Sexton,
W. D. Snodgrass, to name a few—are known to have been in therapy and
were often encouraged to write poetry as part of their treatment. The final section of Robert Lowell's *Life Studies* began as a therapeutic assignment suggested by Lowell's therapist.[15] In an interview with Hilary Holladay, W. D.
Snodgrass responds to the question, "How many years were you in therapy or
analysis all together?": "Oh, I haven't any idea. I've seen a number of doctors
over the years."[16] Likewise, Anne Sexton is quoted as saying that her writing

started, in fact, as therapy: "My analyst told me to write between our sessions about what I was feeling and thinking and dreaming."[17] Confessional poetry was viewed as therapeutic, "equivalent to writing therapy."[18]

Following the emergence of this poetic impulse toward confession in the mid-twentieth century, narrative therapy came into being in the 1970s and 1980s, led by social workers such as Michael White and David Epston. The 1980s also saw the birth of another mode of expressive therapy called writing therapy, which was developed by James W. Pennebaker. In Pennebaker's first seminal study on expressive writing, college students wrote for fifteen minutes on four consecutive days about the most traumatic or upsetting experiences of their entire lives, while controls wrote about superficial topics, such as their room or their shoes. Participants who wrote about their deepest thoughts and feelings reported significant benefits in both objectively assessed and self-reported physical health four months later, with less frequent visits to the health center and a trend toward fewer absences owing to illness.[19] This study yielded the following conclusion: "writing about earlier traumatic experience was associated with both short-term increases in physiological arousal and long-term decreases in health problems."[20] Beginning with the proliferation of psychoanalysis in the early twentieth century, buttressed by the convergence of psychotherapy and confessional poetry in the mid-century, and culminating in the expressive therapy movements, the age of writing to wellness was in full bloom through the last decades of the twentieth century and into the twenty-first century.

Given the conflation of therapeutic writing and literary writing in the decades leading up to the twenty-first century, it seems to be a natural course of events that the first responder to the national anguish following 9/11 turned out to be poetry. But concurrently with this expressive desire, another impulse surfaced: critical repudiation toward expressing or representing the events of 9/11. William Heyen, the editor of the acclaimed anthology of responses to 9/11, *September 11, 2001: American Writers Respond*, recounts his encounter with an unidentified advocate for silence who calls himself or herself "poet"; this person's response to Heyen's prose piece titled "Elegy" declared that this was "no time for talk, for self-aggrandizement, but for quiet resolve," and ended with "Shut the fuck up."[21] As if to counter "September 1, 1939" and the profusion of poems circulated in response to 9/11, some writers would point to W. B. Yeats's poem "On Being Asked for a War Poem":[22]

I think it better that in times like these
A poet's mouth be silent, for in truth
We have no gift to set a statesman right;
He has had enough of meddling who can please
A young girl in the indolence of her youth,
Or an old man upon a winter's night. (1–6)[23]

Yeats wrote this poem partially in response to many mediocre poets speaking up on the eve of the Great War, but it also reveals the other dynamics at play: the express desire to divide the aesthetic from the political. Lines 5–6 present the images of alternatives that Yeats suggests as more acceptable topics of lyric poetry: a young girl's youth, an old man's winter night.[24] The oft-debated but long-held assumption is that lyric poetry is aimed toward the eternal and, as such, contains within it "transhistorical potentialities."[25] Part of these potentialities derives from the assumption that the lyric transcends any particular moment of history and that it stays above the political entanglements that are rooted in the here and now. Political becomes a dirty word in the world of aesthetics; poems and poets branded as political are often seen to lack the transhistorical artistry that withstands the test of time.[26] Even as scholars question this false dichotomy of the political and the aesthetic, it remains, at the visceral level of readerly perceptions, that occasional poems are often terrible and that silence is more appropriate for artists in times of crises, particularly when the poetic utterance risks being perceived as political in one sense or another.

This aesthetic-political struggle is one of the subterraneous undergirds of how Adorno's "no poetry after Auschwitz" statement has been interpreted. One can safely claim that the scholarly community has concluded that the reading of the Adorno statement as a denunciation of poetry, the "impossibility of poetry after the Holocaust,"[27] or "the ultimate argument for silence"[28] are misinterpretations. In introducing Adorno's *Can One Live after Auschwitz?*, Rolf Tiedemann indicates that this statement "was misunderstood . . . by poets" and that it was more an observation of how poetry before Auschwitz and poetry after Auschwitz were separated by an unbridgeable gulf, rather than an admonition that writing poetry is immoral and must be forbidden.[29] In this context, poetry becomes a synecdoche of culture as a whole. Adorno's statement is an expression, in other words, "of the strongest version of a postwar dilemma" shared "by philosophy and criticism" that cultural activities of the mind—whether poetry, philosophy, or criticism—can reside wholly within the realm of the aesthetic:[30] those disciplines must be reflective enough to be aware of the elements of barbarity and taintedness within them, after the same language that they employ has been used to carry out and justify an atrocity of the magnitude of the Holocaust. As Lyn Hejinian puts it, disasters enjoin poets "not to speak the same language as Auschwitz," since "poetry after Auschwitz must indeed be barbarian; it must be foreign to the cultures that produce atrocities."[31] Acknowledging and reflecting on the inherent barbarity of the language has become a requisite for those who write poetry about atrocities and disasters after Auschwitz. The aesthetic-political binary has collapsed; it may have long been defunct, but one can no longer ignore its expiration.

But the real question here is not "what is the correct interpretation of Adorno's declaration?" Misinterpretation is itself a symptom: what does the fact that so many well-meaning and educated people continue to misinterpret this statement, and that those misinterpretations speak to us in the most visceral manner, tell us? Representations of atrocities are fraught with anxieties—anxieties about misrepresentation, cooptation, politicization, as well as the overarching inadequacy of language to heal and console. As Alicia Ostriker notes, almost immediately after the events of 9/11 the debates over "whether poets should or shouldn't, could or couldn't write about public as well as personal events, expressions of patriotism, anti-patriotism" became overwhelming enough to cause exhaustion.[32] The Adorno declaration continues to be misinterpreted because it gives shape to the questions about the limits of literary expression and the ethics of speaking when social customs call for silent prayers, whether those questions surface in Toni Morrison's statement, "I have nothing to say,"[33] or in W. S. Merwin's poetic address to the words—"When it happens you are not there" (1).[34] It speaks, in other words, to poets' collective misgivings: do I have the right to write about this matter?[35]

Poets grapple with multiple layers of ethical anxieties. As Nikki Moustaki's "How to Write a Poem after September 11th" suggests, one source of this unease is the question of whether or not the transformative force of metaphor leads poetry to the path of misrepresentation. Metaphor is central to the function of poetry: as Philip Sidney once posited, poetry is "an art of imitation, . . . a representing, counterfeiting, or figuring forth—to speak metaphorically, a speaking picture—with this end, to teach and delight."[36] Likewise, Paul Ricoeur argues that metaphor, like plot in drama, is at the heart of lyric creativity as a mimetic art.[37] In this context, Moustaki's admonishments like "Don't make a metaphor," "Don't compare the planes to birds," and "Don't call the windows eyes" become expressions of anti-lyricism (9, 11, 12).[38] And this anti-lyric thrust is rooted precisely in the potential that poetic metamorphosis can turn into misrepresentation or cooptation. Stories of fear and terror, stories of healing and recovery, or stories of good and evil may be what some readers and perhaps poets themselves want, but facile reductions feel inappropriate to the writer's sense of professional ethics. The very act of making art out of someone else's suffering feels wrong, in the way that the line "A terrible beauty is born" feels wrong at the sight of the two crumbling towers. The compulsion to speak after tragedies is accompanied by reflective inhibition.

When the urgent personal and political need to speak is met by an equally stringent imperative to silence it, a strange space between speech and silence is born: speaking but not speaking. In this restrictive speech, one of two things happens: either one speaks in codes or finds oneself speaking around taboos. The latter representatively occurs in poems that we may call "falling people" poems in the literature of 9/11. While these poems narrate, describe, and reflect on the victims and their precipitation, they also leave much unsaid.

Along with the sight of the crumbling towers, the images of people falling from the towers were some of the most harrowing representations of 9/11. But they were also some of the most problematic images. In the "Three Years Later" series, *The New York Times* published an article entitled "Falling Bodies, a 9/11 Image Etched in Pain," which describes the situation surrounding the fall victims in the following passage:

> The attack on the World Trade Center was one of the most observed catastrophes in history, and those who fell or jumped from the towers were, briefly, its most public victims. They emerged one or two at a time from a blanket of smoke and fire that rendered mass death virtually invisible. Nearly all the others killed that day—whether high in the trade center, on board the hijacked airplanes or deep inside the Pentagon—were beyond the sight of survivors and witnesses.
>
> Those who came through the windows of the towers provided the starkest, most harrowing evidence of the desperate conditions inside. Since then, though, they have largely vanished from consideration. Newspapers rarely publish images of the falling people. Evacuation studies concentrated on the accounts of survivors.
>
> The 9/11 Commission, which has compiled the most detailed history of the day, mentioned those who jumped only as they affected the people on the streets below.
>
> Even now, there has been less fact-finding than guesswork. Some researchers say more than 200 people most likely fell or jumped to their death. Others say the number is half that, or fewer. None have been officially identified.[39]

The way this article frames the public exposure of the falling victims reveals several critical elements: the visibility of the victims, followed by silence or erasure of those images, and the continuing uncertainties about these victims. The victims were, at first, most visible of all those who passed away in the catastrophe. It owes, in part, to the photographs and footage that were presented to readers and viewers immediately following the attack: those include Richard Drew's "Falling Man," which was published in *The New York Times* on the day after 9/11; Thomas Dallal's "Impending Death," which shows around fifty figures leaning out of the broken windows of the North Tower shortly before its collapse; and a four-second shot of someone jumping, which was aired on CNN in a special report that evening. But after the initial shock, the disappearance occurs; multiple accounts of journalism indicate that the images of falling victims vanished, especially from the U.S. media.[40] In an essay entitled "Still Life: 9/11's Falling Bodies," Laura Frost cites that psychological studies after 9/11 singled out witnessing falling people, live or on TV, as a major predictor of post-traumatic stress disorder.[41] In this sense, it should not be surprising that the force of self-censorship worked to shield viewers from those representations. At least, the sight of crumbling buildings, another image repeatedly shown on various media, does not show people actually dying from the collapses.

As confirmed by the previously cited *New York Times* article, the 9/11 Commission Report says very little on those who fell out of the buildings; the report usually couples them with falling debris, as something to be avoided by the rescue units and survivors on the ground. Samplings of such passages include the following:

> All civilians who reached the lobby were directed by NYPD and PAPD officers into the concourse, where other police officers guided them to exit the concourse and complex to the north and east so that they might avoid falling debris and victims.[42]

> Finally, the jumpers and debris that confronted units attempting to enter the South Tower from its main entrance on Liberty Street caused some units to search for indirect ways to enter that tower, most often through the Marriott Hotel, or simply to remain on West Street.[43]

> In other instances, intangibles combined to reduce what could have been a much higher death total. It is impossible to measure how many more civilians who descended to the ground floors would have died but for the NYPD and PAPD personnel directing them—via safe exit routes that avoided jumpers and debris—to leave the complex urgently but calmly.[44]

There is a stark contrast between the heroism of the rescue officers and the depictions of the fall victims. The latter's equation with debris is disturbing enough. Through the entire Commission Report, the fall victims are mentioned only seven times.[45] Of those seven references, only one affords them much humanity: "conditions were so dire that some civilians on upper floors were jumping or falling from the building."[46] This reticence, in itself, is noteworthy: while a significant minority of the 9/11 victims met their demise in this manner—the widely circulated estimate is 200, although there is no official consensus as to how many there were—their images became objects to be avoided. A profound loss, like the Dickinsonian truth that must be told circuitously, can be too blinding to face directly.

Like the journalistic coverage, in the immediate aftermath of 9/11, numerous poems engaged in one form or another with the portrayal of the images of people falling from the Twin Towers. Wayne Dodd's "The Third Tower" prominently features the themes of falling: the towers, the people, and the time. X. J. Kennedy's "September Twelfth, 2001" narrates an experience of waking up the day after 9/11 with a "selfish thankfulness" that the two people "caught on film / who hurtle from the eighty-second floor, /. . . aren't us" (1–2, 5).[47] Although it is a poem that depicts a sense of uneasy relief that the speaker did not die like those captured and broadcasted, this negative distancing between them and "us" foreshadows the subsequent quarantining of the images of those fall victims. Gail Griffin's fifth poem of "How It Comes" hints at the uneasiness when one refers to those victims as "jumpers" by using a circumlocution, "He calls them."[48] In Miranda Beeson's "Flight," a finch trapped between the screen and pane becomes a diversion from the spectacle of "the man in his business suit / who fell through the air without / the benefit of wings."[49] Diane Seuss's oft-cited "Falling Man" conflates the sense of catastrophe that many people felt in the aftermath of 9/11 with the images of those who are "falling" but who have "not fallen" from the tower: "it is we who are falling, beautifully walling, / we who will be forever falling" (48–49).[50]

The poem that perhaps most squarely engages with the trauma of the "falling people" tragedy is Kimiko Hahn's "Her Very Eyes." This poem describes the inability of the speaker's daughter's friend's sister to close her eyes. The cumbersomeness of the multiple layers of separation—"the speaker's daughter's friend's sister"—is by design: it is a sight that would render one speechless, incapacitated, and anesthetized, if one were to actually witness it. The speaker is able to speak only because she is safely distanced; she is not the witness, not a sister of the witness, not a friend of the witness, and not the parent of the witness. The distance itself suggests the magnitude of the anguish. With this separation, the poem's speaker is able to approach the dumbfounding sight by capturing, however obliquely, the shock of witnessing people falling from the sky, through the eyes of the sister of the friend of the daughter:

she sees bodies falling from the sky,
she sees bodies breaking through the glass atrium
or smashing onto the pavement,
she sees one woman, her skirt billowing out like a manikin's,
and a suited man plunging headfirst.
And she hears them land in front of her
but cannot turn away when she closes her eyes.   (5–11)[51]

The repetition of the phrase, "she sees . . . ," haunts as though to simulate the traumatic flashbacks. As the distant "bodies" turn into real human beings—"one woman, her skirt billowing out," "a suited man plunging head-first"—the anguish becomes more and more acute, enough for the witness to want to liken the victim to something akin to a mannequin, in a self-defensive act. Sigmund Freud has famously suggested that one of the important functions of consciousness is to block out excess stimuli.[52] In the penultimate line, the witness turns off her vision; she does not "see" anymore, but only "hears," in a move simulating a broadcast accident where the screen goes off and it becomes audio only—because the picture should not be shown. Hahn's poem, of the many "falling people" poems that were printed in major publication venues, is one of the very few poems that even talks about the landing aspect of the flight. The witness is spared the sight of the landing, and the poem leaves that part unsaid; it is, nonetheless, a sight that she cannot "turn away" from, even as she closes her eyes.

Hahn's "Her Very Eyes" is an exception rather than the rule; most "falling people" poems depict the people in mid-air, as captured by Richard Drew's photograph and as depicted in Diane Seuss's poem; they censor out the landing, regardless of whether it is oblique or explicit. In fact, many poems go out of their way to blush out the aftermath of the fall, in a seeming countermove to the tide of realism that became prominent in World War I poetry—the soldiers under gas attacks die "guttering, choking, drowning" (16) in Wilfred Owen's "Dulce et Decorum Est," to cite one example—and was sustained through much of the twentieth century. Christine Hartzler's "Diver" starts with the image of a gold-medalist diver, Greg Louganis, which merges with and jars against the "diver" out of the lattice of the skyscraper, folding himself into a breathtaking pike. The poem, as Goldstein notes, is an unrhymed Petrarchan sonnet with octave and sestet inverted, where the second strophe departs from and subverts the first in a radical manner.[53] While readers may appreciate the air of defiance—choosing their destiny, as opposed to being merely killed by the forces that be—and the transformation of a fall victim into the triumphant diver may be seen as more dignifying than the 9/11 Commission Report's treatment of them as something akin to the wreckage and debris, one cannot escape the feeling of discomfort: everyone knows what happened, and no one wants to broach the topic. In the Hartzler poem, the beaming smile of Louganis is so firmly overlaid that the nameless victim disappears, along with his fate. While journalistic labeling of the falling victims as a forbidden subject reaches the threshold of exaggeration—there are too many articles written, too many novels written, too many films made, and too many poems written, to call it an unmentionable topic—one may safely conclude, based on the available literature, that the landing in the aftermath of the fall has become a taboo in the lore of 9/11.

The tabooization of the aftermath of the fall has to do in part with the difficulty of what Pauline Boss calls ambiguous loss. One type of ambiguous loss, physical ambiguous loss, refers to cases involving a missing person or unrecovered body, where the person is considered most likely dead but no confirmation of that fact is available. Ambiguous loss complicates the mourning process, in that unresolved grief makes closure more problematic than it is for normative mourning. In the case of fall victims, it is all but certain that those people captured in the photographs or films are dead, but their identities tend to remain elusive, and the conditions of the bodies, or lack thereof, leave the bereaved in a state of ambivalent mourning.

Taboos are born out of the ethical vexation between the compulsion to speak and the desire to silence it. Wisława Szymborska's "Photograph from September 11" exemplifies and acknowledges these dynamics as it ends with the following stanza: "I can do only two things for them— / describe this flight / and not add a last line" (17–19).[54] The poem is composed of mostly short tercets, interrupted by a single quatrain in the middle and by frequent stops of line breaks, which combine to slow down what is left of the sense of movement in the poem and, in this process, enact the stillness of the photograph. What is apparent to readers is the voice of compassion: unlike the 9/11 Commission Report, those lumped together as "jumpers" are not objectified as debris-like materials that people on the ground must be watchful to avoid. There is an effort to enumerate them—"one, two, a few more" (1)—and the plural "them" is particularized into "each" that is "complete" (7). According to Eva Badowska, the Polish word rendered here as "particular" is "poszczególny," which emphasizes singularity within a group: it considers "each apart from the others."[55] Even as the victims cannot avoid being nameless and unrecognizable, the attempt to speak of them as singular individuals separate from one another is reflected in the language and the form of the poem.

Another characteristic that suggests this poem's attempt to preserve individuality manifests in the form of the relative scarcity of metaphors. This avoidance of metaphor conveys two things. On one level, it signals an aversion to the transformative power of metaphor. Although metaphor is a device that illuminates the tenor and vehicle by transposing the character of each onto the other, this enlightenment comes at a cost: the conflation of the two results in the metamorphosis of both. If the optative aim of elegiac ekphrasis were to keep as much as possible the deceased as they were, metaphor could be regarded as a device that runs counter to this objective. In this sense, the inhibitive use of metaphor functions as an effort to honor the dead, to preserve them and, like embalming, to present them properly for mourning and burial.

On the secondary level, the eschewing of metaphor points to a mechanism similar to Kimiko Hahn's witness closing her eyes before the sight of the fall victims. If, as George Lakoff has established, metaphor is a fundamental mechanism of mind that structures our understanding of experience,[56] the refusal to use metaphor is tantamount to a refusal to think. Seen in this regard, what is communicated through the poem is a sense of sheer bewilderment, an elaborate way of saying, "I don't know what to think." The lack of metaphor, coupled with descriptivism, effects an effacement of reflection.

And self-effacement is the central trope of "Photograph from September 11." The final stanza—"I can do only two things for them— / describe this flight / and not add a last line"—is the only place that mentions the first-person speaker. In her only appearance in the text, the speaker prefers to withhold her words, effectively abnegating the power of her language. This move echoes the multitudinous comments left in the aftermath of 9/11 by writers suggesting that they have no words for this catastrophe, and with it, the poem suspends time, freezing the scene of the fall and leaving it without traces of overbearing writerly intervention.

Another feature that reinforces this moratorium is that the poem takes a form of an ekphrasis based on a photograph. As explored in the previous chapter on Sharon Olds's *The Dead and the Living*, photographs create a curious phenomenon: a space where one's life and death coexist in the same space and where, as long as the artwork lives, it continues to give life to those represented in it, even when they are corporeally dead. That is to say, the life of those portrayed in the artwork can remain "present"—in the sense that things that happen in a book are always retold in the present tense—even as their real-life models might be long "past." It is like a poetic version of Schrödinger's cat. In the original version of the physics experiment, a cat, a flask of poison, and a radioactive source are placed inside a sealed box. There is a monitor inside the box, and if it detects radioactivity, the flask breaks and releases the poison that kills the cat. The Copenhagen interpretation of quantum mechanics—a position that physical systems would not gain definitive properties until they are measured—implies that the cat would remain simultaneously alive and dead until the box is opened, since one can assume the cat would likely die of poison but cannot ascertain that reality unless it is confirmed by the actual results. It is only when one looks inside the box that one sees the cat as either alive or dead, not both alive and dead. Likewise, the photographic halting of the lives heading into certain doom creates this suspension, along with, however wishful, the dual reality—that those people remain alive in the photograph, so long as the poem offers no confirmation of their death and so long as the speaker refuses to add the final line. In this ekphrastic distance and hesitance, the deaths are as engraved as they are ambiguated.

The fall victims' "blood" remains "well hidden" because of this ambiguity. It creates space for a type of magical thinking, the belief that an action or circumstance not logically related to an event can influence its outcome. Magical thinking is one of the frequently observed characteristics of post-9/11 novels,[57] and the same can be said of many of the post-9/11 poems as well, including Szymborska's "Photograph from September 11." In Szymborska's poem, photographic distance, ethical hesitance, and magical thinking combine to enact the elegiacs of equivocation. Equivocation is distinct from previous elegiac modes such as compensatory consolation and anti-elegiac melancholia. Unlike compensatory consolation, equivocation leaves little sense of closure; it ends in suspension, in mid-air. If there is any sense of solace, it derives not from the satisfaction, however ambivalent, of having found or founded some other sign of the deceased, whether it is the religiosity of eternal life or the artistic product as its metonym. Rather, equivocation is born of the acquiescence to ambivalence—a stance one would see in a person who would avoid opening the box with Schrödinger's cat. For, in some instances, ambiguity is preferable to the pronouncement of unacceptable reality.

Elegiacs of equivocation also diverge from anti-elegiac melancholia, in that while both experience difficulties of closure, the sense of melancholy remains much subdued, and there is little of the sense of resistance to or rebellion against the thrust of the elegy itself. According to R. Clifton Spargo, anti-elegy "designates not so much a new form of poetry or a break with the tradition of elegy as a tendency within elegiac poetry to resist consolation by setting a contemporary mourner against past cultural and poetical conventions."[58] Largely conceived as a symptom of twentieth-century modernity, anti-elegy represents the skepticism of commemorative customs, arts, and monuments. The point of divergence between equivocal elegies and anti-elegies is the desire for consolation. In Szymborska's "Photograph from September 11," the refusal to add a last line—with line being the metonym of poetry—may be regarded as anti-elegiac, but the aim of the poem is decidedly commemorative and consolatory. It does not mean a dispelling of skepticism, however: skepticism is deeply and inescapably ingrained in modern sensibilities. Equivocation is a stance that envelops both skepticism and the object of skepticism—namely, consolation—even as its efficacy is questioned. It is a type of magical thinking: if one does not say it, it might not come true.

After the initial deluge, and alongside the continuing flow, of poems explicitly about the events of 9/11, another strain of post-9/11 poetry emerged. Poems in this category tend to represent the disaster more obliquely, constructing the world in which unnamed sorrows loom in the background. Louise Glück's "October" was published first in *The New Yorker* on October 28, 2002, then as a chapbook by Sarabande Books in 2004, before it became a part of her collection *Averno* in 2006. Given that the trauma of 9/11 is inextricably linked to the month of September, October, too, becomes implicated as a month that immediately followed the painful event: October turns into an emblem of mournful remembrance. Several poems from William

Heyen's *American Writers Respond* feature October in this light, including Daniel Bourne's "The First of October, We" and H. Edgar Hix's "October 11, 2001." Likewise, Glück's "October" has also been read in this context, as an oblique evocation of September 11, 2001:[59] the poem was welcomed in 2002 because it "effected a triumph over the Medusa power of September 2001" and insisted upon the perennial rather than the timely.[60] By converting the September attacks into something assimilable to myth, *Averno* exposes the process by which disaster is disguised and even eradicated.[61] This impulse toward effacement is a culmination of the pattern observable in post-9/11 poetry: it starts with an outpouring of explicit mourning, transitions into half-tabooization, and then ends in a cryptonymy that reveals and hides what lies beneath the surfeit of language. And in the case of *Averno*, one sees a form of elegiac equivocation: ambiguous commemoration without closure, consolation that cannot shake off skepticism. What sets *Averno* apart is not only that it embodies the elegiacs of equivocation that surface in post-9/11 poetry but also that it discerns what mobilizes this ambiguation. A closer look at some of the key poems—"The Night Migrations," "October," and "Averno"—reveals the hidden motor of this distancing process in which catastrophic losses are effaced and left behind, even as this diffusion prolongs the unplaced and undefined feeling of disconsolation.

Averno takes its name from a small crater lake ten miles west of Naples, Italy; it was regarded by the ancient Romans as the entrance to the underworld and is also known by its ancient name, Avernus. On the surface, *Averno* is about Persephone. It simulates the Greek myth and its cycle of life, death, and rebirth. In "Psychoanalyzing Persephone: Louise Glück's *Averno*," Uta Gosmann summarizes this story as follows:

> Persephone amuses herself by plucking violets and white lilies in the idyllic landscape of the Sicilian fields of Henna, a valley of eternal spring. Suddenly, Hades, the god of the underworld, appears, ravishes her, and takes her with him to the underworld. Persephone's mother Demeter searches the whole earth for her daughter and, grief-stricken, lays waste to the land. She asks Persephone's father Zeus to force Hades to set Persephone free again, and Zeus consents on the condition that Persephone has eaten nothing that comes from the underworld. But Persephone tasted seven pomegranate seeds, and so will not be allowed to return fully to the earth. She will remain six months of the year with Hades and spend the other six months on earth.[62]

In *The Veiled Mirror and the Woman Poet*, Elizabeth Dodd coins a term, "personal classicism," to describe a poetic mode adopted by many women poets, starting in the nineteenth century and developing throughout the twentieth century: a mode in which personal impulses, such as those that appear in confessional poetry, combine with careful elements of control that allow them to shape, frame, and mute what are at their core romantic, personal poems.[63] With its ability to conceal autobiographical minutiae, the classical trope becomes the vehicle for poems to take on a more universal character, even as they originate from and give shape to parochial urgencies. In Glück's poetry, Greek myths function as the classical element in her brand of personal classicism; underneath the veneer of the Persephone myth are contemporary exigencies.

In addition to the "personal classicism" model of reading *Averno*, Glück's education in psychoanalysis must also be highlighted; from a psychoanalytic perspective, the tale of Persephone connects the "personal unconscious with the mythical unconscious."[64] In Freudian psychoanalysis, trauma arises less from a disruption of the psyche by a traumatic event than from an interaction between the trauma-causing event and the subject's psychic history.[65] In this model, traumatic experience is understood not so much "as a fixed and timeless photographic negative stored in an unlocatable place of the brain" but rather as a point of negotiation between memory and history.[66] In national tragedies, the collective cognition of the traumatic experience interacts with the historical memory of that community, whether it is the bombing of Pearl Harbor or the assassination of Abraham Lincoln. In *Averno*, the cultural memory that 9/11 prompts the reader to revisit is the myth of Persephone; Persephone becomes the returning repression that is belatedly re-cognized, the past trauma where the working-through of the present trauma takes place in a displaced form.[67]

In *Averno*, Glück enacts the elegiacs of equivocation in these half-spaces: speaking but not speaking, mourning but not mourning, being personal but also impersonal. The first poem of the collection, "The Night Migrations," is placed outside of parts I and II, as though to embody a preface or introduction before the book's body chapters begin. The poem, acting like a thesis, sets the tone of this ambiguous mourning by proposing an ambivalent consolation:

What will the soul do for solace then?
I tell myself maybe it won't need
these pleasures anymore;
maybe just not being is simply enough,
hard as that is to imagine.   (9–13)[68]

The feeling of grief arises from the speaker's rumination that the dead will no longer see things like red berries and birds' night migrations in the dark sky—the things we, the living, "depend on" (7). The poetic move toward consolation—"What will the soul do for solace then?"—leads to a kind of stoicism: the dead may not need those things anymore, and for them, their nonexistence might be "simply enough."

This sense of renunciation, however, is unsettled by the repeated expressions of uncertainty—"maybe." Furthermore, the addition of "I tell myself" communicates an element of magical thinking: if I tell myself so, it might become true. This sentiment is reminiscent of the optative ending of the Szymborska poem, which freezes the falling victims in mid-air by not adding the last line, or of Elizabeth Bishop's "One Art," which insists that the loss is no disaster as if to convince oneself that saying so would make it true. The final line reinforces the wavering by suggesting the difficulty of persuading oneself to imagine this possibility: "hard as that is to imagine." Consolation, even as the poem presents it, remains both unsatisfying—does it really console us to think that the dead will not need those sights because they do not exist anymore?—and unconvincing—even if it is satisfying, do we have any way of knowing if it is true?

The speaker derives life pleasure from "seeing" things, but when one examines closely what kind of sights and scenes the poem describes, it becomes questionable if they are actually delightful. The mountain ash forebodes the cataclysmic fire that occurs in the course of *Averno*; the red berries, even if pleasant in and of themselves, become a traumatic reminder of the disaster. Also, the idea of birds migrating at night sounds sufficiently poetic, but in reality, they might not be particularly visible in the dark sky at night. Like the renunciatory solace, the pleasure of living is not as unequivocal as it might seem on the surface of this poem.

"October" reinforces this prevarication by depicting a winter following an unnamed catastrophe, obliquely evoking the specter of September 11. As the poem alternates between seasons—winter in part I, an illusory summer in part II, early spring in part III, autumn in part IV, winter again in part V, and a scene of luminescence in part VI—October comes to signify the passage of time that both blurs and engraves the memories of disaster, inhabiting the halfway space of equivocation. In part I, the first wintry scene begins with what appears to be a minor, personal injury—"didn't Frank just slip on the ice" (I: 2).[69] It sounds simultaneously innocuous enough to be frivolous and ominous enough to function as a miniaturized substitute for the unidentified tragedy.

Much of the poetry with confessional proclivity operates in the half-space between the personal and the universal. While many have pointed to its solipsistic tendencies, confessional poetry at its core is poetry of empathy; it functions through a mechanism of both projection and introjection, a Whitman-like mixture of the incorporation of the other into oneself—"I contain multitudes"—and projection of the self onto the other—"In all people I see myself." These apparatuses engender a state that combines the elements of empathic stages outlined by Theodor Reik and Robert Katz: identification, incorporation, reverberation, and detachment. Confessional poetry works bidirectionally between the personal episode as a springboard for uncovering the universal and the collective episode as impetus for illuminating the personal. This personal-collective amalgamation may be more foregrounded in Sylvia Plath's poetry, but Glück's personal classicism works similarly to meld the personal, the collective, and the mythical. This duplicity of confessional poetry is predisposed to the elegiacs of equivocation, since both reside in the fusion of opposite impulses—the personal and the universal for confessional poetry, and speech and silence for equivocal elegy—without reconciliation or synthesis of them. By saying without saying, Glück's poetry creates a method of committing to both sides of the impulse: the desire to speak and the impulse to suppress it. This halfway space is where one devises the methods to speak after a disaster, for it makes possible the coexistence of the irreconcilable.

The smaller, personal injury sustained by someone named Frank becomes an apt avenue into the empathic ego-expansion of the poet-speaker, and it sets off a series of rhetorical questions, many fixated on the issues of healing, rescue, and safety, which remain illusory and elusive:

didn't he heal, weren't the spring seeds planted . . .

wasn't my body
rescued, wasn't it safe

didn't the scar form, invisible
above the injury

terror and cold,
didn't they just end . . .   (I: 3, 7–12)[70]

Since words take on associative meanings from their contemporary usage, the use of the word "terror" inevitably brings back echoes of September 11, along with the wars on terror that ensued and turned into a drawn-out affair that would characterize much of the lugubrious mood of the 2000s. Lines 3, 7, and 8 suggest the main concerns of these rhetorical questions: healing, a desire for rescue, and a feeling of safety. Scars are tissues that replace normal skin after an injury; as such, they are part of the healing process. But the keyword is "invisible." In one sense, the scar may be invisible because it is a metaphoric one: a spiritual recovery from a psychological trauma. On the other hand, since significant injuries tend to result in visible scars that take years to fade, the invisibility of the scar becomes synonymous with the irrecognition of the injury itself. With this erasure, the loss sustained from this disaster will lose its traces and will turn into a lost loss. All but the last of the questions is left without question marks, and one way to interpret this rhetorical feature is that the speaker does not expect answers to her queries. Another interpretation is that wishes remain unheard, or unfulfilled, like the unanswered cries for comfort and relief in one of Gerard Manley Hopkins's terrible sonnets, "No worst, there is none."

The illusory summer in section II indicates the passage of time since the violent incident. There is some sense of relief—"balm after violence"—but the change is thoroughgoing enough that this belated alleviation is of little help: "it does me no good / to be good to me now" (II: 3–4). Despite that, there is a sense of restoration: "the August sun / returning everything that was taken away" (II: 9–10). Anchoring this oscillation between relief and its inefficacy is skepticism, as evidenced by the repetition of the line "I won't believe you" (II: 24, 26). What underlies this skepticism is the irreversibility of the damage suffered from the disaster: "violence has changed me" (II: 5). Powerlessness against this irreversibility resides in the fact that the only antidote to it is one's own mind's voice: "You hear this voice? This is my mind's voice; / you can't touch my body now" (II: 11–12). Mind over matter is a common self-help concept that has explained the efficacy of placebo and has generated the popular boom of mindfulness. If one were to reductively summarize the history of human thought as the Hegelian dialectical progression from a blind belief in magic and myths, the negativist skepticism of the Enlightenment, to modern reconciliation between belief and skepticism—as exemplified by the Wallace Stevens-like mode of belief in fiction despite awareness of its fictiveness—section II of "October" rebels against the mind trick that enables this fiction-belief. The voice calling attention to the August sun restoring all that has been taken away is the "mind's voice" without substance. Even if the mind says so, the body testifies against it: it has "changed once" (II: 13), has "hardened" (II: 13), and will not "respond again" (II: 14), like Daphne's transformation into a laurel tree with ossified barks, mouthless and mindless.

The illusory summer may be the mind's trick—exposed as such by the bodily evidence that contradicts the mind's wishful restorative thoughts—but the spring in section III is depicted as genuine, unascertainable workings of nature: "Winter was over. In the thawed dirt, / bits of green were showing" (III: 17–18). Spring signals that the calamitous September is now two seasons past. In the pastoral mode, the poet-speaker finds pleasure in the beauty of the world:

Come to me, said the world.
This is not to say
it spoke in exact sentences
but that I perceived beauty in this manner . . . .

Come to me, said the world. I was standing

in my wool coat at a kind of bright portal—
I can finally say
long ago; it gives me considerable pleasure. Beauty
the healer, the teacher—   (III: 3–6, 19–23)

Unlike the illusory voice the poet-speaker hears in section II, the repeated invitations in section III feel authentic. The world does not speak; there is "no voice" (III: 16). Glück's speaker discloses that what she hears is her own interpretation—"This is not to say / it spoke in exact sentences" (III: 4–5). Nonetheless, nature functions as "the healer, the teacher" (III: 23). What anchors this healing—knowledge as healing—is the passage of time; retrospection prompts the poet-speaker to enunciate that the disaster happened "*long ago*" (III: 22). In *Pastoral Elegy in Contemporary British and Irish Poetry*, Iain Twiddy clarifies the distinction between pastoral and non-pastoral elegies as follows: pastoral elegies relinquish the dead to nature and tend to be consolatory, while non-pastoral elegies remain more egalitarian and dispassionate, where pain fades with time rather than through any poetic or philosophical intervention.[71] In the strictest sense, "October" may be neither a pastoral nor an elegy, but its movement incorporates both the pastoral and non-pastoral: there is a sense of consolation through the fading of pain over the passage of time, but the key to this fading is nature—if only for the fact that nature, and its cyclic seasons, lets us know how much time has passed.

This interlude of healing, however, changes the course of mourning. In section IV, the light of autumn, which casts itself differently from that of spring, illuminates what the passage of time actually does to one's trauma; once the sharp edges of melancholia wear off, once one recovers just enough from the trauma, or once one gains a certain amount of distance from the disaster, one is left with little to mourn for. Things change; stages of initial shocks subside, but acceptance continues to be an unreachable prize. The word "acceptance" feels as though it is a misnomer for resignation or repression. The loss becomes inexpressible—"the unspeakable":

The songs have changed; the unspeakable
has entered them . . . .

And yet the notes recur. They hover oddly
in anticipation of silence.
The ear gets used to them.
The eye gets used to disappearances. (IV: 6–7, 18–21)

One of the established tenets of trauma theories is that one's expressivity becomes inhibited by traumatization. The passage of time does not always lead to retrospective clarity: traumas do not become any easier to talk about. Speaking remains difficult even when the blunt force of the traumatic event wears off, precisely because of this distance: when one is temporally removed from the event, to try to mourn would seem inauthentic and overwrought. The line "the songs of morning sound over-rehearsed" (IV: 3), in which "morning" is an obvious pun on "mourning," suggests the difficulty of speaking about distanced trauma: it feels "over-rehearsed" and hence not genuine. Moreover, it instead feels like a further violation of the traumatic event and the traumatized self, now purified and sanctified. With the passage of time, the songs have changed, and events become unmentionable. One speaks around them—the "notes" still "recur," no matter how different the tunes—and words dance into silence. That leads to the illegal burial of trauma in the inaccessible crypt; disappearance is effected. As the ear gets used to silence and the eyes get used to disappearances, one no longer recognizes the absence, which itself becomes absented.

As the unspeakable sets in, silence becomes the theme of section V, which depicts the return of winter. Aside from the icy detachment of the voice, images such as "ornamental lights of the season" (V: 22) portray dutiful Christmas decorations without the substance of celebration. The emphatic one-adjective line defines the mood of the section: "The bland" (V: 6). Speechlessness is not born of traumatic discombobulation but rather from flat affect: the misery in the world of "October" is not excruciating, but characterless. The poet-speaker proclaims that it is "true that I am not competent to restore" beauty in the world (V: 2). Silence dominates—"I am / at work, though I am silent" (V: 4–5), and the efficacy of words is questioned: "the word itself / false, a device to refute / perception (V: 19–21). As the speaker turns silent, so do others around her: they are "not speaking" (V: 10). The abandoned houses and their shuttered rooms become metaphors of the wordlessness of this scene. We may recall many poets questioning the power of words in the aftermath of September 11; one of the previously referenced poems, "To the Word" by W. S. Merwin, is an instance of this skepticism. The poems of September differ markedly from "October," in that the former attempts to capture the immediacy of the event while the latter is squarely situated in retrospection. Nonetheless, both of those face similar challenges. The word feels "false," like a mere ornament: in the September poems, it is because words feel like some diminished homunculi of the real catastrophe that they fail to reproduce; in "October," the words that capture the catastrophic event with the clarity of retrospection come to feel inauthentic as the passage of time dulls one's senses.

In an essay at the end of *Contemporary American Poetry*, Al Poulin Jr. claims that the major difference between modern and contemporary poetry is that the latter is more intimate and personal; contemporary poetry enacts what he terms "personalization of poetry" to attain a voice that sounds genuine.[72] In an interview, Mark Strand explains that the "point of writing a version of plain-style verse, it seems, is to affect as much as possible the naturalness of conversation";[73] it suggests that what ensures the air of authenticity in contemporary poetry is the sound of urgency and the feel of naturalness that derives from the ways in which it disguises poetic contrivances.[74] Although the "contrivances" targeted in these essays refer specifically to aspects of craft from the writer's perspective—poetic devices such as rhymes, images, allusions, and so on—it remains true that signs of artifice sound particularly jarring to readers in elegiac poetry, a genre which is historically seen to engage with emotion, including but not limited to grief, sorrow, anger, and shock, among others. If a natural response to trauma were aphasia, any act of speech would by its own nature sound unnatural; if recapturing trauma after time has half-healed it and left only a trace of it is an impossibility, poetic attempts to do so would seem guileful and inauthentic. Given these dynamics, section V ends with what appears to be a cliché used in countless poems: *"you are not alone"* (V: 27). And the darkness of the tunnel from which it is spoken adumbrates the depth of silence that the poem is ensconced in.

While the poem retreats into darkness, the earth is illuminated by "the fire" in section VI (VI: 3). Light dominates this section; just like September 11, 2001, the day is bright, and the night remains bright as well owing to the fire that sustains its luminescence. But this light is not what sustains life:

My friend the earth is bitter; I think
sunlight has failed her.
Bitter or weary, it is hard to say.

Between herself and the sun,
something has ended.
She wants, now, to be left alone ... (VI: 4–9)

Section VI is decidedly anti-pastoral: the earth wants to be left alone, and the sun becomes distant. If one major source of solace in the pastoral elegy is its simulation of immortality through cyclicality of seasons—flowers may die, but they return the following spring—the failure of sunlight, which is no longer giving, suggestively denies this fertility that underlies prospects of pastoral consolation: the earth becomes an emblem of "bitter disgrace, coldness and barrenness" (VI: 19). There remains beauty in the world—the moon "is beautiful tonight" (VI: 21)—but while section III shows how beauty yields pleasure, in section VI beauty is infused with no redemptive capacity. Whether through bitterness or weariness, consolation becomes impossible as the earth—the one left with the imprint of the fire—becomes distant and indifferent.

"October" moves through its own stages of grief, which can be characterized as follows: questions with no answers; illusions of solace that ironically foster one's awareness of the irreversibility of the change; pleasant beauty that provides temporary reprieve; the tabooization and unspeakability that set in, as time dulls and distances trauma; silence that follows the unspeakable; and the distance that incapacitates mourning processes. Just as proper healing becomes problematic once scar tissues are formed and the changes become permanent, mourning comes to be seen as unnatural and obsolete as the time gap between the disaster and the present widens. In "Averno," a poem placed in the second half of *Averno*, Glück revisits the fire incident and exposes the aggravation of belated mourning: "the earth / didn't know how to mourn, that it would change instead. / And then go on existing without him" (V: 31–33).[75] As suggested by Tennyson's *In Memoriam*, "change" is a way of making "strange"; as the world changes and the loss becomes increasingly more inaccessible, mourning becomes a more contested process. Between the desire for proper mourning and the disavowal of artifice, traumas become unspeakable. The elegiac poetics of equivocation creates a method of speaking in the face of this difficulty of mourning—a method, that is, of speaking under the dominion of the unspeakable. In the process of equivocation, original urges are transformed and extinguished as much as they are given a shape. Equivocation may be non-redemptive, like the beauty of the moon above the cold and barren earth. Nonetheless, it is one of the few avenues left for contemporary elegists to enact authenticity. The salve of post-9/11 poetry derives not so much from the content of its message but rather from the air of verity that it assumes through its personal and ethical engagement with the disappearing loss.

NOTES

1. William Heyen, "Preface," in *September 11, 2001: American Writers Respond*, ed. William Heyen (Silver Spring: Etruscan Press, 2002), xi.

2. Michael Waters, "Fork and Spoon," in *September 11, 2001: American Writers Respond*, ed. William Heyen (Silver Spring: Etruscan Press, 2002), 390.

3. Dennis Loy Johnson and Valerie Merians, "Foreword," in *Poetry after 9/11: An Anthology of New York Poets*, ed. Dennis Loy Johnson and Valerie Merians (Brooklyn: Melville House, 2002), ix.

4. Philip Metres, "Beyond Grief and Grievances: The Poetry of 9/11 and Its Aftermath," *Poetry Foundation*, September 7, 2011, https://www.poetryfoundation.org/features/articles/detail/69737.

5. Laurence Goldstein, "The Response of American Poets to 9/11: A Provisional Report," *Michigan Quarterly Review* 48, no. 1 (Winter 2009), http://hdl.handle.net/2027/spo.act2080.0048.108.

6. Ulrich Baer, *110 Stories: New York Writes after September 11* (New York: New York University Press, 2002), 2.

7. Waters, "Fork and Spoon," 390.

8. Robert Pinsky, "Enormity and the Human Voice," in *September 11, 2001: American Writers Respond*, ed. William Heyen (Silver Spring: Etruscan Press, 2002), 304.

9. Lin Knutson, "Poetic Responses to 9/11 and Adrienne Rich's *The School Among the Ruins*," in *Representing 9/11: Trauma, Ideology, and Nationalism in Literature, Film, and Television*, ed. Paul Petrovic (Lanham: Rowman & Littlefield, 2015), 187.

10. Goldstein, "The Response of American Poets to 9/11."

11. Don DeLillo, *Falling Man: A Novel* (New York: Scribner, 2007), 42.

12. Sascha Pöhlmann, *Future-Founding Poetry: Topographies of Beginnings from Whitman to the Twenty-First Century* (Suffolk: Boydell & Brewer, 2015), 305.

13. Martha Nussbaum, *The Therapy of Desire: Theory and Practice in Hellenistic Ethics* (Princeton: Princeton University Press, 1994), 51.

14. Fredrik Svenaeus, *The Hermeneutics of Medicine and the Phenomenology of Health: Steps Towards a Philosophy of Medical Practice* (Berlin: Springer Science & Business Media, 2013), 15. Svenaeus cites Pedro Lain Entralgo, *The Therapy of the Word in Classical Antiquity*, ed. L. J. Rather and J. M. Sharp (New Haven: Yale University Press, 1970).

15. Ian Hamilton, *Robert Lowell: A Biography* (New York: Faber & Faber, 1982), 220.

16. W. D. Snodgrass and Hilary Holladay, "The Original Confessional Poet Tells All," *Poetry Foundation*, January 14, 2009, https://www.poetryfoundation.org/features/articles/detail/69067.

17. Beatrice Berg, "Oh, I Was Very Sick," *New York Times*, November 9, 1969.

18. Ernest Smith, "Confessional Poetry," in *American Poets and Poetry: From the Colonial Era to the Present*, ed. Jeffrey Gray et al. (Santa Barbara: Greenwood, 2015), 120.

19. Karen A. Baikie and Kay Wilhelm, "Emotional and Physical Health Benefits of Expressive Writing," *Advances in Psychiatric Treatment* 11, no. 5 (September 2005): 338–46.

20. James W. Pennebaker and Sandra K. Beall, "Confronting a Traumatic Event: Toward an Understanding of Inhibition and Disease," *Journal of Abnormal Psychology* 95, no. 3 (August 1986): 280.

21. William Heyen, "The Dragonfly," in *September 11, 2001: American Writers Respond*, ed. William Heyen (Silver Spring: Etruscan Press, 2002), 182.

22. James Longenbach, "A Reason for Keeping Silent?" in *September 11, 2001: American Writers Respond*, ed. William Heyen (Silver Spring: Etruscan Press, 2002), 250.

23. William Butler Yeats, "On Being Asked for a War Poem," in *The Collected Poems of W. B. Yeats*, Revised Second Edition, ed. Richard J. Finneran (New York: Simon & Schuster, 1996), 155–56.

24. John Lyon, "War, Politics, and Disappearing Poetry: Auden, Yeats, Empson," in *The Oxford Handbook of British and Irish War Poetry*, ed. Tim Kendall (Oxford: Oxford University Press, 2007), 288.

25. Heather Dubrow, *The Challenges of Orpheus: Lyric Poetry and Early Modern England* (Baltimore: Johns Hopkins University Press, 2008), 6. Transhistoricity of the lyric is a contested idea, see Gillian White, *Lyric Shame: The "Lyric" Subject of Contemporary American Poetry* (Cambridge: Harvard University Press, 2014), 273.

26. This eschewing of the appearance of the political may explain the uneven reception of anthologies such as *Poets Against the War*, ed. Sam Hamill (New York: Nation Books, 2003), a collection of anti-war poems, many of which were newly composed in protest against the imminent bombing and invasion of Iraq. The collection, which evolved from the aftermath of a canceled White House poetry symposium, was seen to be an explicit attempt—more so than other anthologies such as *September 11, 2001: American Writers Respond* or *Poetry after 9/11*, which, while they contain political aesthetics, were not directly linked to a particular political event or figure—to politicize poetry into public anti-war sentiment.

27. Michael Palmer, "'Dear Lexicon': Interview with David Levi-Strauss and B. Hollander," *Acts* 2, no. 1 (1986): 14, cited in Patrick Pritchett, "How to Write Poetry after Auschwitz: The Burnt Book of Michael Palmer," *Journal of Modern Literature* 37, no. 3 (Spring 2014): 129.

28. Heyen, "Preface," xi.

29. Theodor Adorno, *Can One Live after Auschwitz?: A Philosophical Reader*, ed. Rolf Tiedemann (Stanford: Stanford University Press, 2003), xv, xvi.

30. Robert Kaufman, "Poetry after 'Poetry after Auschwitz,'" in *Art and Aesthetics after Adorno*, ed. Anthony J. Cascardi (Berkeley: Townsend Humanities Center/University of California Press, 2010), 117.

31. Lyn Hejinian, *The Language of Inquiry* (Berkeley: University of California Press, 2000), 325.

32. Alicia Ostriker, "The Window, at the Moment of Flame," in *September 11, 2001: American Writers Respond*, ed. William Heyen (Silver Spring: Etruscan Press, 2002), 295.

33. Quoted in Richard Gray, *After the Fall: American Literature Since 9/11* (Malden: Wiley-Blackwell, 2011), 1.

34. W. S. Merwin, "To the Words," in *September 11, 2001: American Writers Respond*, ed. William Heyen (Silver Spring: Etruscan Press, 2002), 3.

35. For a general discussion on the failure of language after 9/11, see Gray, *After the Fall*, 1–19.

36. Philip Sidney, "The Defence of Poesy," in *Sir Philip Sidney*, ed. Katherine Duncan-Jones (Oxford: Oxford University Press, 1989), 217.

37. Paul Ricoeur, *The Rule of Metaphor: Multi-disciplinary Studies of the Creation of Meaning in Language*, trans. Robert Czerny et al. (Toronto: University of Toronto Press, 1977), 243–46.

38. Nikki Moustaki, "How to Write a Poem after September 11th," in *Poetry after 9/11: An Anthology of New York Poets*, ed. Dennis Loy Johnson and Valerie Merians (Brooklyn: Melville House, 2002), 95–96.

39. Kevin Flynn and Jim Dwyer, "Falling Bodies, a 9/11 Image Etched in Pain," *New York Times*, September 10, 2004, http://www.nytimes.com/2004/09/10/nyregion/nyregionspecial2/falling-bodies-a-911-image-etched-in-pain.html?_r=0.

40. Susie Linfield, "Jumpers," *New York Magazine*, August 27, 2011, http://nymag.com/news/9-11/10th-anniversary/jumpers/.

41. Laura Frost, "Still Life: 9/11's Falling Bodies," in *Literature after 9/11*, ed. Ann Keniston and Jeanne Follansbee Quinn (New York: Routledge, 2013), 180.

42. National Commission on Terrorist Attacks upon the United States (Thomas H. Kean and Lee Hamilton), *The 9/11 Commission Report: Final Report of the National Commission on Terrorist Attacks Upon the United States* (Washington, DC, 2004), 296.

43. Kean and Hamilton, *The 9/11 Commission Report*, 300.

44. Kean and Hamilton, *The 9/11 Commission Report*, 316.

45. According to the present writer's unofficial count.

46. Kean and Hamilton, *The 9/11 Commission Report*, 290.

47. X. J. Kennedy, "September Twelfth, 2001," in *September 11, 2001: American Writers Respond*, ed. William Heyen (Silver Spring: Etruscan Press, 2002), 221.

48. Gail Griffin, "How It Comes," in *September 11, 2001: American Writers Respond*, ed. William Heyen (Silver Spring: Etruscan Press, 2002), 161.

49. Miranda Beeson, "Flight," in *Poetry after 9/11: An Anthology of New York Poets*, ed. Dennis Loy Johnson and Valerie Merians (Brooklyn: Melville House, 2002), 6.

50. Diane Seuss, "Falling Man," in *September 11, 2001: American Writers Respond*, ed. William Heyen (Silver Spring: Etruscan Press, 2002), 350.

51. Kimiko Hahn, "Her Very Eyes," in *September 11, 2001: American Writers Respond,* , ed. William Heyen (Silver Spring: Etruscan Press, 2002), 165.

52. Benjamin, "On Some Motifs in Baudelaire," 317, 319.

53. Goldstein, "The Response of American Poets to 9/11."

54. Wisława Szymborska, "Photograph from September 11," in *Map: Collected and Last Poems*, trans. Clare Cavanagh and Stanisław Barańczak (Boston: Houghton Mifflin, 2015), 344.

55. Eva Badowska, "'My Poet's Junk': Wisława Szymborska in Retrospect," *Parnassus: Poetry in Review* 28, no. 1/2 (2005): 167.

56. George Lakoff and Mark Johnson, *Metaphors We Live By* (Chicago: University of Chicago Press, 1980), 278.

57. Ewa Kowal, *The "Image-Event" in the Early Post-9/11 Novel: Literary Representations of Terror after September 11, 2001* (Krakow: Jagiellonian University Press, 2012), 118–20.

58. R. Clifton Spargo, "The Contemporary Anti-Elegy," in *The Oxford Handbook of the Elegy*, ed. Karen Weisman (Oxford: Oxford University Press, 2010), 415.

59. Ann Keniston, "'Balm after Violence': Louise Glück's *Averno*," *The Kenyon Review* 30, no. 4 (Fall 2008): 178.

60. Goldstein, "The Response of American Poets to 9/11."

61. Keniston, "Balm after Violence," 179.

62. Uta Gosmann, "Psychoanalyzing Persephone: Louise Glück's *Averno*," *Modern Psychoanalysis* 35, no. 2 (2010): 220. The summary of the myth is quoted in full from the Gossman article, in recognition of her original research citing her conversation with Glück; in this conversation, Glück reportedly explained that she wrote about Persephone based on the memories she retained from *D'Aulaires' Book of Greek Myths*, which she read as a child.

63. Elizabeth Dodd, *The Veiled Mirror and the Woman Poet: H.D., Louise Bogan, Elizabeth Bishop, and Louise Glück* (Columbia: University of Missouri Press, 1992), 1.

64. Uta Gosmann, *Poetic Memory: The Forgotten Self in Plath, Howe, Hinsey, and Glück* (Madison: Farleigh Dickinson University Press, 2012), 181. Gossman further details the influence of psychoanalysis on Glück's thinking and writing on pages 181–82.

65. Anna Thiemann, *Rewriting the American Soul: Trauma, Neuroscience and the Contemporary Literary Imagination* (New York: Routledge, 2018), 4: "a blow to the psyche activates previous traumas and early identity-forming experiences, which enter into consciousness and determine how the current event is perceived and remembered."

66. Michelle Balaev, "Trends in Literary Trauma Theory," *Mosaic* 41, no. 2 (June 2008): 151.

67. Louise Glück, *American Originality: Essays on Poetry* (New York: Farrar, Straus and Giroux, 2017), 58: "a work of art can make a kind of mantra: by giving form to devastation, the poem rescues the reader from a darkness without shape or gravity; it is an island in a free fall; it becomes his companion in grief, his rescuer, a proof that suffering can be made somehow to yield meaning." This act of "giving form to devastation" is one of the critical aspects of *Averno*.

68. Louise Glück, "The Night Migrations," in *Averno* (New York: Farrar, Straus and Giroux, 2006), 1.

69. Critics speculate that this Frank refers to Frank Bidart (Daniel Morris, *The Poetry of Louise Glück: A Thematic Introduction* [Columbia: University of Missouri Press, 2006], 11).

70. Glück, "October," *Averno*, 5.

71. Iain Twiddy, *Pastoral Elegy in Contemporary British and Irish Poetry* (London: Continuum, 2012), 5.

72. Al Poulin Jr., ed., *Contemporary American Poetry* (Boston: Houghton Mifflin, 1996), 460.

73. Mark Strand, "A Conversation with Mark Strand," *Ohio Review* 13, no. 2 (1972): 58.

74. Jonathan Holden, "'Affected Naturalness' and the Poetry of Sensibility," *College English* 41, no. 4 (December 1979): 404–6.

75. Glück, "Averno," *Averno*, 69.

Conclusion & Afterword
Lost Loss beyond American Elegiac Poetry

This book is a story of "oddball" elegiac poetry that does not neatly fit conventional thoughts about the genre. The modern and contemporary American poems from Stevens to post-9/11 studied in this book uncover and examine various forms of subtle, unacknowledged, or unconscious losses, which are collectively referred to as "lost loss." These poems do not necessarily involve object-losses, but they are evidence of continued, reorganizational workings of the mind, either before, during, after, or long after a dispossessory incident—or sometimes even in the absence of one—where the loss itself comes to feel inaccessible and "lost."

Lost loss is born of relational, temporal, and cognitive complications in privative experiences. Most reductively speaking, this book is about two variables: distance and gap. The magnitude of one's grief fluctuates based on relational proximity: the death of someone intimate to the griever; of someone who is relationally distant; of someone who is not reliably identified; loss in the recent past; in the distant past; in the future, in one's imagination. The social recognition of those ties, or lack thereof, also impacts one's grief. Beyond relational distance, complications can also arise from uncertainties in one's own perception about what has actually been lost. Sometimes, one finds out more about the deceased after their death—aspects of their personal history, of their character, of their significance to one's life. These perceptual gaps make us wonder just how inaccessible people can be even prior to their death. However ambivalent or faint, the effects of these tenuous dispossessions exist, and their sense of amorphous privation emerges in unpredictable, unanticipated, and unrecognizable forms.

One of the challenges of this project has been to find a suitable methodology for studying a phenomenon that eludes cognition and resists classification. Loss refers to an experience that is premised upon the presence of things or people that we know exists; lost loss—what does it mean, to "lose" loss?—comes with additional layers of complexity. Psychoanalytic apparatuses offer proximate models to analyze hidden and transient phenomena, but they are bound to be, by themselves, insufficient—not only because the approach "has the effect of distancing" elegy from politics and society,[1] but also because there is a nuanced difference between the unconscious and the unaware. Likewise, historicism offers partial answers, since lost loss is not entirely inherent or locatable in a particular cultural moment; the phenomenon is more visible in modernity but not restricted to it. Also, while poetry of lost loss engages with the counter-traditions of elegiac literature, where the orthodoxy has historically been associated with instructive rather than intuitive grief—scholars have debated the gender socialization aspects of mourning, and intuitive grief has been seen to hold a degree of affinity with how women tend to grieve[2]—the representation of women poets and gender theories here may overlap with but does not qualify as gender studies. As the present project moved forward, the methodology began to coalesce into a strategy that aligns loosely with new formalism: a term defined as a combination of close reading with broader critical approaches and contexts,[3] offering reflection upon points of intersection with diverse theoretical approaches ranging from New Criticism to Marxist criticism.[4] New formalism absorbs varying aggregates of disparate schools of theories, and the particular blend of those employed by scholars differs depending on their subjects and their training. When a phenomenon eludes any one set of theories, research turns omnivorous. The risk of such an undertaking is that it may come across as a patchwork, not sufficiently psychoanalytic, historicist, or scientific. Where this project is reliably rooted is the text; in the gaps of existing critical theories, it returns to formalist close reading, albeit a kind that not so much looks inward to a well-wrought urn but rather ravages outward to collect variegated feathers.[5] Although the moral of the story of "The Bird in Borrowed Feathers" has conventionally been understood as an admonition against dressing above one's station, it is an apt emblem for new formalism, a generalist stance that encompasses all because it does not "advocate for any particular theory, method, or scholarly practice."[6]

The findings of this book's enterprise can be summarized as follows: in the Introduction, the book defines its main concept, "lost loss," a condition in which a specific loss is either absent, elusory, or inaccessible, or has become a stand-in or screen for some other unidentifiable dispossession. Based on this formulation, Wallace Stevens's elegiac poetry of the later period uncovers that lost loss is an uncomfortable condition that triggers fiction-making; these fictions overwrite the void, while still maintaining an awareness of their own fictiveness to reconcile belief and disbelief in their invented narratives. In Sylvia Plath's poems of 1963, lost loss manifests in the form of dysthymia, a less forceful but pervasive version of melancholia, highlighting its chronicity in the face of the ambiguity of loss. Elizabeth Bishop's *Geography III* details how lost loss engenders a desire to "un-lose" loss, finding or forging relations in their vacuum whereby the act of writing creates a synthesized space between remembering and forgetting. Sharon Olds's Public sequence in *The Dead and the Living* suggests that one can be ethically empathic toward the suffering of others who are temporally and geographically inaccessible; humanitarianism is refashioned through the imagined connection with the distant other, based on the engagement-detachment apparatus of one's principled compassion. Finally, post-9/11 poetry elucidates the mechanism of lost loss, through which even recent disasters are left behind in a briefer period of time, consigned to the precarious memory space where they are both remembered and forgotten. As examined throughout the book, the concept of "lost loss" is formulated as a way to interpret or make sense of the unexplainable melancholy of the modern and contemporary elegiac poetry. The vagueness or disappearance of the object-loss generates a less acute but chronic disconsolation that persists without clear resolution.

What this book hopes to accomplish is to create a language to speak of ambiguous and ambivalent dispossessions. Because of its amorphous nature, lost loss often ends up unrecognized or misnamed. When loss itself becomes inaccessible, this privation emerges through fiction-making, which is the real project of elegiac literature: when we lose something, we often do not know the full extent of what has actually been lost, and this unknowing necessitates a particular cognitive working-through, of which elegiac poetry models the expressive trace. Elegiac artifices are constructed in response to psychological needs. By becoming meta-aware of this mechanism of the human mind, we may profitably invent more helpful fictions and attenuate less helpful ones, rather than merely debunking previous fictive consolations as "false surmises." While it is unfruitful to try to revive defunct consolatory narratives and to inveigle us into embracing them once again, the realization that a fiction aware of its own fictitiousness can temporarily soothe grievers to get through difficult times may encourage readers as well as writers to move beyond the dichotomy of belief or skepticism. That is to say, whether reading Seamus Heaney's fictive conviction that the burden bequeathed by one's parents can "always be reimagined,"[7] or Amy Clampitt's fancifully sanguine representation of death as one where "the spirit might . . . walk on air,"[8] one would not need to react to these imaginings with disbelief; rather, one can know them to be fiction and still choose to believe them.

Beyond defining the phenomenon of lost loss through modern and contemporary American elegiac poetry, I conclude this book by pointing to its additional stakes: the implications and applicability of its theoretical concepts beyond the immediate confines of elegy studies, both within and outside of literary studies. Within literary studies, there are several subgenres that could be fruitfully examined through the lens of these theories. Two immediately come to mind: poetry of witness and confessional poetry. There is a reason that many of the poets and poems discussed in this book are drawn from these traditions. These two subgenres have close affinity to the elegiac sentiments of the poetry of lost loss. In "Little Gidding," T. S. Eliot suggests that "every poem" is an "epitaph"[9]—so far as "it marks an initiatory moment, pronounces an elegy upon a past artistic self, and announces rebirth of the artist as a poet."[10] In this sense, some aspects of the theories of elegiac poetry are imminently transferable to many other genres of literature.[11] In particular, however, poetry of witness and confessional poetry are ripe targets for the theories of lost loss and dysthymia because of their predispositions.

First, on poetry of witness: in *Precarious Life*, Judith Butler writes on exclusionary consolatory fictions in commemorative practices and rituals, and asserts that these acts are predicated upon the distinction between "grievable" and "non-grievable" lives. Death happens equally, both to those whose lives have been deemed meaningful and to those whose lives have never been acknowledged in the same way. The latter, however, cannot be fully worked through as loss; those people "cannot be mourned because they are always already lost or, rather, never 'were.'"[12] Butler's passage suggests that lost loss can occur at a plainly conscious and social level, through political, cultural, or journalistic manipulations, by design or otherwise.

Writers both in the past and in the present have written to record socially excluded losses. In the contemporary American poetry context, Carolyn Forché's *The Angel of History* stands as one of the landmarks of this effort. In the Notes to the volume, Forché writes the following:

> *The Angel of History* is not about experiences. It is for me the opening of a wound, the muffling and silence of a decade, and it is also a gathering of utterances that have lifted away from the earth and wrapped it in a weather of risen words. These utterances issue from my own encounter with the events of this century but do not represent "it." The first-person, free-verse, lyric-narrative poem of my earlier years has given way to a work which has desired its own bodying forth: polyphonic, broken, haunted, and in ruins, with no possibility of restoration.[13]

Poetry of witness has an affinity to elegiac poetry in that both are literatures of remembrance. What is particularly striking about the above passage is

Forché's insistent use of words like "muffling" and "silence": it communicates a sense of conviction that these utterances had been suppressed, and would remain so, if not for her poetry. What she writes of—"the unlit house / with its breathless windows," the hallucinatory image of a "wooden teahouse / and the corpses of those who slept in it" where no such thing actually exists, or "the child" who "seems . . . as if he had not yet crossed into the world"[14]— are phantasmal hauntings of things that are lost before the possibility of loss and are left beyond restoration. The multiplicity of psychic voices, the hauntings, redemption of things that are forsaken without the possibility of recovery—these are elements that poetry of witness shares with poetry of lost loss: poems of witness present themselves as observers of phantoms, whose voices are coming from what Abraham and Torok call the psychic "crypt" where illegal burials have blotted out the facts of loss. Poetry of witness is driven by the anxiety of lost loss, much as is the case of Bishop's sublimational poetics.

The previously cited Eliot quote—every poem is an epitaph—also recalls confessional poetry, whose chief mechanism is the transformation of the past self into the art form of the present. Confessional poetry is predicated on the death of the biographical self as it is usurped by the artistic self. The act of speaking about the self opens up a gap between the speaking I and the spoken-about I, and this phenomenon is elegiac because it involves a suppression, effacement, or burial of one by the other. Post-confessional poetry assumes that any confession is a fictive narrative; in "Containing Multitudes," David Graham and Kate Sontag comment on Ted Hughes's *Birthday Letters* that the "truth is, strictly speaking, both Hughes's and Plath's poetic versions of their marital problems are fictions . . . . Lyrics have always entangled artifice with confession."[15] The self-loss occurs on two levels: before even the loss is effected by the artistic self's dismantling of the biographical self, this loss is itself deprived, because the biographical self had already been supplanted by its fictionalized version—just as Crusoe's island, left unrediscovered, was obliterated by inaccurate accounts. If loss is inscribed on confessional poetry through the de-facement of autobiography, a loss of loss is consciously ingrained in post-confessional poetry through its awareness of the fictionalization of autobiography.

While the focus of this book is the modern and contemporary period, the transhistoricity of lost loss is evident from the premodern canonical poems, as explored in the Introduction. Transhistorical concepts often entail transnational potentials. This potentiality suggests that the concept of lost loss may be applicable to other national literatures beyond English literature. Just to name a few examples, Charles Baudelaire's causeless melancholia in his "Spleen" poems deserves attention as a precursor of elegiac dysthymia. Heinrich Heine's ethos of "I know not what ails me" points to the difficulty of locating the source of anguish as a cultural condition that has persisted since the nineteenth century. When discussing Sappho's poetry, one cannot go without mentioning that much of her work was actually itself lost, as Anne Carson's translation highlights;[16] the critical implication is that what we see of Sappho's translations is a wish for wholeness that we crave in its absence. Rainer Maria Rilke's poems like "A Roman Sarcophagus" explore ancient loss that requires a mythological story, reminiscent of Stevens's "The Owl in the Sarcophagus." Murano Shiro's oeuvre offers another embodiment of double-loss; in many of his poems, death is taken away from living things, in the sense that they have already been stripped of their individuality and cannot, therefore, be any more "lost." The list may go on, but these are some examples of poets and their works beyond English literature that resonate with the theme of lost loss.

As one specific representative case, Hagiwara Sakutaro's "An Undying Octopus" looms emblematic. This prose poem depicts a starved octopus in the fish tank at an aquarium. In the shadows of underwater rocks, wan lights from the pale ceiling waver like fog. This bleak fish tank has been forgotten, and only the stale seawater reflects the dusty sunlight. The octopus is not dead—it is just hidden—and when it awakes, it endures hunger in the forgotten tank because no one knows it exists and therefore no one feeds it. In the extremity of hunger, the octopus eats one of its own legs, then another. When all its limbs are gone, it reverses its body and eats parts of its innards, bit by bit, until it has eaten all of itself: the skin, the spine, the intestines. One morning, a guard comes and sees the opaque fish tank, empty now save for some seaweed wavering in the same seawater: no living things. The octopus is gone, despite the fact that it still lives in that tank, in half-eternity, as an incarnation of a sense of irresolvable loss.[17]

The poem invites to be read as an allegory of phantasmal haunting: the death of the octopus had already been "lost" by means of oblivion, for the fact that its existence had been forgotten, and its death never registered in anyone's consciousness. Because its demise is never recognized in anyone's perceptual universe, the octopus continues to haunt, as something that is neither alive nor dead, as a thing that embodies irresolution. We are left uncertain whether to characterize the octopus as lost, missing, or absent, and this irrecognition signifies its indeterminate, phantomatic presence.

The drive of the poem has in its roots both a desire to be a witness to this lost loss and a hope to exorcize this phantasmal creature; paradoxically, the act of recording the missing octopus attenuates grief and dissipates the sense of privation, postponing any closure for half-eternity. Hagiwara's poem makes one wonder if the secret objective of the poetry of lost loss may actually be to ward off the phantoms by cataloging the loss of object-loss and giving them a form, so as to calm the raging wraiths and to help them disperse. Remembering is painful; forgetting triggers haunting. The act of recording proves to be the third space of ambiguous mourning, diverging from either remembering or forgetting.

The theory of lost loss can have relevance beyond literary studies, in fields ranging from social psychology, critical race studies, to migration studies. Theories that are central to this book, such as Pauline Boss's ambiguous loss and Nicholas Abraham and Maria Torok's introjection and incorporation, have been implicated in the understanding of the psychology of immigration: the former elucidates the psychological impact of familial disruptions that occur as a result of migration; the latter offers a model of coping with traumas that inhere in the process of transitions and cultural assimilations.[18] Anne Anlin Cheng suggests that melancholia presents a particularly apt paradigm for clarifying the activity and components of racialization in the United States; racialization is enacted and fortified by the spectral drama of the ghostly emptiness of a lost "other." American idealism and its projected self-image as a nation of immigrants have contributed to the historical oscillation between the inclusion and exclusion of the unassimilable racial other; as a result, immigrants—who have historically tended to be classified into the category of the "racial other"—are both present in and lost to the heart of the national narrative.[19] This ambiguous status complicates the sense of loss sustained by immigrants: their grief is at times acknowledged, at other times mythologized, and, on yet other occasions, hidden, denied, or made inaccessible.

In a 2017 anthology *Resist Much / Obey Little: Inaugural Poems to the Resistance*, the poet-activist Margaret Randall contributes a poem entitled "The Morning After." The pretext of the poem is that it is set on the morning after the 2016 U.S. Presidential Election. The poem starts ominously with an image of a polar bear, the symbol of an impending planetary catastrophe that climate change is forecasted to bring about: "It's the morning after and the polar bear / licks blood / from his foot's white fur" (1–3). Repeating the phrase "It's the morning after," the lyric-speaker catalogs the profiles of people whose lives will be upended by this election, and one of those is a girl named Maia, presumed to be from an immigrant family:

Six-year-old Maia tells her mother *Wake me*
when Hillary wins. The next morning
she is afraid to go to school:

If we speak Spanish in the street,
she wants to know,
will they send us away?   (25–30)[20]

    The feeling of shame that immigrants feel about their native language is a common enough experience, especially if they live in a community that values assimilation; they hesitate to speak the language in public, for the fear of reinforcing their self-image as a marginalized "other"—an identity that they prefer to keep at arm's length, in a fit of self-rejection seen in the famous doll test, in which minority children tended to show a preference toward a white doll with yellow hair.[21] Nevertheless, whether or not to speak one's native language in public usually registers in one's mind as a choice; one is not forced by anything other than one's psychological inhibitions. As a result, immigrants often fail to recognize that it is a form of deprivation. This irrecognition triggers an amorphous dejection. In the case of Randall's poem, however, shame is not the only source of this despondency: it is compounded by the threat of deportation. Given the prospect of the loss of one's place in the country that one regards as home, the melancholy of marginalization, as represented by linguistic privation, feels sufficiently trivial that it gets consigned to one's sub-consciousness. The fear of home loss dwarfs all other concerns, leaving language loss and other unfelt deprivations unacknowledged, despite their compounding effect.

    This immigrant girl's plight is acknowledged by Randall's poem; it is not the case that her voice is left unrepresented. But in today's climate, the heart of the debate distills into the question of whose loss counts more. The ideal solution may be to echo Randall's poem, to listen "to the heartland's threatened factory" (38), and to declare that only "together can we resist" (45), in a call for national unity; the implication is that everyone's pain counts. If, however, the issue is complicated by relative deprivation, and if it has to be that when one group's suffering garners attention it necessarily obscures that of other groups—if the process of national grieving has to be a zero-sum game in a grand experiment of a multicultural nation like the United States, at a time in history when it has proved to itself that it is not yet ready to be a post-identity society—then a system of mutual restitution—to "un-lose" loss, as Bishop does in "Poem"—may be one potentially viable path. As the findings in the previous chapters suggest, recognition, understanding, and even imagining can help blunt the dysthymia of denied grief. The pain of loss intensifies in the absence of acknowledgment; lost loss confounds mourning, but a delayed relief is still more desirable than no relief at all. Whatever the case, without an understanding of how unacknowledged loss affects us, the prospect of remedy would continue to feel elusive.

Lost loss, when unrecognized and unprocessed, can have profound personal and social impacts that remain unnoticed or misinterpreted. Loss has been known to be a powerful driving force behind human behavior, and when we fail to recognize what privation is motivating us, it impedes an understanding of our own actions. One reference point in this contention is the theory of the transmission of intergenerational trauma. In the Editor's Notes preceding a chapter in Abraham and Torok's *The Shell and the Kernel* entitled "Secrets and Posterity: The Theory of the Transgenerational Phantom," Nicholas Rand notes that aspects of the idea of the phantom have the potential to illuminate the genesis of social institutions and may provide a new perspective for inquiring into the psychological roots of cultural patterns and political ideology.[22] Rand cites the example of neo-Nazi movements of the 1980s and 1990s in Germany and elsewhere, which appealed to adolescents who obviously had no direct contact with wartime Nazi reality. This phenomenon not only points to the possibility of the generational inheritance of cultural trauma but also reveals how the falsification, disregard, or shaming and silencing of past catastrophes can become a breeding ground for the phantomatic return of a defunct ideology, at the level of individuals, families, communities, and possibly even the entire nation. While there is no question that the collective body politic of Nazism has rightfully been, and should continue to be, discredited and censured, one wonders, when one surveys the present landscape and notices the atavistic resurgence of authoritarian ethno-nationalism in many nations—whether it is the Austrian Freedom Party, Brexit, France's Front National, the neo-fascism in Hungary, Japan's wartime-worshipping Nippon Kaigi, or the post–Civil Rights Movement resurgence of the popularity of the Confederate flag in the American South—if those are side effects of the improper burial of ungrievable ideologies. While these phenomena have complex causes, one of the commonalities among them is the sense of denied grief, the desire to regain what is perceived to have been dispossessed, which inevitably faces disapprobation because their grievances as victims have been regarded as misbegotten and the deprivations they speak of are mythologized and difficult to accept.[23] The legitimization of these ideologies is not a valid remedy, but an understanding of how inadequate processing of historical atrocities could haunt us in the future might prove instructive in mitigating these resurfacings.

Unacknowledged loss has profound effects that are not always easily predicted or deciphered. In connection to immigration and nationalism, the 2016 U.S. Presidential Election and its aftermath are hard to elide. The whole chain of events has an air of inevitability now, but back in 2015, not many people predicted that a candidate who had spent a lifetime in a family business with few civic obligations would assume the highest office in the most powerful nation in the world and continue to maintain a near impregnable block of support from roughly 40 percent of the nation. What is notable is that popular contemporaneous explanations for this denouement often entail an assortment of theories of loss, whether it is globalization and liberalism,[24] loss aversion,[25] risk-taking,[26] or relative deprivation.[27] The merits of these commentaries can be debated, but the receptions of works such as J. D. Vance's *Hillbilly Elegy: A Memoir of a Family and Culture in Crisis* and Arlie Russell Hochschild's *Strangers in Their Own Land: Anger and Mourning on the American Right* during the election year also corroborate the perception of alienation and deprivation among a segment of American society, where some members feel that their hardship is insufficiently recognized. Regardless of whether or not their sentiments are warranted, a sizable portion of the electorate was sufficiently captivated by the narratives of national decline and racial persecution to express a collective approbation of a figure whose prior political engagement had largely come as an advocate of nativist conspiracy theories.

Since this book is a literary analysis, it offers neither policy proposals nor explicit social remedies, but its theoretical findings shed light on the current climate of imagined loss, fiction-belief, and nostalgia, which all surface as symptoms when one feels that one's privations are unrecognized. The underacknowledged loss of the yesteryear that has surfaced in recent years may be the status threat felt by majority group members, who see themselves as forgotten men and women. But the social changes that triggered the push for equality and, consequently, the aforementioned relative deprivation—the civil rights movement, women's liberation, and advocacy for social justice and multiculturalist inclusivity—were also the results of the prior repression of and disregard for those concerns as well. And looking toward the future, one can foresee how the present COVID-19 crisis may turn into a national trauma in which irrecognitions foment unacknowledged psychological disquietude, whether it derives from its massive scale of deaths, various barriers that inhibit our customary mourning practices, disrupted grief, or other less-discussed social or personal deprivations. These are the reasons that the literary enterprise of imagining voices of the voiceless is critical. As we move away from the present moment, we may see more clearly that current unsettlements are manifestations of the invisible loss of the previous era, and that it is instructive to search beneath those for present suppressions and irrecognitions that turn into brewing grounds for future grievances.

The purpose of literature, as has often been said, is to give voice to what does not yet have a voice. The project of this book is to salvage and collect the tentative, vague, attenuated expressive traces of elusive lost loss in modern and contemporary elegiac poetry, for, if not for these expressions that give shape to it, it would be left unnoticed and unrecognized.

What this book uncovers are the remnants of losses that are themselves lost, either to incomprehension—like that of the child-speaker in "First Death in Nova Scotia"—to mythologization—like "The Owl in the Sarcophagus" and its additional layers of loss hidden in the sarcophagus—to stupefaction—like the totalizing privation of "Edge"—to relational distance—like the unnamed girl in "Photograph of the Girl"—or to traumatic oblivion—like the September that is simultaneously erased and preserved in "October."

In the dismal catastrophe of reality, one finds a way to live in the world of imagination: the "fiction" of loss is a product of this human mechanism that is activated when one detects a prospect of lost loss. While I do not advocate for an uncritical embracement of falsehoods—for instance, peddling alternative facts as a type of truth to unsuspecting or unprincipled audiences should be considered problematic, and there is a definitive difference between soothing oneself with a personal contrivance and deceiving others with socially engineered untruths—the present book recognizes fiction as a necessity under specific conditions; oftentimes, one has no choice but to find room for fancies, as a provisional safe space apart from one's recognition of the reality of irrevocable loss. The goal of this study is neither to fetishize fiction, melancholia, or mourning, nor to negate them; rather, the aim is to comprehend their mechanisms, for understanding—the constructionist, fiction-making beings that we are—has its own value.

It is a truism that understanding blunts the force of pain; a pain one comprehends is somehow less stressful than a pain one cannot make sense of. This mental condition might be described as a type of intellectual acquiescence, a state of expediency that places itself in between acceptance and resignation: it is neither a state of acceptance in the sense of the Kübler-Ross model,[28] nor a state of resignation in the sense of a fatalistic concession, the act of giving up, the signing over of one's soul, in passivity.[29] While completing this book, I could not escape the imperative to reflect on my own experience, which I disclose with a certain bashfulness arising from the cultural ambivalence over mixing the academic and the personal. On one bright summer day in August 2012, my father suffered a traumatic brain injury as a result of a car accident that nearly claimed his life. Because of its variability of symptoms, traumatic brain injuries can create ambiguities not unlike those of the personality death of, say, Alzheimer's disease, which is one example of a physically present but psychologically absent case of ambiguous loss.[30] What his injury entailed could be classified as personality change, accompanied by memory loss and diminished cognitive capabilities. On some days, he seemed not much different from what I had always known him to be; on other days, he seemed inorganic, an empty shell. Particularly considering that the brain represented one of his defining personality traits—it was, after all, his desire to study in graduate school that brought him to the United States three decades ago—its decline, at a time when he had just retired and was finally settling down to write a book that he had meant to write, was difficult to process. The result had been a daily confusion over how much of him still actually existed, until he ceased to be on another summery day in August, 2019. During those seven years of unknowing and thereafter, we create one consolatory fiction after another: perhaps, he had had a more peaceful retirement than he could have, being spared of all the quotidian nuisances that might have pained him otherwise; perhaps, these seven years had been more a gift than anything else, given that he could have died in 2012. Theories provide a level of clarity: we know that these stories that we tell ourselves to be fiction. But these are stories that we need in our living.

Poetry of lost loss, by virtue of the fact that the loss has itself been absented, necessitates that we create stories to fill that void. It makes explicit the optative elements in the work of grief and mourning. By becoming aware of the artifices involved in elegiac processes, one gains an ability to cultivate helpful stories, at the same time as discerning away unhelpful, manipulative ones; the process restores agency to the mourner. Poetry allows us to be conscious of the otherwise unconscious premise of lost loss, upon which we construct elegiac fictions.

NOTES

1. David Kennedy, *Elegy* (New York: Routledge, 2007), 104.
2. Mellor, "Anguish No Cessation Knows," 443, see Introduction, Note #19.
3. Connolly, *Grief & Meter*, 15.
4. Verena Theile and Linda Tredennick, *New Formalisms and Literary Theory* (Basingstoke: Palgrave Macmillan, 2013), 6.
5. The young William Shakespeare was once criticized by the elder playwright Robert Greene as being "an upstart crow, beautified with our feathers" (Robert Greene, *A Groat's-worth of Wit Bought with a Million of Repentance* [Public Domain: Ex-classics Project, 2009]), 19. The feather-borrowing crow can be seen to be emblematic of the new formalist methodology.
6. Marjorie Levinson, "What Is New Formalism?" *PMLA* 122, no. 2 (2007): 562.
7. Seamus Heaney, "The Settle Bed," in *Opened Ground: Poems, 1966–1996* (London: Faber and Faber, 1998), 321.
8. Amy Clampitt, "Beethoven, Opus 111," in *The Collected Poems of Amy Clampitt* (New York: Knopf, 1997), 50-52.
9. T. S. Eliot, "Little Gidding," in *The Complete Poems and Plays* (New York: Harcourt, Brace and World, 1971), 144.
10. Celeste Marguerite Schenck, *Mourning and Panegyric: The Poetics of Pastoral Ceremony* (University Park: The Pennsylvania State University Press, 1988), 1.

11. Paul Ricoeur, "Poetry and Possibility," in *A Ricoeur Reader: Reflection and Imagination*, ed. Mario J. Valdés (Toronto: University of Toronto Press, 1991), 452: Ricoeur claims that "the plot of a narrative is a creation of productive imagination which projects a world of its own" and that "the stories are no less poetry than versified literature." By extension, poetic theories can be applicable to other literary forms.

12. Butler, *Precarious Life*, 33.

13. Carolyn Forché, *The Angel of History* (New York: HarperCollins, 1994), 81.

14. The lines are respectively from "Elegy" (19–20), "The Garden Shukkei-en" (12–13), and "The Angel of History" (1).

15. David Graham and Kate Sontag, "Containing Multitudes," in *After Confession: Poetry as Autobiography*, ed. Kate Sontag and David Graham (St. Paul: Graywolf Press, 2001), 7–8.

16. Sappho, *If Not, Winter: Fragments of Sappho*, trans. Anne Carson (New York: Knopf, 2002), xi.

17. Hagiwara Sakutaro, "The Octopus That Does Not Die," in *Howling at the Moon: Poems and Prose of Hagiwara Sakutaro*, trans. Hiroaki Sato (Los Angeles: Green Integer, 2000), 281–82.

18. Anne Anlin Cheng, *The Melancholy of Race: Psychoanalysis, Assimilation, and Hidden Grief* (Oxford: Oxford University Press, 2001), 95–97, 219.

19. Cheng, *The Melancholy of Race*, 10. Cheng suggests that this racialization apparatus affects not only minorities but also dominant white identity, which "operates melancholically—as an elaborate identificatory system based on psychical and social consumption-and-denial." In this environment, those "who do not see the racial problem or those who call themselves nonideological are the most melancholic of all because in today's political climate, as Toni Morrison exclaims in *Playing in the Dark*, 'it requires hard work *not* to see'" (Cheng, *The Melancholy of Race*, 11, and Toni Morrison, *Playing in the Dark: Whiteness and the Literary Imagination* [Cambridge: Harvard University Press, 1992], 17).

20. Margaret Randall, "The Morning After," in *Resist Much / Obey Little: Inaugural Poems to the Resistance*, ed. Michael Boughn et al. (Brooklyn: Spuyten Duyvil, 2017), 516.

21. More details on the doll test can be found in Kenneth B. Clark, *Prejudice and Your Child* (Middletown: Wesleyan University Press, 1988), ix–x. The primary target of Clark's study was African American children, but the core findings of the study have largely been understood to apply to other ethnicities.

22. Nicholas Rand, "Editor's Note," in Abraham and Torok, *The Shell and the Kernel*, 169.

23. Mitch Berbrier, "The Victim Ideology of White Supremacists and White Separatists in the United States," *Sociological Focus* 33, no. 2 (May 2000): 179–86. The claim of victimhood and the attendant sense of unrepaired privation—real or imagined, in the present or in the future—are central to the rhetoric of many of the ethnonationalistic ideologies.

24. Edward Luce, *The Retreat of Western Liberalism* (New York: Grove Press, 2017), 9–11: Luce suggests that the election of Trump is a symptom, though not a cause, of the larger trend of "the age of convergence," in which the world is rapidly

becoming less poor but the West's middle classes are becoming "the biggest losers in a global economy." The implication is that the under-acknowledged loss sustained by the West's middle classes is destabilizing Western liberalism. There certainly are other factors that contributed to the 2016 electoral outcome and its aftermath, whether it is the Russian disinformation campaign as investigated by works such as Kathleen Hall Jamieson's *Cyberwar: How Russian Hackers and Trolls Helped Elect a President—What We Don't, Can't, and Do Know* (Oxford: Oxford University Press, 2018), or the post-truth environment and the transformation of one of the major news networks into a propaganda machine, such as detailed by Jane Mayer's "The Making of the Fox News White House," *New Yorker*, March 11, 2019, https://www.newyorker.com/magazine/2019/03/11/the-making-of-the-fox-news-white-house, and by Yochai Benkler, Robert Faris, and Hal Roberts's *Network Propaganda: Manipulation, Disinformation, and Radicalization in American Politics* (Oxford: Oxford University Press, 2018). While these elements may not be directly linked to the phenomenon of loss, they may be relevant as consequences of fiction-belief, which is one symptom of denied grief.

25. Daniel Kahneman and Amos Tversky, "Choices, Values, and Frames," *American Psychologist* 39, no. 4 (April 1984): 341–50. This concept stipulates that people feel the pain of losses much more than they feel the pleasure of gains; empirical studies suggest that losing is, in general, twice as painful as winning is enjoyable.

26. James Surowiecki, "Losers!" *New Yorker*, May 30, 2016, https://www.newyorker.com/magazine/2016/06/06/losers-for-trump; C. Lawrence Evans, "Trump's Voters are Ready to Risk Everything. Why?" *Washington Post*, March 14, 2016; David Faro, "The Trump Campaign Influenced Voters' Attitudes to Risk, Uncertainty, Loss and Controversy," *London Business School Review*, November 9, 2016.

27. The term is defined as feelings of unfairness accompanied by deprivation (Thomas Pettigrew, "Social Evaluation Theory: Convergences and Applications," in *Nebraska Symposium on Motivation*, Vol. 15, ed. D. Levine [Lincoln: University of Nebraska Press, 1967], 262–63). Since the distinction between feeling deprived as a unique individual and feeling deprived as a representative group member was made clearer in the 1990s, relative deprivation theory regained relevance in concert with related theories such as social identity theory and distributive justice theory (Iain Walker and Heather J. Smith, ed., *Relative Deprivation: Specification, Development, and Integration* [Cambridge: Cambridge University Press, 2002], 2). Relative decline in status prompts one to feel that one's social placement is being threatened, which in turn creates a sense of impasse about one's future—known as temporal relative deprivation. This denial of happiness or wealth in the future one imagines one should have simulates a sensation of loss. The problematic aspect of relative deprivation is that its claims are susceptible to skepticism, particularly when others are experiencing fiercer stringencies. As a result, the sufferers feel as though their grievances are unheard.

28. Elisabeth Kübler-Ross, *On Death and Dying* (New York: Simon and Schuster, 1997), 123–46.

29. Thomas L. Dumm, "Resignation," *Critical Inquiry* 25, no. 1 (Fall 1998): 66.

30. Boss, *Ambigous Loss*, 9.

Bibliography

Abraham, Nicolas, and Maria Torok. *The Shell and the Kernel.* Vol. 1. Edited and translated by Nicholas Rand. Chicago: University of Chicago Press, 1994.

Adorno, Theodor. *Can One Live After Auschwitz?: A Philosophical Reader.* Edited by Rolf Tiedemann. Stanford: Stanford University Press, 2003.

Akiskal, Hagop S., and Giovanni B. Cassano, eds. *Dysthymia and the Spectrum of Chronic Depressions.* New York: The Guilford Press, 1997.

Alexander, Jeffrey C. *Trauma: A Social Theory.* Cambridge: Polity Press, 2012.

Alexiou, Margaret. *The Ritual Lament in Greek Tradition.* Cambridge: Cambridge University Press, 1974.

Altieri, Charles. *Wallace Stevens and the Demands of Modernity: Toward a Phenomenology of Value.* Ithaca: Cornell University Press, 2013.

Anderson, Benedict. *Imagined Communities: Reflections on the Origin and Spread of Nationalism.* London: Verso, 1991.

Anderson, Linda. *Elizabeth Bishop: Lines of Connection.* Edinburgh: Edinburgh University Press, 2013.

Anderson, Linda, and Jo Shapcott, eds. *Elizabeth Bishop: Poet of the Periphery.* Newcastle: Bloodaxe, 2002.

Andrews, Kimberly Quiogue. "Resisting the Intelligence Almost Successfully: Wallace Stevens's 'Academic' Style." *Modernist Cultures* 14, no. 1 (2019): 53–69.

Anselment, Raymond A. "'A Heart Terrifying Sorrow': An Occasional Piece on Poetry of Miscarriage." *Papers on Language & Literature* 33, no. 1 (Winter 1997): 13–46.

Ariès, Philippe. *The Hour of Our Death.* Translated by Helen Weaver. New York: Vintage Books, 1982.

Aristotle. "De Memoria et Reminiscentia." In *Aristotle on Memory*, translated by Richard Sorabji, 47–60. Providence: Brown University Press, 1972.

Aurelius, Marcus. *Meditations.* Translated by Gregory Hays. New York: The Modern Library, 2002.

Axelrod, Steven Gould. "Plath and Torture: Cultural Contexts for Plath's Imagery of the Holocaust." In *Representing Sylvia Plath*, edited by Sally Bayley and Tracy Brain, 67–88. Cambridge: Cambridge University Press, 2011.

———. "The Mirror and the Shadow: Plath's Poetics of Self-Doubt." *Contemporary Literature* 26, no. 3 (Fall 1985): 286–301.

———. "The Poetry of Sylvia Plath." In *The Cambridge Companion to Sylvia Plath*, edited by Jo Gill, 73–89. Cambridge: Cambridge University Press, 2006.

Baddeley, Alan D. *Essentials of Human Memory*. Hove: Psychology Press, 1999.

———. *The Psychology of Memory*. New York: Basic Books, 1976.

Badia, Janet. *Sylvia Plath and the Mythology of Women Readers*. Amherst: University of Massachusetts Press, 2011.

Badowska, Eva. "'My Poet's Junk': Wisława Szymborska in Retrospect." *Parnassus: Poetry in Review* 28, no. 1/2 (2005): 151–168.

Baechler, Lea. "Pre-Elegiac Affirmation in 'To an Old Philosopher in Rome.'" *The Wallace Stevens Journal* 14, no. 2 (Fall 1990): 141–152.

Baer, Ulrich, ed. *110 Stories: New York Writes After September 11*. New York: New York University Press, 2002.

Baikie, Karen A., and Kay Wilhelm. "Emotional and Physical Health Benefits of Expressive Writing." *Advances in Psychiatric Treatment* 11, no. 5 (September 2005): 338–346.

Baker, John E. "Mourning and the Transformation of Object Relationships: Evidence for the Persistence of Internal Attachments." *Psychoanalytic Psychology* 18, no. 1 (Winter 2001): 55–73.

Balaev, Michelle. "Trends in Literary Trauma Theory." *Mosaic* 41, no. 2 (June 2008): 149–166.

Barthes, Roland. *Camera Lucida: Reflections on Photography*. Translated by Richard Howard. New York: Hill & Wang, 1982.

Bassnett, Susan. *Sylvia Plath*. Basingstoke: Macmillan, 1987.

Bates, Milton J. "Stevens's Letters, Notebooks, and Journals." In *Wallace Stevens in Context*, edited by Glen MacLeod, 140–146. Cambridge: Cambridge University Press, 2017.

———. *Wallace Stevens: A Mythology of Self*. Berkeley: University of California Press, 1985.

Bazin, André. *What Is Cinema?* Vol. 1. Translated by Hugh Gray. Berkeley: University of California Press, 2005.

Beckwith, Naomi. "The Necessary Fluster." *Poetry* 200, no. 3 (June 2012): 266–267.

Beeson, Miranda. "Flight." In *Poetry After 9/11: An Anthology of New York Poets*, edited by Dennis Loy Johnson and Valerie Merians, 6. Brooklyn: Melville House, 2002.

Benjamin, Walter. "On Some Motifs in Baudelaire." In *Walter Benjamin: The Selected Writings*. Vol. 4, edited by Howard Eiland and Michael W. Jennings, translated by Edmund Jephcott et al., 313–355. Cambridge: Belknap, 2003.

———. *The Arcades Project*. Translated by Howard Eiland and Kevin McLaughlin. Cambridge: Belknap Press, 1999.

———. *The Origin of German Tragic Drama*. Translated by John Osborne. New York: Verso, 1998.

———. "The Work of Art in the Age of Its Technological Reproducibility." In *Walter Benjamin: The Selected Writings*. Vol. 4, edited by Howard Eiland and Michael W. Jennings, translated by Edmund Jephcott et al., 251–283. Cambridge: Belknap, 2003.

Benkler, Yochai, Robert Faris, and Hal Roberts. *Network Propaganda: Manipulation, Disinformation, and Radicalization in American Politics*. Oxford: Oxford University Press, 2018.

Bennett, Andrew. *Romantic Poets and the Culture of Posterity*. Cambridge: Cambridge University Press, 1999.

Berbrier, Mitch. "The Victim Ideology of White Supremacists and White Separatists in the United States." *Sociological Focus* 33, no. 2 (May 2000): 175–191.

Berg, Beatrice. "Oh, I Was Very Sick." *New York Times*, November 9, 1969.

Berger, Charles. "Bishop's Buried Elegies." In *Elizabeth Bishop in the Twenty-First Century: Reading the New Editions*, edited by Angus Cleghorn, Bethany Hicok, and Thomas Travisano, 41–53. Charlottesville: University of Virginia Press, 2012.

———. *Forms of Farewell: The Late Poetry of Wallace Stevens*. Madison: University of Wisconsin Press, 1985.

———. "The Mythology of Modern Death." In *Wallace Stevens: Modern Critical Views*, edited by Harold Bloom, 165–184. New York: Chelsea House Publishers, 1985.

Berlant, Lauren. "The Female Complaint." *Social Text* 19/20 (1988): 237–259.

Berryman, John. *The Dream Songs*. New York: Farrar, Straus and Giroux, 2014.

Bishop, Elizabeth. *Edgar Allan Poe & the Juke-Box: Uncollected Poems, Drafts, and Fragments*. Edited by Alice Quinn. New York: Farrar, Straus and Giroux, 2006.

———. *Elizabeth Bishop: Poems, Prose, and Letters*. Edited by Lloyd Schwartz and Robert Giroux. New York: Library of America, 2008.

———. *Elizabeth Bishop Papers*. Archives and Special Collections Library, Vassar College Libraries.

———. *The Collected Prose*. New York: Farrar, Straus and Giroux, 1984.

———. *The Complete Poems, 1927–1979*. New York: Farrar, Straus and Giroux, 1983.

———. *Words in Air: The Complete Correspondence Between Elizabeth Bishop and Robert Lowell*. Edited by Thomas Travisano and Saskia Hamilton. New York: Farrar, Straus and Giroux, 2006.

Blessing, Richard. "Theodore Roethke: A Celebration." *Tulane Studies in English* 20 (1972): 169–180.

Bloom, Harold. "Introduction." In *Sylvia Plath*, edited by Harold Bloom, 1–4. New York: Chelsea House Publishers, 1989.

———. *Wallace Stevens: The Poems of Our Climate*. Ithaca: Cornell University Press, 1977.

Bloomfield, Morton W. "The Elegy and the Elegiac Mode: Praise and Alienation." In *Renaissance Genres: Essays on Theory, History, and Interpretation*, edited by Barbara Keifer Lewalski, 147–157. Cambridge: Harvard University Press, 1986.

Bolin, Alice. "Map Quest." *The Paris Review*, September 4, 2012, https://www.theparisreview.org/blog/2012/09/04/map-quest/.

Boltanski, Luc. *Distant Suffering: Morality, Media and Politics*. Translated by Graham D. Burchell. Cambridge: Cambridge University Press, 1999.

Boss, Pauline. *Ambiguous Loss: Learning to Live with Unresolved Grief*. Cambridge: Harvard University Press, 1999.

———. *Loss, Trauma, and Resilience: Therapeutic Work with Ambiguous Loss*. New York: W. W. Norton and Company, 2006.

Bradstreet, Anne. "Here Follows Some Verses Upon the Burning of Our House, July 10th, 1666. Copied Out of a Loose Paper." In *The Making of a Poem: A Norton Anthology of Poetic Forms*, edited by Mark Strand and Eavan Boland, 178–180. New York: W. W. Norton and Company, 2001.

Brain, Tracy. "Fictionalizing Sylvia Plath." In *Representing Sylvia Plath*, edited by Sally Bayley and Tracy Brain, 183–202. Cambridge: Cambridge University Press, 2011.

Braudy, Leo. *The Frenzy of Renown: Fame & Its History*. Oxford: Oxford University Press, 1986.

Brickey, Russell. *Understanding Sharon Olds*. Columbia: University of South Carolina Press, 2016.

Britzolakis, Christina. "*Ariel* and Other Poems." In *The Cambridge Companion to Sylvia Plath*, edited by Jo Gill, 107–123. Cambridge: Cambridge University Press, 2006.

———. *Sylvia Plath and the Theatre of Mourning*. New York: Clarendon, 1999.

Brogan, T. V. F., ed. *The New Princeton Handbook of Poetic Terms*. Princeton: Princeton University Press, 1994.

Bronfen, Elisabeth. *Sylvia Plath*. Oxford: Oxford University Press, 2004.

Bryant, Marsha. "Plath, Domesticity, and the Art of Advertising." *College Literature* 29, no. 3 (Summer 2002): 17–34.

Bryant, William Cullen. "Thanatopsis." In *The Norton Anthology of American Literature*. Shorter Eighth Edition. Vol. I, edited by Nina Baym, 493–494. New York: W. W. Norton and Company, 2013.

Burke, Kenneth. "The Vegetal Radicalism of Theodore Roethke." In *Theodore Roethke*, edited by Harold Bloom, 7–36. New York: Chelsea House Publishers, 1988.

Burt, Stephen. "American Poetry at the End of the Millennium." In *The Cambridge History of American Poetry*, edited by Alfred Bendixen and Stephen Burt, 1144–1166. Cambridge: Cambridge University Press, 2014.

Butler, Judith. *Precarious Life: The Powers of Mourning and Violence*. London: Verso, 2004.

Cameron, Daryl C., and B. Keith Payne. "Escaping Affect: How Motivated Emotion Regulation Creates Insensitivity to Mass Suffering." *Journal of Personality and Social Psychology* 100, no. 1 (2011): 1–15.

Carlson-Bradley, Martha. "Lowell's 'My Last Afternoon with Uncle Devereux Winslow': The Model for Bishop's 'First Death in Nova Scotia.'" *Concerning Poetry* 19 (1986): 117–131.

Carroll, Joseph. "Stevens and Romanticism." In *The Cambridge Companion to Wallace Stevens*, edited by John N. Serio, 87–102. Cambridge: Cambridge University Press, 2007.

———. *Wallace Stevens' Supreme Fiction: A New Romanticism*. Baton Rouge: Louisiana University Press, 1987.
Caruth, Cathy. *Unclaimed Experience: Trauma, Narrative, and History*. Baltimore: Johns Hopkins University Press, 1995.
Cavitch, Max. *American Elegy: The Poetry of Mourning from the Puritans to Whitman*. Minneapolis: University of Minnesota Press, 2007.
Cheng, Anne Anlin. *The Melancholy of Race: Psychoanalysis, Assimilation, and Hidden Grief*. Oxford: Oxford University Press, 2001.
Cikara, Mina, and Jay J. Van Bavel. "The Neuroscience of Intergroup Relation: An Integrative Review." *Perspectives on Psychological Science* 9, no. 3 (2014): 245–274.
Clampitt, Amy. *The Collected Poems of Amy Clampitt*. New York: Knopf, 1997.
Clark, Arthur J. *Empathy in Counseling and Psychotherapy: Perspectives and Practices*. New York: Routledge, 2014.
Clark, Heather. "P(l)athography: Plath and Her Biographers." In *Sylvia Plath in Context*, edited by Tracy Brain, 360–370. Cambridge: Cambridge University Press, 2019.
———. *The Grief of Influence: Sylvia Plath and Ted Hughes*. Oxford: Oxford University Press, 2011.
Clark, Kenneth B. *Prejudice and Your Child*. Middletown: Wesleyan University Press, 1988.
Cleghorn, Angus, Bethany Hicok, and Thomas Travisano, eds. *Elizabeth Bishop in the Twenty-First Century: Reading the New Editions*. Charlottesville: University of Virginia Press, 2012.
Clymer, Lorna. "The Funeral Elegy in Early Modern Britain: A Brief History." In *The Oxford Handbook of the Elegy*, edited by Karen Weisman, 170–186. Oxford: Oxford University Press, 2010.
Coleridge, Samuel Taylor. "Frost at Midnight." In *The Norton Anthology of English Literature*. Ninth Edition. Vol. 2, edited by Stephen Greenblatt, 477–479. New York: W. W. Norton and Company, 2012.
Colwell, Anne. *Inscrutable Houses: Metaphors of the Body in the Poems of Elizabeth Bishop*. Tuscaloosa: University of Alabama Press, 1997.
Connolly, Sally. *Grief & Meter: Elegies for Poets After Auden*. Charlottesville: University of Virginia Press, 2016.
Cook, Eleanor. *Elizabeth Bishop at Work*. Cambridge: Harvard University Press, 2016.
Costello, Bonnie. "Bishop and the Poetic Tradition." In *The Cambridge Companion to Elizabeth Bishop*, edited by Angus Cleghorn and Jonathan Ellis, 79–94. Cambridge: Cambridge University Press, 2014.
———. "Bishop's Impersonal Personal." *American Literary History* 15, no. 2 (July 2003): 334–366.
———. *Elizabeth Bishop: Questions of Mastery*. Cambridge: Harvard University Press, 1991.
———. *The Plural of Us: Poetry and Community in Auden and Others*. Princeton: Princeton University Press, 2017.
Cullen, Countee. "Threnody for a Brown Girl." *Poetry* 26, no. 2 (May 1925): 78–80.

Culler, Jonathan. "Apostrophe." *Diacritics: A Review of Contemporary Criticism* 7, no. 4 (Winter 1977): 59–69.

———. "Changes in the Study of the Lyric." In *Lyric Poetry: Beyond New Criticism*, edited by Chaviva Hošek and Patricia Parker, 38–54. Ithaca: Cornell University Press, 1985.

Darley, John M., and Bibb Latane. "Bystander Intervention in Emergencies: Diffusion of Responsibility." *Journal of Personality and Social Psychology* 8, no. 4 (1968): 377–383.

De Man, Paul. "Autobiography as De-facement." *Modern Language Notes* 94, no. 5 (1979): 919–930.

DeLillo, Don. *Falling Man: A Novel*. New York: Scribner, 2007.

Derrida, Jacques. "*Fors*: The Anglish Words of Nicolas Abraham and Maria Torok." Translated by Barbara Johnson, xi–xlviii. In *The Wolf Man's Magic Word: A Cryptonymy*, edited by Nicholas Abraham and Maria Torok, translated by Nicholas Rand. Minneapolis: University of Minnesota Press, 1986.

———. *Specters of Marx: The State of the Debt, the Work of Mourning, and the New International*. Translated by Peggy Kamuf. New York: Routledge, 1994.

———. *The Work of Mourning*. Edited by Pascale-Anne Brault and Michael Naas. Chicago: University of Chicago Press, 2001.

Deutsch, Helen. "Elegies in Country Churchyards: The Prospect Poem in and around the Eighteenth Century." In *The Oxford Handbook of the Elegy*, edited by Karen Weisman, 187–205. Oxford: Oxford University Press, 2010.

Dickinson, Emily. *The Poems of Emily Dickinson: Reading Edition*. Edited by R. W. Franklin. Cambridge: Belknap Press, 1999.

Didion, Joan. *The White Album*. New York: Farrar, Straus and Giroux, 1979.

Diehl, Joanne Feit. *Elizabeth Bishop and Marianne Moore: The Psychodynamics of Creativity*. Princeton: Princeton University Press, 1993.

Dodd, Elizabeth. *The Veiled Mirror and the Woman Poet: H. D., Louise Bogan, Elizabeth Bishop, and Louise Glück*. Columbia: University of Missouri Press, 1992.

Doka, Kenneth J. "Disenfranchised Grief and Trauma." In *Handbook of Traumatic Loss: A Guide to Theory and Practice*, edited by Neil Thompson, Gerry R. Cox, and Robert G. Stevenson, 377–386. New York: Routledge, 2017.

———., ed. *Disenfranchised Grief: Recognizing Hidden Sorrow*. Lexington, Massachusetts: Lexington Books, 1989.

Dolan, John. "'The Warmth I Had Forgotten': Stevens' Revision of 'First Warmth' and the Dramatization of the Interpersonal." *The Wallace Stevens Journal* 21, no. 2 (1997): 162–174.

Doreski, C. K. *Elizabeth Bishop: The Restraints of Language*. New York: Oxford University Press, 1993.

Dubrow, Heather. *The Challenges of Orpheus: Lyric Poetry and Early Modern England*. Baltimore: Johns Hopkins University Press, 2008.

Dumm, Thomas L. "Resignation." *Critical Inquiry* 25, no. 1 (Fall 1998): 56–76.

Dunn, Allen. "In the Shadow of Central Man: Self-Transcendence and Self-Discovery in Charles Altieri's Reading of Stevens." *The Wallace Stevens Journal* 39, no. 1 (Spring 2015): 56–64.

Edkins, Jenny. *Trauma and the Memory of Politics*. Cambridge: Cambridge University Press, 2003.
Eliot, Thomas Stearns. *The Complete Poems and Plays*. New York: Harcourt, Brace and World, 1971.
Ellenbogen, Josh. "On Photographic Elegy." In *The Oxford Handbook of the Elegy*, edited by Karen Weisman, 682–700. Oxford: Oxford University Press, 2010.
Ellis, Jonathan. *Art and Memory in the Work of Elizabeth Bishop*. Burlington: Ashgate, 2006.
Epicurus. "Letter to Menoeceus." In *Stoic and Epicurean*, translated by Robert Drew Hicks, 168–173. New York: C. Scribner's Sons, 1910.
Evans, C. Lawrence. "Trump's Voters Are Ready to Risk Everything. Why?" *Washington Post*, March 14, 2016.
Faro, David. "The Trump Campaign Influenced Voters' Attitudes to Risk, Uncertainty, Loss and Controversy." *London Business School Review*, November 9, 2016.
Figlerowicz, Marta. *Spaces of Feeling: Affect and Awareness in Modernist Literature*. Ithaca: Cornell University Press, 2017.
Filreis, Alan. "Review of *Wallace Stevens and the Question of Belief: Metaphysician in the Dark* by David R. Jarraway." *The Wallace Stevens Journal* 17, no. 2 (Fall 1993): 251–253.
Flynn, Kevin, and Jim Dwyer. "Falling Bodies, a 9/11 Image Etched in Pain." *New York Times*, September 10, 2004, http://www.nytimes.com/2004/09/10/nyregion/nyregionspecial2/falling-bodies-a-911-image-etched-in-pain.html?_r=0.
Forché, Carolyn. *The Angel of History*. New York: HarperCollins, 1994.
Fortuny, Kim. *Elizabeth Bishop: The Art of Travel*. Boulder: University Press of Colorado, 2003.
Forty, Adrian, and Susanne Küchler, ed. *The Art of Forgetting*. Oxford: Berg, 1999.
Fosso, Kurt. *Buried Communities: Wordsworth and the Bonds of Mourning*. Albany: State University of New York Press, 2004.
Fountain, Gary, and Peter Brazeau. *Remembering Elizabeth Bishop: An Oral Biography*. Amherst: University of Massachusetts Press, 1994.
Frazer, James George. *The Golden Bough: A Study in Magic and Religion*. Abridged Edition. New York: Macmillan, 1943.
Freud, Sigmund. *Beyond the Pleasure Principle*. Translated by James Strachey. London: Hogarth Press, 1950.
———. "Constructions in Analysis." In *The Standard Edition of the Complete Psychological Works of Sigmund Freud*. Vol. XXIII, edited and translated by James Strachey, 257–269. London: Hogarth Press, 1964.
———. "Mourning and Melancholia." In *General Psychological Theory: Papers on Metapsychology*, edited by Philip Rieff, 161–178. New York: Simon & Schuster, 1991.
———. "Negation." In *General Psychological Theory: Papers on Metapsychology*, edited by Philip Rieff, 217–221. New York: Simon & Schuster, 1991.
———. "On Transience." In *The Standard Edition of the Complete Psychological Works of Sigmund Freud*. Vol. XIV, edited and translated by James Strachey, 305–307. London: Hogarth Press, 1957.

———. *Letters of Sigmund Freud*. Edited by Ernst L. Freud. Translated by Tania and James Stern. New York: Basic Books, 1960.

Frost, Laura. "Still Life: 9/11's Falling Bodies." In *Literature After 9/11*, edited by Ann Keniston and Jeanne Follansbee Quinn, 180–208. New York: Routledge, 2013.

Frow, John. *Genre: The New Critical Idiom*. New York: Routledge, 2006.

Frye, Northrop. *The Anatomy of Criticism: Four Essays*. Princeton: Princeton University Press, 1957.

Fuss, Diana. *Dying Modern: A Meditation on Elegy*. Durham: Duke University Press, 2013.

———. "How to Lose Things: Elizabeth Bishop's Child Mourning." *Post 45*, September 23, 2013, http://post45.org/2013/09/how-to-lose-things-elizabeth-bishops-child-mourning/.

Galvin, Rachel. *News of War: Civilian Poetry 1936–1945*. Oxford: Oxford University Press, 2017.

Gilbert, Sandra M., ed. *Inventions of Farewell: A Book of Elegies*. New York: W. W. Norton and Company, 2001.

Glück, Louise. *American Originality: Essays on Poetry*. New York: Farrar, Straus and Giroux, 2017.

———. *Averno*. New York: Farrar, Straus and Giroux, 2006.

———. "Invitations and Exclusion." In *Proofs and Theories: Essays on Poetry*, 113–123. New York: Ecco, 1994.

Goldensohn, Lorrie. *Elizabeth Bishop: The Biography of a Poetry*. New York: Columbia University Press, 1992.

Goldstein, Laurence. *Ruins and Empire: The Evolution of a Theme in Augustan and Romantic Literature*. Pittsburgh: University of Pittsburgh Press, 1977.

———. "The Response of American Poets to 9/11: A Provisional Report." *Michigan Quarterly Review* 48, no. 1 (Winter 2009), http://hdl.handle.net/2027/spo.act2080.0048.108.

Gopnik, Adam. "What Meditation Can Do for Us, and What It Can't." *New Yorker*, July 31, 2017, https://www.newyorker.com/magazine/2017/08/07/what-meditation-can-do-for-us-and-what-it-cant.

Gosmann, Uta. *Poetic Memory: The Forgotten Self in Plath, Howe, Hinsey, and Glück*. Madison: Farleigh Dickinson University Press, 2012.

———. "Psychoanalyzing Persephone: Louise Glück's Averno." *Modern Psychoanalysis* 35, no. 2 (2010): 219–239.

Graham, David, and Kate Sontag. "Containing Multitudes." In *After Confession: Poetry As Autobiography*, edited by Kate Sontag and David Graham, 3–8. St. Paul: Graywolf Press, 2001.

Gray, Richard. *After the Fall: American Literature Since 9/11*. Malden: Wiley-Blackwell, 2011.

Gray, Thomas. "Elegy Written in a Country Churchyard." In *The Making of a Poem: A Norton Anthology of Poetic Forms*, edited by Mark Strand and Eavan Boland, 180–183. New York: W. W. Norton and Company, 2001.

Green, Harvey. "Review of *On Photography* by Susan Sontag." *Winterthur Portfolio* 14, no. 2 (Summer 1979): 209–211.
Greene, Robert. *A Groat's-worth of Wit Bought with a Million of Repentance*. Public Domain: Ex-classics Project, 2009.
Gregerson, Linda. *Negative Capability: Contemporary American Poetry*. Ann Arbor: University of Michigan Press, 2001.
Griffin, Gail. "How It Comes." In *September 11, 2001: American Writers Respond*, edited by William Heyen, 160–163. Silver Spring: Etruscan Press, 2002.
Hagiwara, Sakutaro. "The Octopus That Does Not Die." In *Howling at the Moon: Poems and Prose of Hagiwara Sakutaro*, translated by Hiroaki Sato, 281–282. Los Angeles: Green Integer, 2000.
Hahn, Kimiko. "Her Very Eyes." In *September 11, 2001: American Writers Respond*, edited by William Heyen, 165. Silver Spring: Etruscan Press, 2002.
Hamelman, Steven. "Bishop's 'Crusoe in England.'" *Explicator* 51, no. 1 (Fall 1992): 50–53.
Hamill, Sam, ed. *Poets Against the War*. New York: Nation Books, 2003.
Hamilton, Ian. *Robert Lowell: A Biography*. New York: Faber and Faber, 1982.
Hammond, Jeffrey. "New World Frontiers: The American Puritan Elegy." In *The Oxford Handbook of the Elegy*, edited by Karen Weisman, 206–223. Oxford: Oxford University Press, 2010.
Han, Gül Bilge. *Wallace Stevens and the Poetics of Modernist Autonomy*. Cambridge: Cambridge University Press, 2019.
Harris, Darcy L., and Eunice Gorman. "Grief from a Broader Perspective: Nonfinite Loss, Ambiguous Loss, and Chronic Sorrow." In *Counting Our Losses: Reflecting on Change, Loss, and Transition in Everyday Life*, edited by Darcy L. Harris, 1–14. New York: Routledge, 2010.
Hartman, Geoffrey. *Wordsworth's Poetry, 1787–1814*. New Haven: Yale University Press, 1964.
Hastings, Mark E., Lisa M. Northman, and June P. Tangney. "Shame, Guilt, and Suicide." In *Suicide Science: Expanding the Boundaries*, edited by Thomas Joiner and M. David Rudd, 67–79. Berlin: Springer, 2002.
Heaney, Seamus. *Opened Ground: Poems, 1966–1996*. London: Faber and Faber, 1998.
Heidegger, Martin. *Being and Time*. Translated by John Macquarrie and Edward Robinson. London: SCM Press, 1962.
Hejinian, Lyn. *The Language of Inquiry*. Berkeley: University of California Press, 2000.
Helle, Anita. "Women's Elegies, 1834–Present: Female Authorship and the Affective Politics of Grief." In *The Oxford Handbook of the Elegy*, edited by Karen Weisman, 463–480. Oxford: Oxford University Press, 2010.
Heyen, William, ed. *September 11, 2001: American Writers Respond*. Silver Spring: Etruscan Press, 2002.
Hill, Patricia Wonch, Joanne Cacciatore, Karina M. Shreffler, and Kayla M. Pritchard. "The Loss of Self: The Effect of Miscarriage, Stillbirth, and Child Death on Maternal Self-Esteem." *Death Studies* 41, no. 4 (2017): 226–235.

Hochschild, Arlie Russell. *Strangers in Their Own Land: Anger and Mourning on the American Right*. New York: The New Press, 2016.

Holden, Jonathan. "'Affected Naturalness' and the Poetry of Sensibility." *College English* 41, no. 4 (December 1979): 398–408.

Holland, Patricia. *What Is a Child?: Popular Images of Childhood*. London: Virago, 1992.

Hopkins, Gerard Manley. *Poems and Prose of Gerard Manley Hopkins*. London: Penguin Books, 1985.

Howe, Irving. "The Plath Celebration: A Partial Dissent." In *Sylvia Plath*, edited by Harold Bloom, 5–16. New York: Chelsea House Publishers, 1989.

Hughes, Ted. "Introduction." In *The Collected Poems of Sylvia Plath*, edited by Ted Hughes, 13–17. New York: Harper Perennial, 1992.

Ions, Veronica. *Egyptian Mythology*. New York: Hamlyn, 1965.

Jackson, Virginia. *Dickinson's Misery: A Theory of Lyric Reading*. Princeton: Princeton University Press, 2005.

Jacobs, Joseph. "The Dying of Death." *The Fortnightly Review* 66 (August 1899): 264–269.

Jamieson, Kathleen Hall. *Cyberwar: How Russian Hackers and Trolls Helped Elect a President: What We Don't, Can't, and Do Know*. Oxford: Oxford University Press, 2018.

Jarraway, David R. *Wallace Stevens Among Others: Diva-Dames, Deleuze, and American Culture*. Ithaca: McGill-Queen's University Press, 2015.

Jenkins, Lee M. *Wallace Stevens: Rage for Order*. Portland: Sussex Academic Press, 2000.

John, Eileen. "Poetry and Cognition." In *A Sense of the World: Essays on Fiction, Narrative, and Knowledge*, edited by John Gibson, Wolfgang Huemer, and Luca Pocci, 219–232. New York: Routledge, 2007.

Johnson, Dennis Loy, and Valerie Merians, eds. *Poetry After 9/11: An Anthology of New York Poets*. Brooklyn: Melville House, 2002.

Jonson, Ben. *Epigrams and the Forest*. Edited by Richard Dutton. New York: Routledge, 2003.

Kahneman, Daniel, and Amos Tversky. "Choices, Values, and Frames." *American Psychologist* 39, no. 4 (April 1984): 341–350.

Kalstone, David. *Becoming a Poet: Elizabeth Bishop with Marianne Moore and Robert Lowell*. New York: Farrar, Straus and Giroux, 1989.

Katz, Robert L. *Empathy: Its Nature and Uses*. New York: Free Press of Glencoe, 1963.

Kaufman, Robert. "Poetry After 'Poetry After Auschwitz.'" In *Art and Aesthetics After Adorno*, edited by Anthony J. Cascardi, 116–181. Berkeley: Townsend Humanities Center/University of California Press, 2010.

Kean, Thomas H., and Lee Hamilton. *The 9/11 Commission Report: Final Report of the National Commission on Terrorist Attacks Upon the United States*. Washington, D.C.: National Commission on Terrorist Attacks upon the United States, 2004, https://www.9-11commission.gov/report/911Report.pdf.

Keniston, Ann. "'Balm After Violence': Louise Glück's *Averno*." *The Kenyon Review* 30, no. 4 (Fall 2008): 177–187.

———. *Overheard Voices: Address and Subjectivity in Postmodern American Poetry*. New York: Routledge, 2006.

Kennedy, David. *Elegy*. New York: Routledge, 2007.

Kennedy, X. J. "September Twelfth, 2001." In *September 11, 2001: American Writers Respond*, edited by William Heyen, 221. Silver Spring: Etruscan Press, 2002.

Kessler, Edward. *Images of Wallace Stevens*. New Brunswick: Rutgers University Press, 1972.

Knutson, Lin. "Poetic Responses to 9/11 and Adrienne Rich's *The School Among the Ruins*." In *Representing 9/11: Trauma, Ideology, and Nationalism in Literature, Film, and Television*, edited by Paul Petrovic, 187–198. Lanham: Rowman & Littlefield, 2015.

Kowal, Ewa. *The "Image-Event" in the Early Post-9/11 Novel: Literary Representations of Terror After September 11, 2001*. Krakow: Jagiellonian University Press, 2012.

Kristeva, Julia. *Black Sun: Depression and Melancholia*. New York: Columbia University Press, 1989.

———. "On the Melancholic Imaginary." In *Discourse in Psychoanalysis and Literature*, edited by Shlomith Rimmon-Kenan, 104–123. London: Routledge, 1987.

Kübler-Ross, Elisabeth. *On Death and Dying*. New York: Simon and Schuster, 1997.

Lacan, Jacques. "Desire, and the Interpretation of Desire in *Hamlet*." In *Literature and Psychoanalysis: The Question of Reading Otherwise*, edited by Shoshana Felman, 11–52. Baltimore: Johns Hopkins University Press, 1982.

LaCapra, Dominick. "Trauma, Absence, Loss." *Critical Inquiry* 25, no. 4 (Summer 1999): 696–727.

Lain Entralgo, Pedro. *The Therapy of the Word in Classical Antiquity*. Edited by L. J. Rather and J. M. Sharp. New Haven: Yale University Press, 1970.

Laing, Ronald David. *The Divided Self*. London: Pelican Books, 1965.

Lakoff, George, and Mark Johnson. *Metaphors We Live By*. Chicago: University of Chicago Press, 1980.

Lambert, Ellen Zetzel. *Placing Sorrow: A Study of the Pastoral Elegy Convention from Theocritus to Milton*. Chapel Hill: University of North Carolina Press, 1976.

Lefkovitz, Lori Hope. "Inherited Memories and the Ethics of Ventriloquism." In *Shaping Losses: Cultural Memory and the Holocaust*, edited by Julia Epstein and Lori Hope Lefkovitz, 220–230. Champaign: University of Illinois Press, 2001.

Leggett, B. J. *Late Stevens: The Final Fiction*. Baton Rouge: Louisiana State University Press, 2005.

Leighton, Angela. "Poetry of Knowing: So What Do We Know?" In *The Philosophy of Poetry*, edited by John Gibson, 162–182. Oxford: Oxford University Press, 2015.

Lensing, George S. *Making the Poem: Stevens' Approaches*. Baton Rouge: Louisiana State University Press, 2018.

Levinas, Emmanuel. *Dieu, la mort et le temps*. Paris: Grasset, 1993.

Levinson, Marjorie. *Thinking Through Poetry: Field Reports on Romantic Lyric.* Oxford: Oxford University Press, 2018.

———. "What Is New Formalism?" *PMLA* 122, no. 2 (2007): 558–569.

———. *Wordsworth's Great Period Poems: Four Essays.* Cambridge: Cambridge University Press, 1986.

Linfield, Susie. "Jumpers." *New York Magazine*, August 27, 2011, http://nymag.com/news/9-11/10th-anniversary/jumpers/.

Litz, A. Walton. *Introspective Voyager: The Poetic Development of Wallace Stevens.* New York: Oxford University Press, 1972.

Locke, John. *The Locke Reader: Selections from the Works of John Locke with a General Introduction and Commentary.* Edited by John W. Yolton. Cambridge: Cambridge University Press, 1977.

Lombardi, Marilyn May. *The Body and the Song: Elizabeth Bishop's Poetics.* Carbondale: Southern Illinois University Press, 1995.

Longenbach, James. "A Reason for Keeping Silent?" In *September 11, 2001: American Writers Respond*, edited by William Heyen, 248–250. Silver Spring: Etruscan Press, 2002.

———. *The Resistance to Poetry.* Chicago: University of Chicago Press, 2004.

———. "The World After Poetry: Revelation in Late Stevens." *The Wallace Stevens Journal* 23, no. 2 (Fall 1999): 187–193.

Louis, Margot Kathleen. *Swinburne and His Gods: The Roots and Growth of an Agnostic Poetry.* Kingston: McGill-Queen's University Press, 1990.

Luce, Edward. *The Retreat of Western Liberalism.* New York: Grove Press, 2017.

Lyon, John. "War, Politics, and Disappearing Poetry: Auden, Yeats, Empson." In *The Oxford Handbook of British and Irish War Poetry*, edited by Tim Kendall, 279–298. Oxford: Oxford University Press, 2007.

Machova, Mariana. *Elizabeth Bishop and Translation.* Lanham: Lexington Books, 2017.

Malkin, Rachel. "American Philosophy." In *Wallace Stevens in Context*, edited by Glen MacLeod, 217–226. Cambridge: Cambridge University Press, 2017.

Marshall, Megan. *Elizabeth Bishop: A Miracle for Breakfast.* Boston: Houghton Mifflin Harcourt, 2017.

Martin, Terry L., and Kenneth J. Doka. *Men Don't Cry... Women Do: Transcending Gender Stereotypes of Grief.* Philadelphia: Brunner/Mazel, 2000.

Martindale, Charles. *Redeeming the Text: Latin Poetry and the Hermeneutics of Reception.* New York: Cambridge University Press, 1993.

Matlak, Richard E. "Captain John Wordsworth's Death at Sea." *The Wordsworth Circle* 31, no. 3 (2000): 127–133.

Matthews, Samantha. *Poetical Remains: Poets' Graves, Bodies, and Books in the Nineteenth Century.* New York: Oxford University Press, 2004.

Mayer, Jane. "The Making of the Fox News White House." *New Yorker*, March 11, 2019, https://www.newyorker.com/magazine/2019/03/11/the-making-of-the-fox-news-white-house.

McCabe, Susan. "Bishop's 'Crusoe in England.'" *Explicator* 48, no. 1 (Fall 1989): 57–59.

———. *Elizabeth Bishop: Her Poetics of Loss*. University Park: Pennsylvania State University Press, 1994.
McCann, Janet. *Wallace Stevens Revisited: "The Celestial Possible."* New York: Twayne Publishers, 1995.
McFarland, Thomas. *Romanticism and the Forms of Ruin: Wordsworth, Coleridge, and Modalities of Fragmentation*. Princeton: Princeton University Press, 1981.
McKendrick, Jamie. "Bishop's Birds." In *Elizabeth Bishop: Poet of the Periphery*, edited by Linda Anderson and Jo Shapcott, 123–142. Newcastle: Bloodaxe Books, 2002.
Mellor, Anne K. "'Anguish No Cessation Knows': Elegy and the British Woman Poet, 1660–1834." In *The Oxford Handbook of the Elegy*, edited by Karen Weisman, 442–462. Oxford: Oxford University Press, 2010.
———. *English Romantic Irony*. Cambridge: Harvard University Press, 1980.
Melville, Joan. "'Inventions of Farewell': Wallace Stevens' 'The Owl in the Sarcophagus.'" *The Wallace Stevens Journal* 16, no. 1 (Spring 1992): 3–21.
Merwin, William Stanley. "To the Words." In *September 11, 2001: American Writers Respond*, edited by William Heyen, 3. Silver Spring: Etruscan Press, 2002.
Metres, Philip. "Beyond Grief and Grievances: The Poetry of 9/11 and Its Aftermath." *Poetry Foundation*, September 7, 2011, https://www.poetryfoundation.org/articles/69737/beyond-grief-and-grievance.
Meyers, Jeffrey. "The Background of Theodore Roethke's 'Elegy for Jane.'" *Resources for American Literary Study* 15, no. 2 (Autumn 1985): 139–144.
Mill, John Stuart. "What Is Poetry?" In *Essays on Poetry by John Stuart Mill*, edited by F. Parvin Sharpless, 3–27. Columbia: University of South Carolina Press, 1976.
Miller, Nancy K. "Reporting the Disaster." In *Trauma at Home: After 9/11*, edited by Judith Greenberg, 39–47. Lincoln: University of Nebraska Press, 2002.
Millier, Brett C. *Elizabeth Bishop: Life and the Memory of It*. Berkeley: University of California Press, 1993.
Milton, John. "Lycidas." In *The Norton Anthology of English Literature*. Ninth Edition. Vol. 1, edited by Stephen Greenblatt, 1791–1796. New York: W. W. Norton and Company, 2012.
Monteiro, George, ed. *Conversations with Elizabeth Bishop*. Jackson: University Press of Mississippi, 1996.
Morey, Tracy Crowe, and Cristina Santos. "*Las Madres Guerreras*: Testimonial Writing on Militant Motherhood in Latin America." In *Motherhood and War: International Perspectives*, edited by Dana Cooper and Claire Phelan, 61–84. New York: Palgrave, 2014.
Morris, Daniel. *The Poetry of Louise Glück: A Thematic Introduction*. Columbia: University of Missouri Press, 2006.
Morrison, Toni. *Playing in the Dark: Whiteness and the Literary Imagination*. Cambridge: Harvard University Press, 1992.
Moustaki, Nikki. "How to Write a Poem After September 11th." In *Poetry After 9/11: An Anthology of New York Poets*, edited by Dennis Loy Johnson and Valerie Merians, 95–96. Brooklyn: Melville House, 2002.

Murphy, Charles M. *Wallace Stevens: A Spiritual Poet in a Secular Age*. New York: Paulist Press, 1997.

Nagy, Gregory. "Ancient Greek Elegy." In *The Oxford Handbook of the Elegy*, edited by Karen Weisman, 13–45. Oxford: Oxford University Press, 2010.

Naimou, Angela. "Double Vision: Refugee Crises and the Afterimages of Endless War." *College Literature* 43, no. 1 (Winter 2016): 226–233.

Narbeshuber, Lisa. *Confessing Cultures: Politics and the Self in the Poetry of Sylvia Plath*. Victoria: ELS Editions, 2009.

Newman, Charles. "Candor Is the Only Wile: The Art of Sylvia Plath." In *The Art of Sylvia Plath, a Symposium*, edited by Charles Newman, 21–55. London: Faber and Faber, 1970.

Nietzsche, Friedrich. *The Gay Science*. Translated by Walter Kaufmann. New York: Vintage Books, 1974.

Nussbaum, Martha C. *The Therapy of Desire: Theory and Practice in Hellenistic Ethics*. Princeton: Princeton University Press, 1994.

Olds, Sharon. *The Dead and the Living*. New York: Knopf, 1984.

Orchard, Andy. "Not What It Was: The World of Old English Elegy." In *The Oxford Handbook of the Elegy*, edited by Karen Weisman, 101–117. Oxford: Oxford University Press, 2010.

Ostriker, Alicia. "The Window, at the Moment of Flame." In *September 11, 2001: American Writers Respond*, edited by William Heyen, 294–295. Silver Spring: Etruscan Press, 2002.

Page, Barbara. "Elizabeth Bishop: Stops, Starts and Dream Divagations." In *Elizabeth Bishop: Poet of the Periphery*, edited by Linda Anderson and Jo Shapcott, 12–30. Newcastle: Bloodaxe, 2002.

———. "Home, Wherever That May Be: Poems and Prose of Brazil." In *The Cambridge Companion to Elizabeth Bishop*, edited by Angus Cleghorn and Jonathan Ellis, 124–140. Cambridge: Cambridge University Press, 2014.

Palmer, Michael. "Dear Lexicon." Interview with David Levi-Strauss and B. Hollander. *Acts* 2, no. 1 (1986): 8–35.

Pancer, S. Mark, Linda M. McMullen, Randal A. Kabatoff, Kent G. Johnson, and Carole A. Pond. "Conflict and Avoidance in the Helping Situation." *Journal of Personality and Social Psychology* 37, no. 8 (1979): 1406–1411.

Parini, Jay. *Theodore Roethke: An American Romantic*. Amherst: University of Massachusetts Press, 1979.

Parker, Robert Dale. *The Unbeliever: The Poetry of Elizabeth Bishop*. Urbana: University of Illinois Press, 1988.

Pennebaker, James W., and Sandra K. Beall. "Confronting a Traumatic Event: Toward an Understanding of Inhibition and Disease." *Journal of Abnormal Psychology* 95, no. 3 (August 1986): 274–281.

Pensky, Max. *Melancholy Dialectics: Walter Benjamin and the Play of Mourning*. Amherst: University of Massachusetts Press, 1993.

Perloff, Marjorie G. "On the Road to *Ariel*: The 'Transitional' Poetry of Sylvia Plath." *The Iowa Review* 4, no. 2 (Spring 1973): 94–110.

———. *Poetic License: Essays on Modernist and Postmodernist Lyric*. Evanston: Northwestern University Press, 1990.

Perrine, Laurence, and James M. Reid. *100 American Poems of the Twentieth Century*. New York: Harcourt Brace, 1966.

Perry, Laura. "Plath and the Culture of Hygiene." In *Sylvia Plath in Context*, edited by Tracy Brain, 191–200. Cambridge: Cambridge University Press, 2019.

Pettigrew, Thomas F. "Social Evaluation Theory: Convergences and Applications." In *Nebraska Symposium on Motivation*. Vol. 15, edited by David Levine, 241–311. Lincoln: University of Nebraska Press, 1967.

Pinch, Adela. *Strange Fits of Passion: Epistemologies of Emotion, Hume to Austen*. Stanford: Stanford University Press, 1996.

Pinsky, Robert. "Enormity and the Human Voice." In *September 11, 2001: American Writers Respond*, edited by William Heyen, 303–306. Silver Spring: Etruscan Press, 2002.

Plath, Sylvia. *Ariel: The Restored Edition*. New York: Harper Collins Publishers, 2004.

———. *The Collected Poems*. Edited by Ted Hughes. New York: Harper Perennial, 1992.

———. *The Letters of Sylvia Plath, Vol. 2: 1956–1963*. Edited by Peter K. Steinberg and Karen V. Kukil. New York: Harper Collins, 2018.

———. *The Unabridged Journals of Sylvia Plath*. Edited by Karen V. Kukil. New York: Anchor Books, 2000.

Pöhlmann, Sascha. *Future-Founding Poetry: Topographies of Beginnings from Whitman to the Twenty-First Century*. Suffolk: Boydell & Brewer, 2015.

Pollak, Vivian R. *Our Emily Dickinsons: American Women Poets and the Intimacies of Difference*. Philadelphia: University of Pennsylvania Press, 2017.

Poulet, Georges. "Exploding Poetry: Baudelaire." In *Charles Baudelaire*, edited by Harold Bloom, 63–80. New York: Chelsea House Publishers, 1987.

Poulin, Jr., A., ed. *Contemporary American Poetry*. Boston: Houghton Mifflin, 1996.

Pritchett, Patrick. "How to Write Poetry After Auschwitz: The Burnt Book of Michael Palmer." *Journal of Modern Literature* 37, no. 3 (Spring 2014): 127–145.

Rae, Patricia, ed. *Modernism and Mourning*. Lewisburg: Bucknell University Press, 2007.

Ragg, Edward. *Wallace Stevens and the Aesthetics of Abstraction*. Cambridge: Cambridge University Press, 2010.

Ramazani, Jahan. "'Daddy, I Have Had to Kill You': Plath, Rage, and the Modern Elegy." *PMLA* 108, no. 5 (October 1993): 1142–1156.

———. *Poetry of Mourning: The Modern Elegy from Hardy to Heaney*. Chicago: University of Chicago Press, 1994.

Randall, Margaret. "The Morning After." In *Resist Much/Obey Little: Inaugural Poems to the Resistance*, edited by Michael Boughn, Kent Johnson, and Anne Waldman, 516–517. Brooklyn: Spuyten Duyvil, 2017.

Ravinthiran, Vidyan. *Elizabeth Bishop's Prosaic*. Lewisburg: Bucknell University Press, 2015.

Regan, Stephen. "The Art of Losing: American Elegy Since 1945." In *American Poetry Since 1945*, edited by Eleanor Spencer, 183–202. Basingstoke: Palgrave, 2017.

Ricciardi, Alessia. *The Ends of Mourning: Psychoanalysis, Literature, Film*. Stanford: Stanford University Press, 2003.

Ricoeur, Paul. "Poetry and Possibility." In *A Ricoeur Reader: Reflection and Imagination*, edited by Mario J. Valdés, 448–462. Toronto: University of Toronto Press, 1991.

———. *The Rule of Metaphor: Multi-disciplinary Studies of the Creation of Meaning in Language*. Translated by Robert Czerny, Kathleen McLaughlin, and John Costello. Toronto: University of Toronto Press, 1977.

Riddel, Joseph N. *The Clairvoyant Eye: The Poetry and Poetics of Wallace Stevens*. Baton Rouge: Louisiana State University Press, 1965.

Riddle, Karen. "Always on My Mind: Exploring How Frequent, Recent, and Vivid Television Portrayals Are Used in the Formation of Social Reality Judgments." *Media Psychology* 13, no. 2 (2010): 155–179.

Roberts, Neil. "English Elegies." In *A Companion to Poetic Genre*, edited by Erik Martiny, 77–92. Hoboken: Wiley-Blackwell, 2011.

Roethke, Theodore. *The Collected Poems*. New York: Doubleday, 1975.

Rollyson, Carl. *American Isis: The Life and Art of Sylvia Plath*. New York: St. Martin's Press, 2013.

Rose, Jacqueline. *On Not Being Able to Sleep: Psychoanalysis and the Modern World*. Princeton: Princeton University Press, 2003.

———. *The Haunting of Sylvia Plath*. London: Virago, 1991.

Ross-Bryant, Lynn. *Theodore Roethke: Poetry of the Earth, Poet of the Spirit*. Port Washington: Kennikat Press, 1981.

Sacks, Kenneth S. "Stoicism in America." In *The Routledge Handbook of the Stoic Tradition*, edited by John Sellars, 331–345. New York: Routledge, 2016.

Sacks, Peter M. *The English Elegy: Studies in the Genre from Spenser to Yeats*. Baltimore: Johns Hopkins University Press, 1985.

Said, Edward. *Beginnings: Intention and Method*. New York: Basic Books, 1975.

Sampson, Fiona. "After Plath: The Legacy of Influence." In *Sylvia Plath in Context*, edited by Tracy Brain, 350–359. Cambridge: Cambridge University Press, 2019.

Samuels, Peggy. "Bishop and Visual Art." In *The Cambridge Companion to Elizabeth Bishop*, edited by Angus Cleghorn and Jonathan Ellis, 169–182. Cambridge: Cambridge University Press, 2014.

Sappho. *If Not, Winter: Fragments of Sappho*. Translated by Anne Carson. New York: Knopf, 2002.

Schenck, Celeste Marguerite. *Mourning and Panegyric: The Poetics of Pastoral Ceremony*. University Park: Pennsylvania State University Press, 1988.

Schillace, Brandy. *Death's Summer Coat: What the History of Death and Dying Teaches Us About Life and Living*. New York: Pegasus Books, 2016.

Schor, Esther. *Bearing the Dead: The British Culture of Mourning from the Enlightenment to Victoria*. Princeton: Princeton University Press, 1994.
Schwartz, Lloyd. "Back to Boston: *Geography III* and Other Late Poems." In *The Cambridge Companion to Elizabeth Bishop*, edited by Angus Cleghorn and Jonathan Ellis, 141–154. Cambridge: Cambridge University Press, 2014.
Schwartz, Lloyd, and Sybil P. Estess, eds. *Elizabeth Bishop and Her Art*. Ann Arbor: University of Michigan Press, 1983.
Seager, Allan. *The Glass House: The Life of Theodore Roethke*. Ann Arbor: University of Michigan Press, 1991.
Seuss, Diane. "Falling Man." In *September 11, 2001: American Writers Respond*, edited by William Heyen, 350–351. Silver Spring: Etruscan Press, 2002.
Shah, Siddharth Ashvin. "Mental Health Emergencies and Post-traumatic Stress Disorder." In *Emergency Public Health: Preparedness and Response*, edited by Girish Bobby Kapur and Jeffrey P. Smith, 493–516. Sudbury: Jones & Bartlett Learning, 2011.
Shakespeare, William. "Sonnet #18." In *The Norton Shakespeare*, edited by Stephen Greenblatt, 1929. New York: W. W. Norton and Company, 1997.
Shaw, W. David. *Elegy & Paradox: Testing the Conventions*. Baltimore: Johns Hopkins University Press, 1994.
Shigley, Sally Bishop. *Dazzling Dialectics: Elizabeth Bishop's Resonating Feminist Reality*. New York: Peter Lang, 1997.
Shklar, Judith N. *American Citizenship: The Quest for Inclusion*. Cambridge: Harvard University Press, 1991.
Shneidman, Edwin S. *The Suicidal Mind*. New York: Oxford University Press, 1996.
Sidney, Philip. "The Defence of Poesy." In *Sir Philip Sidney*, edited by Katherine Duncan-Jones, 212–250. Oxford: Oxford University Press, 1989.
Simmel, Georg. "The Metropolis and Mental Life." In *Rethinking Architecture: A Reader in Cultural Theory*, edited by Neil Leach, 69–79. New York: Routledge, 1997.
Sircy, Jonathan. "Bishop's 'One Art.'" *Explicator* 63, no. 4 (Summer 2005): 241–244.
Smith, Adam. *The Theory of Moral Sentiments*. Edited by Knud Haakonssen. Cambridge: Cambridge University Press, 2002.
Smith, Ernest. "Confessional Poetry." In *American Poets and Poetry: From the Colonial Era to the Present*. Vol. 1, edited by Jeffrey Gray, Mary McAleer Balkun, and James McCorkle, 120–124. Santa Barbara: Greenwood, 2015.
Snodgrass, W. D., and Hilary Holladay. "The Original Confessional Poet Tells All." *Poetry Foundation*, January 14, 2009, https://www.poetryfoundation.org/articles/69067/the-original-confessional-poet-tells-all.
Sontag, Susan. "Looking at War." *New Yorker*, December 9, 2002, https://www.newyorker.com/magazine/2002/12/09/looking-at-war.
———. *On Photography*. New York: RosettaBooks, 2005.
———. *Regarding the Pain of Others*. New York: Picador, 2003.

Spargo, R. Clifton. "The Contemporary Anti-Elegy." In *The Oxford Handbook of the Elegy*, edited by Karen Weisman, 413–429. Oxford: Oxford University Press, 2010.

———. *The Ethics of Mourning: Grief and Responsibility in Elegiac Literature*. Baltimore: Johns Hopkins University Press, 2004.

Stein, Dan J., David J. Kupfer, and Alan F. Schatzberg, eds. "Dysthymic Disorder." In *The American Psychiatric Publishing Textbook of Mood Disorders*, 551–553. Washington, D.C.: American Psychiatric Publishing, Inc., 2006.

Stevens, Wallace. *Collected Poetry and Prose*. Edited by Frank Kermode and Joan Richardson. New York: Library of America, 1997.

———. *Letters of Wallace Stevens*. Edited by Holly Stevens. Berkeley: University of California Press, 1966.

———. *Opus Posthumous*. New York: Knopf, 1957.

Stevenson, Anne. *Bitter Fame: A Life of Sylvia Plath*. London: Viking, 1989.

———. *Elizabeth Bishop*. New York: Twayne Publishers, 1966.

Stever, Gayle S. "Fan Behavior and Lifespan Development Theory: Explaining Para-Social and Social Attachment to Celebrities." *Journal of Adult Development* 18, no. 1 (March 2011): 1–7.

Stewart, Susan. *Poetry and the Fate of the Senses*. Chicago: University of Chicago Press, 2002.

Strand, Mark. "A Conversation with Mark Strand." *Ohio Review* 13, no. 2 (1972): 54–71.

Strand, Mark, and Eavan Boland, eds. *The Making of a Poem: A Norton Anthology of Poetic Forms*. New York: W. W. Norton and Company, 2001.

Styron, William. *Darkness Visible: A Memoir of Madness*. New York: Vintage Books, 1992.

Sukenick, Ronald. *Wallace Stevens: Musing the Obscure*. New York: New York University Press, 1967.

Surowiecki, James. "Losers!" *New Yorker*, May 30, 2016, https://www.newyorker.com/magazine/2016/06/06/losers-for-trump.

Svenaeus, Frederik. *The Hermeneutics of Medicine and the Phenomenology of Health: Steps Towards a Philosophy of Medical Practice*. Berlin: Springer Science & Business Media, 2013.

Swinburne, Algernon Charles. "Ave atque Vale." In *The Norton Anthology of English Literature*. Ninth Edition. Vol. 2, edited by Stephen Greenblatt, 1531–1537. New York: W. W. Norton and Company, 2012.

Szymborska, Wisława. "Photograph from September 11." In *Map: Collected and Last Poems*, translated by Clare Cavanagh and Stanisław Barańczak, 344. Boston: Houghton Mifflin, 2015.

Tate, William. "Shades of Bliss: Imagining Heaven in Wallace Stevens and Richard Wilbur." *Christianity & Literature* 68, no. 2 (March 2019): 252–271.

Taxidou, Olga. *Tragedy, Modernity and Mourning*. Edinburgh: Edinburgh University Press, 2004.

Taylor, Charles. *Sources of the Self: The Making of the Modern Identity*. Cambridge: Harvard University Press, 1989.

Thase, Michael E., and Susan S. Lang. *Beating the Blues: New Approaches to Overcoming Dysthymia and Chronic Mild Depression*. Oxford: Oxford University Press, 2004.

Theile, Verena, and Linda Tredennick. *New Formalisms and Literary Theory*. Basingstoke: Palgrave Macmillan, 2013.

Thiemann, Anna. *Rewriting the American Soul: Trauma, Neuroscience and the Contemporary Literary Imagination*. New York: Routledge, 2018.

Tóibín, Colm. *On Elizabeth Bishop*. Princeton: Princeton University Press, 2015.

Toida, Michizou. *The Structure of Forgetting*. Tokyo: Chikuma Shobou, 1984.

Tomlinson, Charles. "Elizabeth Bishop's New Book." Review of *Questions of Travel*, by Elizabeth Bishop. *Shenandoah* 17 (Winter 1966): 88–91.

Travisano, Thomas. *Elizabeth Bishop: Her Artistic Development*. Charlottesville: University Press of Virginia, 1988.

———. *Midcentury Quartet: Bishop, Lowell, Jarrell, Berryman, and the Making of a Postmodern Aesthetic*. Charlottesville: University Press of Virginia, 1999.

Trinidad, David. "'Two Sweet Ladies': Sexton and Plath's Friendship and Mutual Influence." *The American Poetry Review* 35, no. 6 (November–December 2006): 21–29.

Tussman, Malka Heifetz. "Cellars and Attics." Translated by Kathryn Hellerstein. In *American Yiddish Poetry: A Bilingual Anthology*, edited by Benjamin Harshav and Barbara Harshav, 607–611. Berkeley: University of California Press, 1986.

Tversky, Amos, and Daniel Kahneman. "Availability: A Heuristic for Judging Frequency and Probability." In *Judgment Under Uncertainty: Heuristics and Biases*, edited by Daniel Kahneman, Paul Slovic, and Amos Tversky, 163–178. Cambridge: Cambridge University Press, 1982.

Twiddy, Iain. *Cancer Poetry*. Basingstoke: Palgrave Macmillan, 2015.

———. *Pastoral Elegy in Contemporary British and Irish Poetry*. London: Continuum, 2012.

Van Dyne, Susan R. *Revising Life: Sylvia Plath's Ariel Poems*. Chapel Hill: University of North Carolina Press, 1993.

Vendler, Helen. "Domestication, Domesticity, and the Otherworldly." In *Elizabeth Bishop*, edited by Harold Bloom, 83–96. New York: Chelsea House, 1985.

———. *Last Looks, Last Books: Stevens, Plath, Lowell, Bishop, Merrill*. Princeton: Princeton University Press, 2010.

———. *On Extended Wings: Wallace Stevens' Longer Poems*. Cambridge: Harvard University Press, 1969.

———. *The Music of What Happens: Poems, Poets, Critics*. Cambridge: Belknap Press, 1988.

———. *Wallace Stevens: Words Chosen Out of Desire*. Knoxville: University of Tennessee Press, 1984.

Vickery, John B. *The Literary Impact of the Golden Bough*. Princeton: Princeton University Press, 1973.

———. *The Modern Elegiac Temper*. Baton Rouge: Louisiana State University Press, 2006.

Waldoff, Leon. *Wordsworth in His Major Lyrics: The Art and Psychology of Self-Representation*. Columbia: University of Missouri Press, 2001.

Walker, Cheryl. *Masks Outrageous and Austere: Culture, Psyche, and Persona in Modern Women Poets*. Bloomington: Indiana University Press, 1991.

Walker, Iain, and Heather J. Smith, ed. *Relative Deprivation: Specification, Development, and Integration*. Cambridge: Cambridge University Press, 2002.

Waters, Michael. "Fork and Spoon." In *September 11, 2001: American Writers Respond*, edited by William Heyen, 389–391. Silver Spring: Etruscan Press, 2002.

Waters, William. *Poetry's Touch: On Lyric Address*. Ithaca: Cornell University Press, 2003.

Weinrich, Harald. *Lethe: The Art and Critique of Forgetting*. Translated by Steven Rendall. Ithaca: Cornell University Press, 1997.

Weisman, Karen, ed. *The Oxford Handbook of the Elegy*. Oxford: Oxford University Press, 2010.

West, Candace, and Don H. Zimmerman. "Accounting for Doing Gender." *Gender & Society* 23, no. 1 (2009): 112–122.

———. "Doing Gender." *Gender & Society* 1, no. 2 (1987): 125–151.

White, Gillian. *Lyric Shame: The "Lyric" Subject of Contemporary American Poetry*. Cambridge: Harvard University Press, 2014.

Whiting, Anthony. *The Never-Resting Mind: Wallace Stevens' Romantic Irony*. Ann Arbor: University of Michigan Press, 1996.

Whitman, Walt. *Leaves of Grass*. New York: Vintage, 1992.

———. "When Lilacs Last in the Dooryard Bloom'd." In *The Norton Anthology of Modern and Contemporary Poetry*. Third Edition. Vol. 1, edited by Jahan Ramazani, Richard Ellmann, and Robert O'Clair, 23–29. New York: W. W. Norton and Company, 2003.

Wilson, Edmund. "Santayana at the Convent of the Blue Nuns." *New Yorker* 22, no. 6 (April 1946): 59–67.

Winnicott, Donald Woods. "Communicating and Not Communicating Leading to a Study of Certain Opposites." In *The Maturational Processes and the Facilitating Environment: Studies in the Theory of Emotional Development*, 179–192. New York: International Universities Press, 1965.

———. *Playing and Reality*. New York: Routledge, 1971.

Withycombe, Shannon. *Lost: Miscarriage in Nineteenth-Century America*. New Brunswick: Rutgers University Press, 2018.

Witten, Barrett. "Poetics and the Question of Value; or, What Is a Philosophically Serious Poet?" *The Wallace Stevens Journal* 39, no. 1 (Spring 2015): 84–101.

Woodward, Kathleen. "Late Theory, Late Style: Loss and Renewal in Freud and Barthes." In *Aging and Gender in Literature: Studies in Creativity*, edited by Anne Wyatt-Brown and Janice Rossen, 82–101. Charlottesville: University of Virginia Press, 1993.

Wordsworth, William. "Elegiac Stanzas, Suggested by a Picture of Peele Castle, in a Storm, Painted by Sir George Beaumont." In *The Norton Anthology of English Literature*. Ninth Edition. Vol. 2, edited by Stephen Greenblatt, 343–344. New York: W. W. Norton and Company, 2012.

———. "Lines: Composed a Few Miles Above Tintern Abbey, on Revisiting the Banks of the Wye During a Tour, July 13, 1798." In *The Norton Anthology of English Literature*. Ninth Edition. Vol. 2, edited by Stephen Greenblatt, 288–292. New York: W. W. Norton and Company, 2012.

———. "My Heart Leaps Up When I Behold." In *The Norton Anthology of English Literature*. Ninth Edition. Vol. 2, edited by Stephen Greenblatt, 335. New York: W. W. Norton and Company, 2012.

———. "Ode: Intimations of Immortality from Recollections of Early Childhood." In *The Norton Anthology of English Literature*. Ninth Edition. Vol. 2, edited by Stephen Greenblatt, 337–341. New York: W. W. Norton and Company, 2012.

———. *The Prose Works of William Wordsworth*. Vol. 2. Edited by W. J. B. Owen and Jane Worthington Smyser. Oxford: Clarendon Press, 1974.

Wordsworth, William, and Dorothy Wordsworth. *The Letters of William and Dorothy Wordsworth, Vol. 1: The Early Years, 1787–1805*. Edited by Ernest de Selincourt and Chester L. Shaver. Oxford: Clarendon Press, 1967.

Wright, Carolyn. "Review of *the Dead and the Living*." *Iowa Review* 15, no. 1 (Winter 1985): 151–161.

Yeats, William Butler. *The Collected Poems of W. B. Yeats*. Revised Second Edition. Edited by Richard J. Finneran. New York: Scribner, 1996.

Zaki, Jamil. "Empathy: A Motivated Account." *Psychological Bulletin* 140, no. 6 (2014): 1608–1647.

Zapedowska, Magdalena. "Dickinson's Delight." *The Emily Dickinson Journal* 21, no. 1 (2012): 1–24.

Zeiger, Melissa F. *Beyond Consolation: Death, Sexuality, and the Changing Shapes of Elegy*. Ithaca: Cornell University Press, 1997.

Acknowledgments

My debts are many. This project was first conceived at the University of Michigan, under the guidance of Laurence Goldstein, Adela Pinch, Yopie Prins, and John Whittier-Ferguson; I thank them profusely for their generous support at the inception of this study. Without naming each one of them, I also express gratitude to my professors and colleagues at the University of Michigan, Cornell University, and Dartmouth College who advised and supported me in the formative years of my scholarship; without them, this project would never have begun.

For its development, this study principally relied on the collections in many great libraries. I am grateful to the University of Washington for granting me access to its immense resources as a visiting scholar every summer since 2016, during the crucial period of my composition of this manuscript: I would like to thank their faculty, staff, and librarians, in particular, Brian Reed, who for many years kindly sponsored my visits; Anis Bawarshi, who generously continues to do the same; and Carolyn Busch, who has been a great help in making sure that my stays go smoothly. I would also like to thank Smith College for providing me with access to the Sylvia Plath collection, and Karen V. Kukil for her help during my visit; Vassar College for access to the Elizabeth Bishop papers, and Dean Rogers for his help; Marietta College for access to the William Heyen papers, and Linda Showalter for her help.

I gratefully acknowledge the sources that supported the writing of this book. This work was supported by JSPS Grant Number JP17K02575. I also express my gratitude to the Fukuhara Memorial Fund for the Studies of English and American Literature.

I would like to thank the editors and staff at Lexington Books who assisted me through the publication phase of this project: Aimee Pozorski and Nicholas Ealy, for kindly welcoming my book to the Reading Trauma and

Memory series; Holly Buchanan, for her help, advice, and patience throughout the publishing process; Jessica Thwaite, for her enthusiastic endorsement of this book at the beginning phases of the publishing process; Megan Conley, for her attentive assistance; and Monica Sukumar for shepherding me through the production process. Several anonymous readers offered detailed and insightful suggestions during the revision of this manuscript; I cannot thank them enough for helping me find clarity and improve this book. I also thank Ayumi Matsuo, who has been a source of valuable mentorship, along with Hiroko Uno, Nigel Duffield, Ben Railton, Iain Twiddy, and many other friends and colleagues in the United States and around the world, to whom I feel indebted.

Editors of the following journal have kindly granted permission to reprint in revised form my previously published article: "Modern Elegy and the Fiction and Creation of Loss: Wallace Stevens's 'The Owl in the Sarcophagus,'" copyright © 2010 Johns Hopkins University Press. This article first appeared in *ELH: English Literary History*, Volume 77, Issue 1, Spring 2010, pages 45–70. Published with permission by Johns Hopkins University Press.

Grateful acknowledgment is given to the following publishers and individuals for permission to reprint the poems that appear in this book. Every attempt has been made to locate the copyright holders. "The Owl in the Sarcophagus," copyright © 1950 by Wallace Stevens; "To an Old Philosopher in Rome" and "As You Leave the Room" from *The Collected Poems of Wallace Stevens* by Wallace Stevens, copyright © 1954 by Wallace Stevens and copyright renewed 1982 by Holly Stevens. Used by permission of Alfred A. Knopf, an imprint of the Knopf Doubleday Publishing Group, a division of Penguin Random House LLC. Excerpts from "Morning Song," "Sheep in Fog," "Paralytic" from *The Collected Poems*, Sylvia Plath. Copyright © 1960, 1965, 1971, 1981 by the Estate of Sylvia Plath. Used by permission of HarperCollins Publishers. "Photograph of the Girl" and "Nevsky Prospekt" from *The Dead and the Living* by Sharon Olds, copyright © 1975, 1978, 1979, 1980, 1981, 1982, 1983 by Sharon Olds. Used by permission of Alfred A. Knopf, an imprint of the Knopf Doubleday Publishing Group, a division of Penguin Random House LLC. *September 11, 2001: American Writers Respond*, copyright © 2002 by William Heyen. Used by permission of Etruscan Press. "How It Comes," copyright © 2002 by Gail Griffin. Used by permission of Etruscan Press. "Her Very Eyes," copyright © 2002 by Kimiko Hahn; first appeared in *The Clarion: Newspaper of the Professional Staff Congress/CUNY*. Used by permission of Etruscan Press. "September Twelfth, 2001," copyright © 2002 by X. J. Kennedy. Used by permission of Etruscan Press. "Falling Man," copyright © 2002 by Diane Seuss. Used by permission of Etruscan Press. "Elegy for Jane," copyright © 1950 by Theodore Roethke; copyright © 1966 and renewed 1994 by Beatrice

Lushington; from *Collected Poems* by Theodore Roethke. Used by permission of Doubleday, an imprint of the Knopf Doubleday Publishing Group, a division of Penguin Random House LLC. All rights reserved.

As one last note, I would like to thank my parents, Yoshiko and Heijiro Komura, to whom I dedicate this book. Finally, my heartfelt thanks go to Lily Komura, who has grown with the progress of this book and has been a delightful presence in our lives; and to Kelly Komura, who has given me as much encouragement and support as anyone can hope for, while sharing insights and reading every word of my manuscript in all stages of revision through the finish line.

Index

Abraham, Nicholas, 12–15, 22, 31n43, 52, 80, 181–83
Adagia (Stevens), 35–36, 65
Adorno, Theodor, 24, 149, 153–54
Aesop's crow, 45, 176
"Aesthetics of the Shah" (Olds), 129
affective syncopation, 120n9
"After great pain, a formal feeling comes" (Dickinson), 150
AIDS crisis, 11
allegory, 40, 50–52, 56
"All the Dead Dears" (Plath), 77
ambiguous loss, 2, 9; absence of, 185; Boss on, 11, 73, 158–59, 181; melancholia as reaction, 74; naming of, 11; in "Parliament Hill Fields," 79; Plath and, 23, 74–76, 89; in post-9/11 elegiac poetry, 158–59; resolution and, 73
Ambiguous Loss (Boss), 11, 73
ambivalence, 113, 141, 161; ambivalent loss, 10, 22; betrayed, in elegiac poetry, 21; cultural, 185; in "Edge," 87; in "Elegy for Jane," 4; in "Lycidas," 17–18; Stevens and, 70n64
The Angel of History (Forché), 178–79
anticipatory grief, 12, 26
anti-elegy, 9, 15; of Bishop, 98; "Daddy" as, 78; "Lady Lazarus" as, 78; "The Owl in the Sarcophagus" as, 37, 42; of Plath, 8, 22, 77–78, 91n21; post-9/11 elegiac poetry and, 161; Spargo on, 161
aphasia, 169
Ariel (Plath), 76–78, 80–83, 88–89
Ariès, Philippe, 11
Aristotle, 104
assimilation, 181–82
"As You Leave the Room" (Stevens), 22, 62–64
Auden, W. H., 115, 150
aura, 130–31, 140
Aurelius, Marcus, 55
The Auroras of Autumn (Stevens), 35
Auschwitz, 24, 149, 153
"The Author to Her Book" (Bradstreet), 85
"Autobiography as De-facement" (de Man), 63
"Ave atque Vale" (Swinburne), 57
Averno (Glück), 25, 161–63, 170
"Averno" (Glück), 162, 170

Badowska, Eva, 159
Baer, Ulrich, 150
"Balloons" (Plath), 86–87
Barthes, Roland, 12, 130–31, 140
Baudelaire, Charles, 179
Bazin, André, 146n25

Beat literature, 84
Beaumont, George, 18–20
Beeson, Miranda, 157
Benjamin, Walter, 39–40, 51–52, 133;
    on aura, 130–31, 141; Benjaminian
    melancholia, 67n27; on collection,
    108; on isolated experience, 100
Berger, Charles, 50
Berkeley, George, 107
Berryman, John, 8, 140
Binswanger, Ludwig, 7
Birthday Letters (Hughes), 179
Bishop, Elizabeth, 1, 151, 164;
    ambiguous melancholy and, 23; anti-
    elegy of, 98; breakdown of, 33n80;
    childhood and, 100; on confessional
    poetry, 119n6; elegy for, 97–98;
    indirection and, 104–5; lost loss and,
    97–98, 119n1; melancholia and, 97;
    as politically engaged, 105; privacy
    and, 121n32; sublimation and, 97–
    98, 102, 113, 118, 179; third space
    of, 97–98, 102–3, 117; translational
    poetics of, 105, 121n30; un-losing
    loss and, 118, 126, 177, 182
Bloom, Harold, 45, 57
Boland, Eavan, 6
Boltanski, Luc, 125, 127
Bonanno, George, 10
Boss, Pauline, 11, 23, 73, 158–59, 181
Bourne, Daniel, 162
Bradstreet, Anne, 15–16, 20, 85
Breughel, Pieter, 115
Brogan, T. V. F., 6
Brontë, Emily, 89
Bryant, William Cullen, 16
Buddhism, 84
Butler, Judith, 11, 23, 75, 178

Camera Lucida (Barthes), 130–31, 140
canonical elegy, 21, 53
"Captain John Wordsworth's Death at
    Sea" (Matlak), 19–20
Carson, Anne, 179–80
causeless melancholia, 179

"Cellars and Attics" (Tussman), 2–3, 20
Cheng, Anne Anlin, 181
"The Circus Animals' Desertion"
    (Yeats), 88
Clampitt, Amy, 177
Coleridge, Samuel Taylor, 102
collective trauma, 25, 163
"The Colossus" (Plath), 74, 77
The Colossus and Other Poems (Plath),
    75, 77, 81, 87–89
Colwell, Anne, 103–4
"The Comedian as the Letter C"
    (Stevens), 35
community trauma, 24, 127, 163
compassion: collapse of, 142; fatigue,
    137
compensation/compensatory
    consolation, 7–9, 28n15, 161;
    elegies and, 28n18; *In Memoriam*
    and, 95n62; in "The Owl in the
    Sarcophagus," 36, 50–51
confessional poetry, 81, 163, 178;
    Bishop on, 119n6; empathy and,
    164; mechanism of, 179; Plath and,
    92n37, 151, 165; as writing therapy,
    152
consolation, 4; in elegy, 6; healing
    and, 25; in "Lycidas," 17–18;
    melancholia as new, 8; in "The Night
    Migrations," 163–64; rejection of, 8;
    of Stevens, 41–42
consolatory fiction, 37, 50, 178, 185
"Containing Multitudes" (Graham and
    Sontag, K.), 179
"Contusion" (Plath), 86, 87
Costello, Bonnie, 61
Covid-19 crisis, 11, 184
"Crusoe in England" (Bishop), 23, 104;
    collector instinct in, 110–11; drafts
    of, 106, 123n48; indirection in, 117;
    left out objects in, 106–7; lost loss
    in, 105, 113; object-loss in, 107; pain
    of loss in, 116; removed objects in,
    112–13, 118; self-pity in, 109, 111
cryptonymy, 52, 56, 162

Cullen, Countee, 25
Culler, Jonathan, 46

"Daddy" (Plath), 8, 23, 74, 78, 88
Dallal, Thomas, 155
Daphne myth, 49, 55, 118
The Dead and the Living (Olds), 24, 177; ekphrastic representations in, 127–29, 140; empathy and, 143; ethics and, 137, 143–44
death: Covid-19 deaths, 11, 184; disappearance of, 11; as linguistic predicament, 41; photography and, 130, 140, 160; second death, 20; ungrievable, 26
"The Death of a Soldier" (Stevens), 36, 66n12
"The Death of Marilyn Monroe" (Olds), 129, 143; vicarious traumatization in, 136–37, 139
Defoe, Daniel, 106, 123n45
DeLillo, Don, 150–51
de Man, Paul, 41, 63, 140
denied grief, 1, 5, 182, 188n24
Derrida, Jacques: on ghost, 111; proleptic loss and, 11–12, 22, 67n23
Dickinson, Emily, 17, 20–21, 150; renunciation and, 85; stoicism of, 84
Didion, Joan, 50
diffusion of responsibility, 142
disenfranchised grief, 10–11, 26, 79
Disenfranchised Grief (Doka), 79
disenfranchised loss, 75
disrupted grief, 51, 184
distant loss, 1, 11, 25; in "Elegy for Jane," 4; Olds and, 24; spectator and, 126–27; subjective feeling of, 126; un-losing of, 9
distant suffering, 125–27
Distant Suffering (Boltanski), 125
"Diver" (Hartzler), 158
Dodd, Elizabeth, 162–63
Dodd, Wayne, 157
doing gender, 133
Doka, Kenneth J., 75, 79

Doreski, C. K., 100
"Dream Song #384" (Berryman), 8
The Dream Songs (Berryman), 140
Drew, Richard, 155, 158
"Dulce et Decorum Est" (Owen), 158
Dying Modern (Fuss), 8
"The Dying of Death" (Jacobs), 11
dysthymia, 97; of absence mourning, 89; defined, 81, 90n11; of denied grief, 182; dispossession and, 8, 12–13; lost loss as, 8–9, 97, 176–78; as mood disorder, 90n11; Plath and, 22–23, 75, 81, 89

"Easter, 1916" (Yeats), 150
Ebbinghaus, Hermann, 104
"Edge" (Plath), 23, 86–88, 184
ekphrasis, 18, 115; in *The Dead and the Living*, 127–29, 140; in "Nevsky Prospekt," 135; of Olds, 141; in "Photograph of the Girl," 134; photography and, 144; in "Poem," 113
"Electra on Azalea Path" (Plath), 74, 77
elegiac poetry: ambivalence betrayed in, 21; equivocation and, 2, 9, 161; inconclusive loss and, 1; lost loss in American and British traditions, 14–22; new subgenre for, 2; reflection in, 6
elegiac poetry, post-9/11: ambiguous loss in, 158–59; anti-elegy and, 161; disappearing loss in, 170; falling man poems, 149, 157–60; fall victims and, 155–56; as first responder, 152; lost loss in, 177; profusion of, 149–50; unnamed sorrows in, 161–62
"Elegiac Stanzas" (Wordsworth, W.), 18–19, 20
elegy: for Bishop, 97–98; canonical elegy, 21, 53; compensation and, 28n18; consolation in, 6; contradictory elements of, 21; conventional, 7; defining, 5–10; funeral, 7; for living, 64; as

mechanism of creation, 56; need for, 25; new meanings and, 118; pastoral elegy, 6, 15, 17, 167, 169; as poem of mourning, 6; repetition in, 67n29; variations in, 6
"Elegy" (Heyen), 152
"Elegy for Jane" (Roethke), 20, 76, 115; ambivalence in, 4; critical reception for, 27n4; debate over, 27n6; distant loss in, 4; lost loss in, 3–5; reticence in, 86; tone of, 116
"Elegy Written in a Country Churchyard" (Gray), 15, 20
Eliot, T. S., 178–79
empathy, 9; as automatic reflex, 142; choice of, 143; confessional poetry and, 164; *The Dead and the Living* and, 143; ethical, 128, 138, 141, 144, 147n40; of Olds, 138; photography and, 135; poetry of, 24, 164; stages of, 164–65; theory of, 135–36; in "Things That Are Worse Than Death," 139
Empathy (Katz), 135
"The Emperor of Ice-Cream" (Stevens), 36
"The End of March" (Bishop), 23, 117
Epicurus, 128
epitaphs, 18–19, 23, 75; Eliot on poems as, 178–79; poets writing self, 140
Epston, David, 152
equivocation: in "As You Leave the Room," 64; in *Averno*, 162–63; as communication, 13; elegiac poetry and, 2, 9, 161; *Geography III* and, 23; Glück and, 25; loss as, 14
Essays upon Epitaphs (Wordsworth, W.), 18
"Esthétique du Mal" (Stevens), 35–36
ethical empathy, 128, 138; consequentialist, 147n40; defined, 141; deontological obligations of, 141; photography and, 144
ethics: *The Dead and the Living* and, 137, 143–44; ethics of representation, 154; of photography, 141; professional, 154
The Ethics of Mourning (Spargo), 29n22
"The Eye-Mote" (Plath), 77

Falling Man (DeLillo), 150–51
"Falling Man" (Seuss), 157–58
falling man poems, 149, 157–60
"Fever 103°" (Plath), 78
fiction-making, 42; as access to loss, 89, 177; belief and, 60, 64, 166, 184; consolatory fiction, 37, 50, 178, 185; loss as fiction, 37–38, 55–56, 64, 88; loss masked through, 60, 64; loss-salvaging through, 35–36; lost loss and, 89, 177; restorative fiction, 135; Stevens and, 35–37, 55, 57, 60, 63, 68n32, 176; supreme fiction, 35–36, 68n32, 71n78
"Final Soliloquy of the Interior Paramour" (Stevens), 22, 60–61, 63
"First Death in Nova Scotia" (Bishop), 112; capturing remembering and forgetting, 98, 104; comprehension and incomprehension in, 101; objects in, 105; readings of, 102–3; repetition in, 99; self-meanings in, 118; speaker projecting self in, 100, 184; whiteness in, 103, 115
"The First of October, We" (Bourne), 162
"First Warmth" (Stevens), 62
"Flight" (Beeson), 157
Forché, Carolyn, 24, 144, 178–79
Forty, Adrian, 104
Freud, Sigmund, 7–8, 37, 54; on excess stimuli, 158; Freudian negation, 52; mourning theory of, 10, 70n64; screen memory of, 53; on self-knowledge, 69n48; on transience, 86
Frost, Laura, 156
"Frost at Midnight" (Coleridge), 102
Frow, John, 6
frozen grief, 74, 87
Frye, Northrop, 45

"Full Fathom Five" (Plath), 74, 77, 85
funeral elegy, 7
Fuss, Diana, 8, 33n80

gendering of mourning, 129, 135, 138–39
Genovese, Kitty, 142
Geography III (Bishop): cognitive reorganization in, 116–17; Colwell on, 103–4; equivocation and, 23; lost loss in, 23, 113; thesis of, 118; un-losing loss in, 177
Gilbert, Sandra, 116
Glück, Louise, 1, 25, 149–50, 161; healing and, 167, 170; personal classicism of, 162–63, 165
Goldstein, Laurence, 19, 150, 151, 158
Gosmann, Uta, 162
Graham, David, 179
Gray, Thomas, 15, 20
grief: anticipatory grief, 12; cultural norms of, 5; denied grief, 1, 5, 182, 188n24; disrupted grief, 51, 184; of explicit loss, 2; frozen grief, 74, 87; stages of, 170; studies of, 10; suppressed, 25. *See also* inaccessible grief
Griffin, Gail, 157
Gunn, Thom, 6

Hagiwara, Sakutaro, 180
Hahn, Kimiko, 157–58, 159
Harmonium (Stevens), 35
Hartman, Geoffrey, 19
Hartzler, Christine, 158
healing, 154; consolation and, 25; Glück and, 167, 170; language of, 150–52; in "October," 165–67; poetry of healing, 105, 150–51
Heaney, Seamus, 177
Hejinian, Lyn, 153
"Here Follows Some Verses upon the Burning of Our House, July 10, 1666" (Bradstreet), 15–16, 20
"Her Very Eyes" (Hahn), 157–58

Heyen, William, 152, 161–62
Hillbilly Elegy (Vance), 183
Hix, H. Edgar, 162
Hochschild, Arlie Russell, 183–84
Holocaust, 2–3, 10, 153
Hopkins, Gerard Manley, 43, 166
The Hour of Our Death (Ariès), 11
"How It Comes" (Griffin), 157
"How to Write a Poem after September 11th" (Moustaki), 154
Hughes, Ted, 74, 80, 179
humanitarianism, 128, 134, 143, 177

"The Idea of Order at Key West" (Stevens), 35
Ideas of Order (Stevens), 35
"Ideographs" (Olds), 128, 131, 143
idyll, 13–14, 26
imaginary loss, 11, 16
"Imagination as Value" (Stevens), 58, 59
immigration, 26, 144, 183; assimilation and, 181–82; Plath and, 74
inaccessible grief, 2–3, 8, 13, 89, 170, 181; language for, 26; in "Photograph of the Girl," 134
In Memoriam (Tennyson), 107, 170; compensatory consolation and, 95n62
intergenerational trauma, 182
"In the Waiting Room" (Bishop), 23, 33n80, 117, 118
Inventions of Farewell (Gilbert), 116
isolated experience, 100
"The Issues" (Olds), 137–38

Jacobs, Joseph, 11
Jonson, Ben, 15

Kalstone, David, 101
Katz, Robert L., 135, 138, 164
Keats, John, 45, 89, 133
Kennedy, X. J., 157
Knutson, Lin, 150
Kristeva, Julia, 69n48, 93n39

Kübler-Ross, Elisabeth, 10, 185
Küchler, Susanne, 104

Lacan, Jacques, 77
"Lady Lazarus" (Plath), 23, 78
Lain Entralgo, Pedro, 151
Lakoff, George, 159–60
"Landscape with the Fall of Icarus" (Breughel), 115
language: of healing, 150–52; for inaccessible grief, 26; linguistic insufficiency, 52–53; of love, 61; of mourning, 46
"Large Bad Picture" (Bishop), 114
Levinson, Marjorie, 19
Lincoln, Abraham, 16, 163
Listening with the Third Ear (Reik), 135–36
"Little Gidding" (Eliot), 178
Locke, John, 133–34
Longenbach, James, 40
"Looking at War" (Sontag, S.), 130
"Lorelei" (Plath), 77
loss: ambivalent loss, 10, 22; as amorphous, 5; as equivocation, 14; as fiction, 37–38, 55–56, 64, 88; fiction-making as access to, 89, 177; imaginary loss, 11, 16; inconclusive, in elegiac poetry, 1; loss aversion, 183; in photography, 131; theorization of, 10–14; unacknowledged loss, 1–2, 183–84; under-acknowledged loss, 187n24. *See also* phantom loss; proleptic loss
lost loss: in American and British elegiac poetry, 14–22; beyond American elegiac poetry, 175–86; awareness of in poetry, 186; Bishop and, 97–98, 119n1; in "Cellars and Attics," 2–3; in "Crusoe in England," 105, 113; defined, 2; as dysthymia, 8–9, 97, 176–78; in "Elegy for Jane," 3–5; fiction-making and, 89, 177; in *Geography III*, 23, 113; inaccessible, 25, 149, 176; beyond literature, 181; "The Owl in the Sarcophagus" and, 38–40; Plath and, 88–89; in "Poem," 116; in post-9/11 elegiac poetry, 177; Stevens and, 60, 176; theorization of, 10–14; as under-acknowledged, 11; un-losing of, 23, 126; unrecognized, 182
Lowell, Robert, 151
"Lycidas" (Milton), 17–18, 20
lyric sentimentalism, 21
lyric voice, 76

magical thinking, 160–61
The Making of a Poem (Strand and Boland), 6
Marxist criticism, 176
Matlak, Richard, 19–20
maximization of consciousness, 103
"Mayflower" (Plath), 85, 86
meaning-assignation, 103, 110, 115
melancholia: Benjaminian melancholia, 67n27; Bishop and, 97; causeless melancholia, 179; as maximization of consciousness, 103; as new consolation, 8; Plath and, 23, 90n6; racialization and, 181, 187n19; as reaction to ambiguous loss, 74; Stevens and, 36, 39–40, 47; value in, 29n22
melancholic mourning, 7, 29n22, 51, 91n21, 116
Mellor, Anne K., 36–37
memorialization, 17, 104
"The Men That Are Falling" (Stevens), 36
Merwin, W. S., 154, 168
"Metaphor" (Plath), 87
Mill, J. S., 76
Miller, Nancy K., 16
Miłosz, Czesław, 149
Milton, John, 15, 17–18, 20
"The Missing All—Prevented Me" (Dickinson), 17, 20–2
The Modern Elegiac Temper (Vickery), 9
modified naturalism, 139

"The Moon and the Yew Tree" (Plath), 87
"The Moose" (Bishop), 23, 104–5, 117, 151
moratorium, 160
"The Morning After" (Randall), 181–82
"Morning Song" (Plath), 82–83, 87
mother of the dead, 40–41
mother of us all, 46–47, 56
mourning, 4, 126; in *Averno*, 170; collective mourning, 25; dysthymia of absence, 89; elegy as poem of, 6; Freud's theory of, 10, 70n64; language of, 46; melancholic mourning, 7, 29, 29n22, 51, 91n21, 116; politicization of, 154; spiritual mourning, 16
Moustaki, Nikki, 154
"The Munich Mannequins" (Plath), 23, 82–84, 87
Murano, Shiro, 180
"Musée des Beaux Arts" (Auden), 115
"Mystic" (Plath), 85
mythology, 50, 162; mythologization, 70n64, 184

narrative therapy, 152
Nazism, 78, 142, 183
near-sentimentalism, 120n9
"Nevsky Prospekt" (Olds), 128–29, 143; ekphrasis in, 135; restoration of individual in, 135–36; silence in, 136
New Criticism, 176
new formalism, 176
The New Princeton Handbook of Poetic Terms (Brogan), 6
Nietzsche, Friedrich, 42, 66n7, 68n34
"The Night City" (Bishop), 23
"The Night Migrations" (Glück), 163–64
9/11 attacks, 16, 24–25. *See also* elegiac poetry, post-9/11
"North Haven" (Bishop), 97
"Notes Toward a Supreme Fiction" (Stevens), 35–36

Nussbaum, Martha C., 151

objective poetry, 97
object-loss, 5, 8, 175; in "Crusoe in England," 107; "The Owl in the Sarcophagus" and, 38–39; Plath and, 77–78, 80–81, 83, 89
"Objector" (Stafford), 150
"Objects & Apparitions" (Bishop), 117
"O Captain! My Captain!" (Whitman), 16–17
"October" (Glück), 25, 149–50, 170, 184; healing in, 165–67; light in, 169; mind's trick in, 166; as mournful remembrance, 161–62; pastoral and non-pastoral in, 167; unspeakable in, 167–68; winter depiction in, 164
"October 11, 2001" (Hix), 162
"Ode on a Grecian Urn" (Keats), 133
Olds, Sharon, 1, 177; distant loss and, 24; ekphrasis of, 141; empathy of, 138; gendering images of, 138–39; modified naturalism and, 139; privacy of, 143; ungrievable life and, 24. *See also The Dead and the Living*
"On Being Asked for a War Poem" (Yeats), 152–53
"One Art" (Bishop), 97, 117–18, 124n56, 164
"On My First Son" (Jonson), 15
On Photography (Sontag, S.), 130
"On Some Motifs in Baudelaire" (Benjamin), 100
Orchard, Andy, 9
Orpheus, 42, 68n36
Ostriker, Alicia, 154
Ovid, 6
Owen, Wilfred, 6, 158
"The Owl in the Sarcophagus" (Stevens), 22, 25, 180; as allegory, 50–52, 56; as anti-elegy, 37, 42; apostrophe in, 48; compensatory consolation in, 36, 50–51; discovery in, 53–54; layers of loss in, 184; lost

loss and, 38–40; mother of the dead in, 40–41; mother of us all in, 46–47, 56; object-loss and, 38–39; peace in, 39, 44–45, 56; romantic irony of, 36–37; self-awareness in, 48–50; sleep in, 44–45, 56; underground journey in, 42–43; as uninterpretable, 45–46; unplaceability of sorrow and, 38

The Oxford Handbook of the Elegy (Weisman), 6

Pancer, S. Mark, 142
"Paralytic" (Plath), 85, 87
Parker, Robert Dale, 99
"Parliament Hill Fields" (Plath), 23; ambiguous loss in, 79; phantom loss in, 80
pastoral elegy, 6, 15, 17, 167, 169
Pastoral Elegy in Contemporary British and Irish Poetry (Twiddy), 167
peace, 39, 44–45, 56
"Peele Castle" (Wordsworth, W.), 17–20
Pennebaker, James W., 152
Perloff, Marjorie, 79
Persephone, 162–63, 174n62
personal classicism, 162–63, 165
personalization of poetry, 169
Phaedrus (Plato), 151
phantom loss, 11, 13–14, 22, 26; defined, 52; in "Parliament Hill Fields," 80
Philomela, 45
"Photograph from September 11" (Szymborska), 25, 149, 159–61
"Photograph of the Girl" (Olds), 128, 143, 184; ekphrasis in, 134; gaze in, 131–32; gendering images in, 129, 132–35; inaccessible grief in, 134
photography, 24–25; death and, 130, 140, 160; ekphrasis and, 144; as embalming dead, 146n25; empathy and, 135; ethical empathy and, 144; ethics of, 141; loss in, 131; as violence, 141

Plath, Sylvia, 1, 87; ambiguous loss and, 23, 74–76, 89; ambivalent loss and, 22; anti-elegies of, 8, 22, 77–78, 91n21; confessional poetry and, 92n37, 151, 165; cultural ethos of, 85; dysthymia and, 22–23, 81, 89; immigration and, 74; lost father and, 83; lost loss and, 88–89; melancholia and, 23, 90n6; mirror images of, 94n53; object-loss and, 77–78, 80–81, 83, 89; resigned despair of, 80; Roethke compared to, 76, 86; self-elegy and, 75; suicide of, 80, 88, 93n39; surrealism of, 76; violence and, 75
Plato, 151
Playing and Reality (Winnicott), 55
"Poem" (Bishop), 23, 104–5; ekphrasis in, 113; left out objects in, 114, 118; lost loss in, 116; as sudden recognition, 115; un-losing loss in, 126, 182; use of useless concern, 114–15
"Poetic Responses to 9/11" (Knutson), 150
poetry: awareness of lost loss, 186; objective poetry, 97; personalization of, 169; poetics of misery, 21; poetry of healing, 105, 150–51; poetry of witness, 178–79; post-confessional poetry, 179; as safe forgetting, 98. *See also* confessional poetry; elegiac poetry; elegy
"Poetry as Confession" (Rosenthal), 151
Poetry of Mourning (Ramazani), 7–8
politicization of mourning, 154
"Poppies in July" (Plath), 87
"Portrait of a Child" (Olds), 128, 143
post-confessional poetry, 179
poszczególny, 159
Poulet, Georges, 103
Poulin, Al, Jr., 168–69
Precarious Life (Butler), 11, 178
The Prelude (Wordsworth, W.), 140
proleptic loss, 1, 57; Derrida and, 11–12, 22, 67n23

prosopopoeia, 103, 140
"Psychoanalyzing Persephone" (Gosmann), 162

quantum mechanics, 160
Questions of Travel (Bishop), 23, 98, 103, 118
The Quest for Inclusion (Shklar), 9

"Race Riot, Tulsa, 1921" (Olds), 128, 134, 143
racialization, melancholia and, 181, 187n19
Ramazani, Jahan, 7–8
Rand, Nicholas, 182–83
Randall, Margaret, 24, 138–39, 144, 181–82
reality-making, 38, 55
Regarding the Pain of Others (Sontag, S.), 125, 130
Reik, Theodor, 135–36, 138, 164
relative deprivation, 26, 182, 183, 184, 188n27
restorative fiction, 135
Rich, Adrienne, 150
"Richard Cory" (Robinson), 6
Ricoeur, Paul, 154, 186n11
Rilke, Rainer Maria, 180
risk-taking, 183
Robinson, E. A., 6
"The Rock" (Stevens), 61
Roethke, Theodore, 3–4, 10, 20, 115, 116; Plath compared to, 76, 86
"A Roman Sarcophagus" (Rilke), 180
romantic irony, 36–37, 57–58, 136
Romantic poets, 44–46, 49, 140
Rosenthal, M. L., 151
Ruins and Empire (Goldstein), 19

Santayana, George, 57–60, 71n73
Sappho, 179–80
The School Among the Ruins (Rich), 150
Schrödinger's cat, 160
screen loss, 53, 57

screen memory, 53
screen sorrow, 53
"The Second Coming" (Yeats), 85
secret trauma, 13
self-elegy, 62–63, 70n59, 75, 120n10
self-loss, 47–48, 87, 179
self-mourning, 53–54, 70n59
self-reflexivity, 6, 15–16; of Stevens, 53, 66n12
self-spectralization, 98, 103, 116, 117
"September 1, 1939" (Auden), 150
"September Twelfth, 2001" (Kennedy), 157
Seuss, Diane, 157–58
Sexton, Anne, 151–52
Shakespeare, William, 128, 140
"Sheep in Fog" (Plath), 88; "Morning Song" compared to, 82–83
The Shell and the Kernel (Abraham and Torok), 12–15, 181–82
Shklar, Judith, 9
Sibbes, Richard, 16
Sidney, Philip, 154
sleep, 44–45, 56
Smith, Adam, 127, 141–42
Snodgrass, W. D., 151
"Song of Myself" (Whitman), 47, 69n46
Sontag, Kate, 179
Sontag, Susan, 125, 130–31, 141, 145n14
Spargo, R. Clifton, 29n22, 161
speech as cryptonymy, 31n43
spiritual mourning, 16
Stafford, William, 150
Stevens, Wallace, 1, 22, 25, 88, 166, 180; ambivalence and, 70n64; on fiction, 55; fiction-making and, 35–37, 57, 60, 63, 68n32, 176; fragile consolation of, 41–42; on funeral practices, 36; language of love and, 71; lost loss and, 60, 176; melancholia and, 36, 39–40, 47; mythology and, 50, 70n64; Nietzsche and, 42, 66n7; pensive style of, 65, 72n90; portraying collapse of

temporal into spatial, 43; as Roman Catholic, 60; Romantic poets and, 44–46, 49; Santayana admired by, 58–60, 71n73; self-reflexivity of, 53, 66n12; supreme fiction and, 35–36, 68n32, 71n78; synesthesia of, 42
Stewart, Susan, 40
"Still Life" (Frost), 156
Strand, Mark, 6, 169
Strangers in Their Own Land (Hochschild), 183–84
stupefaction, 184
sublimation, 97–98, 102, 113, 118, 179
suicide, 11
"Sunday Morning" (Stevens), 59, 65n4, 69n39
surrealism, 76
Swenson, May, 150
Swinburne, Algernon Charles, 57
synesthesia, 42, 136
Szymborska, Wisława, 25, 149, 159–61

taboos, 24, 155, 159
temperance, 151
Tennyson, Alfred Lord, 95n62, 107, 170
"Thanatopsis" (Bryant), 16
The Theory of Moral Sentiments (Smith), 127, 141–42
theory of secret, 12–14, 31n43
"Things That Are Worse Than Death" (Olds), 129, 137–39
third space: of Bishop, 97–98, 102–3, 117; of Hagiwara, 180
"The Third Tower" (Dodd, W.), 157
Thoreau, Henry David, 84
"Threnody for a Brown Girl" (Cullen), 25
Tiedemann, Rolf, 153
"Tintern Abbey" (Wordsworth, W.), 18, 44
"To an Old Philosopher in Rome" (Stevens), 22; alliterative verse of, 58; as anticipatory elegy, 57–58; apostrophes in, 59; lyricism of, 59;

romantic irony of, 57–58; theme in, 61
"Too Big for Words" (Swenson), 150
Torok, Maria, 12–15, 22, 31n43, 52, 80, 181–83
"Totem" (Plath), 81
"To the Word" (Merwin), 168
transience, 86–87
transitional objects, 37, 64
translation, 114, 117; translational poetics, 105, 121n30
Transport to Summer (Stevens), 35
trauma, 3; as breach of trust, 74, 127; collective trauma, 25, 163; community trauma, 24, 127, 163; intergenerational trauma, 182; secret, 13; theories, 167–68; traumatic brain injury, 185; vicarious traumatization, 136–37, 139
Trump, Donald, 187n24
Tussman, Malka Heifetz, 2–3, 10, 18, 20
Twiddy, Iain, 167
"Two Illustrations That the World Is What You Make of It" (Stevens), 60

unacknowledged loss, 1–2, 183–84
under-acknowledged loss, 187n24
"An Undying Octopus" (Hagiwara), 180
unexperienced loss, 26
ungrievable death, 26
ungrievable life, 11; grievable life compared to, 178; Olds and, 24
ungrievable loss, 75, 178
universalization, 131, 134, 139, 141
unrecognized loss, 3, 21, 26, 177, 182, 184
unresolved grief, 73, 159; as frozen grief, 74

Vance, J. D., 183
Van Dyne, Susan R., 87
The Veiled Mirror and the Woman Poet (Dodd, E.), 162–63
Vendler, Helen, 101

vicarious traumatization, 136–37, 139
Vickery, John B., 9
violence, 166; photography as, 141; Plath and, 75

Walden (Thoreau), 84
Waters, William, 4, 48
Weinrich, Harald, 98
Weisman, Karen, 6
"What We See Is What We Think" (Stevens), 60
"When Lilacs Last in the Dooryard Bloom'd" (Whitman), 16
White, Michael, 152
Whitman, Walt, 16–17, 47, 49, 69n46

Winnicott, D. W., 22, 37, 38, 55, 64
The Witness of Poetry (Miłosz), 149
"Words" (Plath), 82, 85
Wordsworth, John, 18–20
Wordsworth, William, 17–20, 44, 46, 60, 140
"The Work of Art in the Age of Its Technological Reproducibility" (Benjamin), 130
The Work of Mourning (Derrida), 12
"The Worm at Heaven's Gate" (Stevens), 36
writing therapy, 152

Yeats, W. B., 85, 88, 140, 150, 152–53

About the Author

Toshiaki Komura is a scholar of modern and contemporary American poetry; he is also a published poet. He is associate professor of English at Kobe College and holds a PhD in English Literature from the University of Michigan at Ann Arbor and an MFA in poetry from Cornell University. His work has appeared in a number of academic and literary journals, including *ELH: English Literary History*, *European Romantic Review*, and *The Louisville Review*.

www.ingramcontent.com/pod-product-compliance
Lightning Source LLC
Chambersburg PA
CBHW050904300426
44111CB00010B/1367